The American Exploration and Travel Series

Exploring the Great Basin

EXPLORING THE GREAT BASIN

by Gloria Griffen Cline

UNIVERSITY OF OKLAHOMA PRESS • NORMAN

Library of Congress Catalog Card Number 63–8988

Copyright 1963 by the University of Oklahoma Press, Publishing Division of the University. Composed and printed at Norman, Oklahoma, U.S.A., by the University of Oklahoma Press. First edition.

To my Mother and Father

FOREWORD

By George P. Hammond

Until 1844, a scant 125 years ago, men knew little of the great American West, as we call it, or the interior of western North America. It was not fully realized until that year that the vast area between the Sierra Nevada of California and the Wasatch Range in central Utah, stretching for nearly six hundred miles from east to west and almost nine hundred from north to south, was an inland basin, with no outlet to the sea. So primitive was knowledge of this vast region that men had envisioned mythical kingdoms in its midst or conjured up great river systems, leading through the continent and linking America to the Orient, that had no basis in reality.

John C. Frémont, at the end of his second great exploration of the West, during which he had literally circled this vast interior domain looking for the fabled San Buenaventura River or other outlets to the sea, at last came to the inevitable conclusion necessitated by geographic reality and in his report to his government applied to this region one of history's great names: "The Great Basin."

In the exploration of North America, this basin was indeed the last part of the continent to reveal its secrets, except for the Arctic north. Spaniards, contemporaries of Cortés, conqueror of Mexico, sought fabled kingdoms in the Northern Interior. Hernando de Soto roamed through the southeastern United States in a vain search for Indian empires, and Francisco Vásquez Coronado did the same farther west. He heard of numerous realms, one of which, Quivira— thought to be a golden treasure—he sought in present Kansas, but found the land inhabited by simple Plains Indians, innocent of any knowledge of the white man's gold or silver. Defeated in this search for "other Mexicos" in the Northern Interior, the Spaniards for nearly two centuries satisfied themselves with the occupation of New Mexico and the conversion and civilization of its Pueblo people.

Eventually (though not till the eighteenth century) some adventurous spirits, friars and soldiers in New Mexico, revived the ancient dream of exploring that mysterious interior, partly under the stimulus of Spanish occupation of California, with which they wished to establish contact. In 1776, two friars, Domínguez and Escalante, with soldier escort set out from Santa Fe, made a great reconnaissance into western Colorado that took them on to Utah Lake, then returned home by a circuitous route through northeastern Arizona, the first white men to penetrate the interior basin. A desert barrier had prevented them from reaching California. They had learned but little of that land, and that little was disappointing, so the Spanish era was to pass away with the Interior Basin and the Indians who dwelt there almost as much a mystery as in past centuries.

Meantime, other forces precipitated action in western North America, a dramatic and relentless search for treasure—not gold or silver ores, but fur-bearing animals. From Canada, past the Great Lakes, up the Saskatchewan and Missouri rivers and into mountains beyond the prairies, adventurers probed and pushed their way, French, British, and American. Leading the way in this search for furs was the Northwest Company, later merged in the Hudson's Bay Company, whose daring and energetic vanguard crossed the continent and reached British Columbia in the Pacific Northwest before 1800. Caught by an imaginative vision of the new country and the possibility of finding a River of the West that would provide a route to the Pacific Ocean, President Thomas Jefferson sent Lewis and Clark to investigate. Their route up the Missouri and into the basin of the Columbia River took the two captains well north of the Great Basin, and their detailed reports fired the imagination of American traders and merchants, like John Jacob Astor, eager to exploit the western fur trade. Still there was no clear idea of the nature and extent of the vast western empire, especially those parts of it south of the country Lewis and Clark had seen.

Paving the way for ultimate solution of the puzzle, fur traders, singly or in companies and brigades, invaded the interior West. Men like Jedediah Smith or Peter Skene Ogden, representing American and British interests, and a host of others pursued the fur trade with extraordinary zeal. In their quest for beaver they explored rivers, mountains, and lakes, a fascinating chapter in the history of the continent, in which the lineaments of the Great Basin for the first time were made visible.

Other expeditions followed, and, like that of Captain Bonneville, added to the growing knowledge of the West, and in particular of its Interior Basin. Finally, Lieutenant J. C. Frémont, on his second exploration, in 1844, came to realize the true geographical facts, and made them known to the world the next year in his published report.

The story of the Great Basin through the centuries is the theme of Mrs. Cline's book. It is told with a sweep and zest from Indian and Spanish days down to the very eve of Mormon migration and gold discovery. The overland immigrants of later days could not have made their way into and across the West without the knowledge gathered by the men who preceded them. This book is the dramatic record of their deeds.

PREFACE

As an inhabitant of the Great Basin since childhood, I early developed an interest in the history of the land of interior drainage—the states lying between the Wasatch and Sierra Nevada Mountains—upon which Spanish, English, and American explorers converged while following adjacent river systems to their headwaters during the eighteenth and nineteenth centuries. Recent attention has been focused upon this region by geologists and anthropologists, but other academicians have failed to recognize the rich historical background of this geographically semi-arid region.

In the preparation of this book, a preoccupation for many years, I am indebted to a number of people. However, I especially wish to acknowledge with gratitude my indebtedness to the Governor and Committee of the Hudson's Bay Company for their courtesy in allowing me access to their archival collections. Without the valuable Peter Skene Ogden journals, this book would present an unbalanced history of the Great Basin. I am also greatly indebted to Miss A. M. Johnson, archivist of the Hudson's Bay Company, for taking time away from her many duties to read chapters six and seven of this manuscript and for making valuable suggestions pertaining thereto. To W. Kaye Lamb, Dominion archivist, and his staff of the National Archives of Canada, I give thanks for their gracious presentation of Hudson's Bay Company materials and for providing a most pleasant environment for study. Too, I am indebted to Willard E. Ireland, Provincial archivist of British Columbia, for making pertinent materials available to me.

Through the years, I have been a habitué of Bancroft Library, and I, therefore, wish to express my gratitude to Director George P. Hammond and his staff, John Barr Tompkins, Robert Becker, Julia

xiii

Macleod, Helen Bretnor, and others for their patience, graciousness, and courtesy. To Dale L. Morgan, the erudite Jedediah Smith biographer and western historian, I wish to express my appreciation for his helpful suggestions.

Within the Great Basin, a number of people were of assistance; I refer specifically to David E. Miller of the University of Utah—a fellow Peter Skene Ogden enthusiast; to Russell L. Mortensen, former director of the Utah Historical Society; to Clara Beatty, director of the Nevada Historical Society; and to J. J. Hill, retired director of the University of Nevada Library.

To Lawrence Kinnaird, I owe a debt of thanks for his stimulating seminars, sagacious counsel, and illuminating suggestions regarding this book. Others who are especially remembered for their encouragement, advice, and counsel or for reading all or parts of the manuscript are C. Gregory Crampton, Department of History, University of Utah; John S. Galbraith, Department of History, University of California at Los Angeles; George P. Hammond, Bancroft Library; James J. Parsons, chairman, Department of Geography, University of California; and O. O. Winther, Department of History, University of Indiana.

Gloria Griffen Cline

SACRAMENTO, CALIFORNIA
JANUARY 21, 1963

CONTENTS

ILLUSTRATIONS

following page 46

Map of Domínguez-Escalante Expedition, 1776
Humboldt's Map of 1811
Las Mejores autoridades, 1828
Map of Ogden's 1828–29 Snake Country Expedition
Brué Map of 1834
Burr's Map of 1840
Preuss Map of Great Salt Lake

following page 142

Governor Simpson
Dr. McLoughlin
Alexander Ross
Peter Skene Ogden
Old Fort Walla Walla (Nez Percés)
Fort Vancouver
Captain Bonneville
Joseph Reddeford Walker
Pyramid Lake

Exploring the Great Basin

MAPS

Exploring the Great Basin

1

THE LAND OF INTERIOR DRAINAGE

WITH THE COLUMBUS VOYAGE IN 1492, exploration of North America was begun, and within the next 250 years expeditions coasted the Atlantic and Pacific littorals or plodded overland, revealing most of the physical characteristics of the continent. By 1750 only one large area still lay unknown to the white man: the Great Basin, lying in the heart of the Trans-Mississippi West between latitudes 34 and 42 degrees. This region, which encompasses the western half of the present state of Utah, the southwest corner of Wyoming, the southeast corner of Idaho, a fairly large area in southeastern Oregon, part of Southern California, and almost all of Nevada, stands in marked contrast to other parts of the United States, chiefly because it is an area of interior drainage and, therefore, without an outlet to the sea. Undoubtedly because of the internal-drainage aspect, its harsh physical conditions, and the adjacent pattern of settlement, the Great Basin was the last large area in North America south of Arctic latitudes to be explored; however, quite paradoxically, it was in this land of interior drainage that explorers searched for the San Buenaventura, the mythical waterway between the Rocky Mountains and the Pacific Ocean, and trappers searched for rich beaver-bearing streams.

The Great Basin deserves in many ways the name that John Charles Frémont applied to it in 1844. The adjective "great" is appropriate in that the basin encompasses an area of approximately 210,000 square miles; it measures 880 miles in length from north to south and nearly 572 miles in width at its broadest part. In spite of the implication of its name, however, the Great Basin is not a single cup-shaped depression surrounded by mountains. Instead, it is a series of more than 90 basins separated from each other by more than 160 ranges which have a north-south trend and vary in length from

3

thirty to about one hundred miles. The higher basin ranges reach altitudes of from eight thousand to ten thousand feet and are separated by broad desert plains or basins lying at altitudes varying from sea level or a little less in the southwest[1] to four thousand to five thousand feet in the north. Many of these basins have their own interior drainage, and thus playa lakes are formed on the valley floors. These are shallow sheets of water which cover many square miles in the winter season but evaporate during the summer, leaving their beds a hard, smooth alkali plain.

Although the Great Basin is divided into a large number of interior-drainage areas or hydrographic basins, two—Bonneville and Lahontan—are so large that they deserve special attention. These basins were carved out by long tongues of ice which during the Pleistocene period extended into the Great Basin along the eastern flank of the Sierra Nevada Mountains and the western flank of the Wasatch mountains at Bell and Little Cottonwood canyons near the site of present Salt Lake City. With the subsequent climatic changes that ended the expansion of the ice sheets and caused them to disappear, the ancient lakes of the Great Basin were formed about 30,000 to 35,000 years ago.[2]

Bonneville Lake and Basin drained an approximately 54,000-square-mile area in northern and western Utah, together with small portions of Idaho, Wyoming, and Nevada. At its highest stage, the lake had an intricate shore line which was a succession of promontories and deep bays. Today one may see this shore line about one thousand feet above the present level of Great Salt Lake. The general outline of Bonneville Lake, which had a north-south orientation, was that of a pear, and at the present time is denoted by the Great Salt Lake Desert and the Sevier Desert, while the stem of the pear is occupied by Escalante Desert.

The lowest depression in Bonneville Basin is located along its eastern border and today is filled by Great Salt Lake, a remnant of the once expansive Lake Bonneville. This body of water is a broad,

1 Death Valley is a good example of a southern depression in the Great Basin. Bad Water, Death Valley, lies at an elevation of 280 feet below sea level and marks the lowest point in the Western Hemisphere. Extremes in topographical formations are found in this area, for a short distance north of Bad Water towers Mount Whitney, the highest peak in the United States.

2 Ernst Antlevs, "On the Pleistocene History of the Great Basin," *Quaternary Climates,* 51–114.

Three Centuries of Exploration

shallow sheet which extends 80 miles in a northwest-southeast direction, has a breadth of 35 miles, and covers an area of 2,360 square miles. Great Salt Lake is an unusual lake, since it receives much fresh water from four important Utah rivers—the Bear, the Ogden, the Weber, and the Jordan—yet has no outlet to the sea. Its water level is stabilized greatly by the tremendous amount of evaporation, which also contributes to one of the most striking characteristics of the lake —its high content of mineral salts and the resulting pungent bitterness of its waters. This quality was to confound explorers for many years, for, like Jim Bridger, its discoverer, they believed this salty lake must be an arm of the sea. Even as the shores of the lake became known, explorers refused, because of its saline features, to believe that it had no connection with the ocean. In December, 1826, *Niles' Register* reported that the Great Salt Lake "was coasted last spring by a party of gen. Ashley's men in canoes, who were occupied four and twenty days, in making its circuit. They did not exactly ascertain its outlet but passed a place where they supposed it must have been."[3] Fifteen years later explorers were still attempting to explain the source of the salt in the Great Salt Lake, as Frémont's *Report* attests: "It was generally supposed that it has no visible outlet; but among the trappers, including those in my own camp, were many who believed that somewhere on its surface was a terrible whirlpool, through which its waters found their way to the ocean by some subterranean communication."[4]

Of the four streams that are largely responsible for the maintenance of Great Salt Lake, Bear River is perhaps the most significant geographically and historically. Its main branch heads in the Uinta Mountains and follows a circuitous course, proceeding through Cache Valley and the narrow passage between precipitous walls of limestone known as "the Gates" before entering the Great Salt Lake. As early as 1818, Donald Mackenzie at the head of a party of Nor'westers trapped the upper courses of this river, while seven years later Jim Bridger discovered the Great Salt Lake by following this stream to its mouth. The valleys through which this river flows were enjoyed on many occasions by British and American trapping expeditions and were also the site of several picturesque rendezvous.

---

3 *Niles' Register,* December 9, 1826, p. 229.

4 John Charles Frémont, *Report of the Exploring Expedition to the Rocky Mountains,* 132. (Hereafter referred to as Frémont, *Report.*)

To the south of Bear River and the Great Salt Lake lies Utah Lake. The drainage of the southern portion of the Wasatch Mountains and an area on the southwestern slopes of the Uinta Range provide the sustenance for this body of water. The surplus from Utah Lake flows by way of the Jordan River to the Great Salt Lake, which lies about thirty miles to the north at an elevation almost three hundred feet lower than that of Utah Lake. The shores of Utah Lake are similar to those of its northern neighbor, for they are flat and shallow, particularly along the eastern side where the valley slope from the foothills of the Wasatch Mountains to the water is even less than in Salt Lake Valley.

To the west of the Great Salt Lake and the desert of the same name is a region of high, narrow mountain ridges which have a north-south trend and are separated by broad, nearly level valleys, which present, in a less pronounced manner, most of the arid, desolate features of the Great Basin itself. From the desert westward, the mountain ranges increase in height and importance as far as the East Humboldt Range, which is not only the main range of central Nevada but also the most prominent uplift between the Sierra Nevada and the Wasatch mountains. The valleys west of the East Humboldt Range contribute to the drainage system of the Humboldt River, which flows from east to west across the several basin ranges in central Nevada. A number of tributaries flowing from the north and from the south, following the intermontane valleys, serve to produce this anomalous stream. The Humbolt River is of great significance, for it is the only river within the Great Basin which traverses the area from east to west for such a distance, running from its source near present Wells, Nevada, nearly 290 miles before disappearing into the Humboldt Sink west of modern Lovelock, Nevada. This river, although sometimes cursed for its rather brackish waters, was the principal guide for Indians, fur trappers, and emigrants crossing through this maze of basins and ranges. It well deserves the name "Highroad of the West" which Dale Morgan has applied to it.

The Humboldt River deposits its waters in Humboldt Sink, or, as it is sometimes called, Humboldt Lake. This lake is typical of the lakes in the Great Basin. During a good part of the year it is a dry, flat bed, yet during the spring its stark form embraces the melting snows and, on occasion, overflows to Carson Lake or Sink, where its waters are evaporated. The wash created by the overflow from the

7

Humboldt Sink to the Carson Sink became an important link in the route from the Humboldt River to the Sierra Nevada Mountains by way of Carson Sink and its supplier, the Carson River. This avenue was not only followed by trappers but was much used in the middle of the nineteenth century by emigrants following the Overland Trail to California.[5]

The Humboldt Sink was a favorite camping place for Indians, and large numbers of them congregated here, especially in the late spring. It was in the lower course of the Humboldt River and along the shores of the Humboldt Sink that the first two recorded Great Basin clashes between Caucasians and Indians took place. Peter Skene Ogden's Snake Country Expedition of 1828–29 encountered a large, hostile Indian population in this region when they camped near the mouth of the Humboldt River on May 28, 1829, and in his diary and on the map which accompanied this journal, Ogden mentions that his party while examining "Unknown Lake" (Humboldt Sink) was surrounded by approximately 250 Indians, whom Ogden records as being "more daring and bold Indians seldom as ever I have seen."[6] Several years later the Walker-Bonneville party under the command of Joseph Reddeford Walker encountered a similar group of Indians in the same area and engaged in the first significant Great Basin Indian battle, which has been eloquently described by Washington Irving.

It is little wonder that the Indians congregated in this region, for water is extremely scarce in the Great Basin, especially in the central and southern portions. The Humboldt River is the only stream that has its source and terminus well within the area of interior drainage. The other principal streams of the Great Basin—such as the Bear, Weber, and Sevier rivers—have their sources in the Wasatch Mountains, while the melting snows of the Sierra Nevada bring into being the Truckee, Carson, and Walker rivers. As these streams proceed from the mountains which form the eastern and western boundaries of the Great Basin, however, their volume decreases until they are reduced to a trickle and disappear into the desert sands. This phenomenon is even more pronounced in the southern portions of the

[5] S. F. Emmons, "Lake Region," *Report of the Geological Exploration of the Fortieth Parallel* (ed. by Clarence King), 441.

[6] "Journal of Peter Skene Ogden's Snake Country Expedition, 1828–29," Hudson's Bay Company Archives (hereafter referred to as H.B.C.A.), B. 202/a/8, p. 48.

Great Basin, which is so dry that interior drainage is insufficient to support any significant rivers or lakes. On the eastern border of the Great Basin, Sevier Lake, located at 39 degrees north latitude, is the most southerly permanent body of water in the region,[7] while on the west, Owens Lake, which lies between the 36th and 37th parallels, is the most southern lake in the Great Basin sustained by the Sierra Nevada Mountains. Then for three hundred miles evaporation becomes supreme; this is the land where playas abound, springs are rare, and streams are almost unknown; those that do exist are exotic, such as the Mojave and Amargosa rivers.

Because of the meager amount of precipitation within the Great Basin, flora is not especially prolific and is primarily xerophytic. Broad plains and hills gray with sagebrush and shadscale, interspersed on the basin ranges with scanty forests of junipers and piñon pine, constitute the most typical aspect of the region. Southward, where the precipitation decreases and evaporation increases, this flora dwindles and gives place to barren gravelly wastes, dotted with scattered shrubs of creosote brush, greasewood, mesquite, and cacti, as well as picturesque stands of the yucca or Joshua tree. However, in the high mountains in the north, fir, pine, and spruce are found, while the rivers are fringed with willows and cottonwoods.

The presence or absence of water systems in various areas of the Great Basin had a profound effect upon the distribution of the Indian population. Although the Paiutes, the Shoshonis, and the Utes, the principal tribes inhabiting the Great Basin, roamed throughout large areas of the interior-drainage basin, their population concentration was far greater in areas where there was water. Therefore, it was not unusual for large groups of Indians, such as those encountered by Peter Skene Ogden and Joseph Walker, to congregate along the banks of the Humboldt River or other northern Great Basin streams in an attempt to catch fish to vary their meager diet. As the Great Basin is extremely arid and nearly all the lakes are alkaline, such fish as were found were very small, and only in a few streams were they large enough to be useful as food. Thus rodents and birds, with the exception of birds of prey, were important foods, while ants, ant eggs, larvae, crickets, and locusts were considered

7 Because of the large-scale use for irrigation purposes of the water of Sevier River, the chief source of Sevier Lake, the Sevier Lake bed is no longer filled with water all year round.

9

delicacies. On occasion, when the large, black "Mormon cricket" invaded the eastern portion of the Great Basin, this insect which creeps across the ground unable to fly became another important source of food.

As a whole, big game was relatively scarce in the Great Basin, and thus the Indians generally suffered from a lack of meat, especially for storage. Few animals of considerable size appear; however, again the higher mountains of the basin are an exception, bear, mountain lion, bighorn sheep, and deer being found there. Deer inhabited the rugged mountains in most parts of the Great Basin except for a few of the more southern basin ranges, while antelope lived in the valleys and foothills of the central and northern parts of this province. Although deer and antelope were commonly found, the rabbit and the rodent appeared in great numbers in the wide, flat basins and formed the preponderant animal life.

In the region to the north and west of the Great Salt Lake buffalo were found in limited numbers, and their presence helps to account for the fact that north-central Utah was one of the favorite winter quarters for the explorers of the Great Basin. Although fossil species of buffalo have been discovered in the present state of Nevada,[8] it seems difficult to believe that during the period of Caucasian exploration of the Great Basin the buffalo ranged this far to the west. The diaries and journals of the 1820's, 1830's, and 1840's kept by individuals traveling through large areas of the northern Great Basin make frequent mention of buffalo in the Bear River Valley and the region immediately adjacent to it, but say nothing about these animals in other basin areas. Thus explorers who were likely to be overtaken by winter in the western Great Basin and who did not have an appetite for the Indian diet of rodents and insects evacuated this area in the late fall in favor of the buffalo country of northern Utah. The Ogden Snake country expeditions are classic examples of the desertion of the Humboldt River area during the winter months for a region of more plentiful game. Such removal to more favorable areas accounts, in part, for the slowness of exploration of what is now western Nevada.

The buffalo were hunted for food and clothing by the Indians of the eastern Great Basin. The Utes who occupied the entire central

[8] Frank Gilbert Roe, *The North American Buffalo*, 257–82.

and western parts of Colorado and the eastern sections of Salt Lake Valley and Utah Valley lived within the buffalo country, and thus were able to take advantage of the presence of these animals. Although the Paiutes lived farther to the west, outside the buffalo range, there is evidence that bands of these Indians traveled to the area north and west of the Great Salt Lake to participate in buffalo hunts. The Utes and the Paiutes came into possession of the horse at quite an early date, undoubtedly by 1700,[9] an acquisition which gave them greater mobility and allowed them to exploit the buffalo to a greater degree. Although the Indians hunted large game such as buffalo, deer, and antelope, their weapons were primitive, primarily the bow and arrow.

Most of the Indian groups of the Great Basin used the bow and arrow for hunting rather than for war. The absence of elaborate war equipment is explained by the infrequency of battles between the tribes of the Great Basin. The Utes, however, appear to have been a warlike people, and the acquisition of the horse seems to have intensified their aggressive character.[10] There is evidence that the Utes caused Spanish traders moving northward from Santa Fe toward and into the Great Basin some difficulty during the latter part of the eighteenth century, although when Domínguez and Escalante visited these Indians in 1776, they found them to be peaceful and informative; and generally this seems to have been the experience of later visitors to the Utah Lake–Great Salt Lake region.

It is difficult to make generalizations regarding Great Basin Indians since marginal portions of the basin are strongly stamped with traits of the Indians of neighboring areas. The Wyoming Shoshonis are a Plains people, and even the eastern Idaho Shoshonis and Utah Utes possess such Plains characteristics as horse travel, the tipi, the travois, and interest in warfare. The Northern Paiutes of eastern California and western Nevada resemble the California tribes in many positive traits, while some of the Southern Paiutes and Utes possess some horticulture which relates them to certain southwestern tribes. Only the Shoshonis of central Nevada had no direct contact with neighbor-

[9] Frank Gilbert Roe, *The Indian and the Horse*, 79.

[10] Frederick Webb Hodge, *Handbook of American Indians North of Mexico*, II, 874–75.

ing areas and consequently had a culture little affected by influences outside of the Great Basin.[11]

As a whole, the Paiutes and the Shoshonis who ranged over a large portion of the Great Basin were more reticent and timid than the Utes. Although the "daring and bold" Indians whom Ogden encountered at the Humboldt Sink in the late spring of 1829 were probably Paiutes, their ranks were undoubtedly strengthened and encouraged by members of the more warlike Bannock tribe of southern Idaho, who visited northern Nevada often and on many occasions intermarried with the Paiutes. On the whole, however, the Indians of the Great Basin may be considered a peaceful lot and not a deterrent to exploration.

Speaking positively, the Indians of the Great Basin were of assistance to the explorers of the region, for they provided two services: first, the trails that the Indians had blazed could be followed by Caucasians; and, second, in some areas the Indians could be prevailed upon to act as guides. In the Sierra region there were a number of trails, many of them worn several feet deep through long use prior to Caucasian entry. Other trails were not as easily distinguishable and were marked by various means. According to several authorities,[12] the Miwoks[13] sometimes marked an obscure trail by throwing sticks on the ground, and in the treeless high Sierra it is alleged that they marked the trail over rocks with pine needles. It is even purported to be true that the Miwoks would hang a dead skunk along a difficult trail so that the scent could guide the traveler.

Although there seems to have been little intercourse between the Indians of the Great Basin and the Indians of the Pacific Slope, some did exist. In the central region the Washos who ranged about Lake Tahoe and the present towns of Carson City, Reno, and Minden, Nevada, traded with the California foothill tribes, especially since the orientation of this group was to the west after they had been

[11] Julian H. Steward, "Culture Element Distributions: XIII. Nevada Shoshoni," *Anthropological Records,* Vol. IV, No. 2, p. 216.

[12] S. A. Barrett, "The Washo Indians," *Publications* of the Museum of the City of Milwaukee, *Bulletin 2,* No. 1 (1910); Stephen Powers, *Tribes of California.*

[13] The Miwoks occupied the territory that was bounded on the north by the Cosumnes River, on the east by the Sierra Nevada Mountains, on the south by Fresno Creek, and on the west by the San Joaquin River. Hodge, *Handbook of American Indians,* II, 913.

driven from the valleys farther to the east by the Paiutes, with whom a chronic state of ill-feeling existed. The Washos traded with the Maidus, living at the head of the south fork of the American River, raw obsidian, pine nuts which were found on the basin ranges and formed an important part of the Washo diet, and rabbit skins, while the latter gave papam bulbs and skins in exchange.[14] The Miwoks also supplied the Washos with acorns, as well as with shell beads and redbud bark for weft and sewing material important to the geometric designs in Washo baskets. This trade seems to have taken place during all seasons, for when Frémont crossed the summit of the Sierra in the vicinity of the south fork of the American River in the winter of 1844, he observed several Washos crossing to the west.

The Paiutes, too, took part in this trade, acquiring acorns, clamshell beads, blankets, arrows, and various types of berries from these foothill and mountain people, and in return gave raw obsidian, salt, arrows, fish spears, rabbit-skin blankets, and pine nuts. The Paiutes, the eastern neighbors of the Washos, constitute one of the most important tribes of Indians inhabiting the Great Basin and occupied at the time of Caucasian penetration a large area in what is now western Nevada, southwestern Idaho, southeastern Oregon, and eastern California. Paiute bands roamed an area from Malheur Lake in the north to Owens Lake in the south, with the exception of the small area occupied by the Washos, and moved out into the basin as far east as present Battle Mountain and Austin, Nevada.

Although the western boundary of Paiute territory was the Sierra Nevada, the Paiutes traveled over the mountains to visit the Miwoks and the Western Monos, with whom they traded and intermarried. Intermarriage with the Maidus also occurred, especially when bands of Paiutes wintered in the Yosemite region in the years when there was a scarcity of pine nuts on the Nevada ranges. Trade was not one-sided; there is evidence that people crossed from both sides of the mountains, generally making hurried trips.

Through the trade and cultural relations of the Washos and the Paiutes with the coastal tribes, most of the important passes over the Sierra Nevada Mountains were discovered before the appearance of the white man. Miss Sample points out that the natural passes such as Beckwourth, Donner, Carson, Ebbetts, Sonora, and Walker were

[14] Laetitia Sample, "Trade and Trails in Aboriginal California," University of California *Archaeological Survey Report No. 8,* map opposite p. 23.

no doubt known to the Indians and used by them.[15] The only significant pass over the Sierra Nevada Mountains south of Beckwourth Pass[16] that was not used by the Indians was Tioga Pass.[17]

Although Tioga Pass was not used by the Indians, it has become popular in recent years, being utilized greatly today by tourists following U. S. Highway 120 into the eastern portions of Yosemite National Park. The Indians visited what is now the modern park area on many occasions but developed other trails as alternatives to the Tioga Pass route. Tributary trails ran through Walker Canyon, into Bloody Canyon, and over Mono Pass to the Tuolumne River and Meadows. One branch followed the modern Sunrise Trail over Cathedral Pass to Little Yosemite, which was a favorite Paiute summer hunting camp. From the modern Bishop, California, area, a Sierra trail proceeded up Bishop Creek and over Paiute Pass to the south fork of the San Joaquin River and down to Western Mono territory, while from the site of present Big Pine, California, a trail utilized Taboose Pass to reach the south fork of Kings River and the San Joaquin Valley.

Farther to the south, the Mojave Indians, who were perhaps the greatest travelers in California, had also established a trail across the Sierra to the coast. These Indians, who inhabited what is now the Mojave Desert region of California and the adjacent arid area in western Arizona, developed an active trade between the coastal Indians of Southern California and the Pueblo Indians of the Southwest. Father Garcés, traveling in the Mojave Desert region in 1776, mentions that Mojave Indians were willing to guide him across the desert by way of their trade route to the coast. While following this Mojave trail, Garcés met two groups of Mojave Indians returning from the west with shells, and was amazed to find they were making the trip without provisions or weapons to hunt. Garcés was informed by the Indians that without burdens of this kind, they could cross the desert in four days. The Mojave Trail was utilized by Jedediah Smith in his treks to California in 1826 and 1827 and became the most im-

15 *Ibid.*

16 Beckwourth Pass is located about thirty-five miles to the north and west of Reno, Nevada.

17 Julian H. Steward, "Ethnography of the Owens Valley Paiute," University of California *Publications in American Archaeology and Ethnology,* 329.

portant route through the southern Great Basin in the guise of the Old Spanish Trail.

Although the discovery and use of these mountain-pass trails by the Indians facilitated exploration, they did so to a lesser degree than would appear at first examination, for exploration of the Great Basin came generally from two directions, the north and the south, this orientation being determined by the adjacent pattern of settlement. The first Caucasian penetrations of the Great Basin came from the south and were made by individuals ranging out from the Spanish settlements of Santa Fe and Tucson, while the northern incursions were made by British trappers representing the North-West and Hudson's Bay fur companies of the Columbia drainage basin. Although the Spaniards had established themselves immediately to the west of the Great Basin as early as 1769, their California settlements were confined to the coastal region, and thus they did not utilize the Indian knowledge of the Sierra or attempt to penetrate the Great Basin from this direction. It was not until 1827 when Jedediah Smith crossed the Sierra Nevada Mountains from west to east, and, more particularly, when Captain Walker entered California from the east by surmounting the Sierra, that Caucasian east-west travel between the Great Basin and California began. This travel, which came to be monopolized by Americans, had a profound effect upon political developments in Mexican California in the next decade.

As a whole, trails were not as numerous in the northern and eastern sections of the Great Basin as they were in the Sierra Nevada region; however, a number of trails were developed by the Owens Valley Paiutes, who traveled from their homes around Owens Lake into the pine-nut country to the east. Farther to the east lived the Shoshonis, who inhabited the country in eastern Nevada and western Utah. They ranged as far west as Reese River Valley and Battle Mountain and probably as far south as Spring Valley in southern White Pine County, and Hot Creek, Belmont, Tybo, and Big Smoky, all of which are in the present state of Nevada. The Shoshonis of central Nevada, with few exceptions, had no direct contact with neighboring tribes, and thus there was not a network of trails from the eastern Great Basin to the western portion. However, the Shoshonis did develop trails within their own territory, especially in the Ruby and Reese River Valley section leading northward to the Humboldt River. The region north of the Humboldt River was not generally inhabited by the Paiutes or the Shoshonis in the winter, for frequently at this time of the year the thermometer would drop to thirty or forty degrees below zero. Even today many of the lowest winter temperatures recorded in the nation are reported from this region. In the summer the Northern Paiutes and Shoshonis were numerous in this area. Peter Skene Ogden mentions in his 1828–29 Snake Country Journal the prevalence of Indians and the abundance of trails in what is now northern Nevada. Undoubtedly, some of the trails encountered by Ogden between the Snake River drainage and the Humboldt region were blazed by Bannocks or Snakes who on occasion crossed over this northern rim of the Great Basin.

Although it is a generally accepted fact that there was little intercourse between the Shoshonis and the Utes of the eastern Great Basin and thus there was no well-established trail between their territories, Indian trails between water holes and creek beds did exist in this area. In most cases, these Indian tracks were numerous and confusing, and, therefore, trappers making the journey from the headwaters of the Humboldt River to the Great Salt Lake had to depend upon Indian guides or upon Indian information to find their way through this portion of the Great Basin.

The Indians of the Great Basin, as a whole, did not think in terms of maps, but they could often draw a map when asked for directions.[18] There are frequent mentions in the Frémont journal of getting cartographic information from Indians, and it seems that Frémont utilized this source more than any other Great Basin explorer.[19] In 1844, when Frémont was encamped at Pyramid Lake in what is now northern Nevada, the Northern Paiutes must have supplied the party with cartographic information, for Frémont writes: "They made on the ground a drawing of the [Truckee] river which they represented as issuing from another lake [Tahoe] in the mountains three or four days distant, in a direction a little west of south; beyond which, they drew a mountain [Sierra Nevada]; and further still, two rivers [Sacramento and/or Feather or American or San Joaquin] on which they told us that people like ourselves travelled."[20]

Although the Indians of the land of interior drainage were gen-

18 Robert F. Heizer, "Aboriginal California and Great Basin Cartography," University of California *Archaeological Survey Report No. 41.*

19 Frémont, *Report,* 206.

20 *Ibid.,* 219.

erally peaceful and were of some material aid to Caucasian exploration, the Great Basin's rather inhospitable environment delayed movement into the region. But it was not completely neglected in exploration, and its history displays great continuity if one considers the major trends in the development of North America. It was here in the land of interior drainage, paradoxical as it may seem, that the search for the mythical took place; it was here that one of the most significant chapters in the annals of the North American fur trade was written; and it was here that the Mormons said "three Hosannahs and a Hail Mary" and settled down to develop an oasis out of the parched earth.

2

WATER PASSAGE, FURS,
AND A LEGION OF LEGENDS

THE FASCINATION AND ATTRACTION OF THE ORIENT impelled much of
the pioneer exploration of the New World, particularly of North
America, which stood as a barrier between Europe and Asia. From
the time of discovery to the middle of the nineteenth century the
search was for a practical route through the American continent to
serve the needs of commerce. Spain led off with the first westward
crossings, and was stimulated in her efforts by the reports of legendary
lands of wealth—other Mexicos and Perus—waiting to be con-
quered. But it was the English, French, and later the Americans who
moved into the heart of the continent, beaver skins paying their way.
Thus the water passage, the fur trade, and the legends of lands of
wealth which were largely responsible for the unveiling of the North
American continent were also very important in the history of the
Great Basin, for these three motivating forces, either singly or combined, prompted the exploration of the basin of interior drainage.

With the Columbus voyages, a new continent was revealed, and
man quickly attempted to discover the secrets of this new land.
Equipped both with theory based upon limited information and
with myth, the result of two milleniums of romance and fairy tales,
explorers made incursions into the surrounding territories. With the
realization that the East Indies had not been reached, the quest for
a water route to China began, and occupied men's resources and
energies for almost four centuries. Although many of the names and
situations that are inextricably involved in the search for a "waterway
to Cathay" are, no doubt, familiar to the reader, little seems to have
been done in synthesizing the results of these explorations, and even
less seems to have been accomplished in developing perspective on

18

this significant search that permeated the history of almost every area in the Western Hemisphere.

The Cabots, sailing for Henry VII in 1497 and 1498, coasted the east side of Greenland, passed on to Labrador and south to Delaware via Newfoundland and Nova Scotia. Although they made known a large extent of the northeastern coast, it was Spain who led off with the first westward crossing. In 1513, Balboa standing "silent, upon a peak in Darien," first viewed the *Mar del Sur* and aroused Spain to renew her efforts to find a water route to India. His discovery was an important factor in leading to Magellan's voyage, greatest of the voyages of discovery in the sixteenth century.

As adventurers converged upon the new continent and gradually penetrated its façade, geographers and cosmographers were busily engaged in incorporating this new discovery into geographical knowledge. Realization of the existence of the Strait of Magellan, which was known to separate the main continent of America from land to the south, seems to have been the principal basis for the belief that a corresponding passage existed to the north of America. This belief manifested itself in a number of ways, as is illustrated in the works of several leading contemporary geographers. Gemma Phrysius conceived the New World to be a series of islands and terra firma separated from northeast Asia by a strait which led to the South Sea,[1] whereas Franciscus Monachus presented another view, soon adopted by such notables as Orontius Finaeus, Vopellius, Ruscelli, and Moletus. He portrayed the New World as a great peninsular extension of Asia partly separated from it by Ptolemy's Sinus Magnus.

In 1569, Mercator advanced his view of the Western Hemisphere, which seemed to be one of the most accurate and achieved the greatest vogue. His conception, concurred in by Ortelius, depicted America as a great continent having open water to the north and separated from Asia by the Strait of Anían in the extreme west.[2]

This first concrete conception of the strait that manifested itself in the form of Anían and was to figure heavily in the annals of explora-

[1] The influence of Gemma's views as expressed on his globe map were given even wider circulation by their adoption by Sebastian Munster for the world map in the Basel Ptolemy of 1540.

[2] The Mercator map of 1569 is reproduced by Justin Winsor in *Narrative and Critical History of America*, II, 452. Also see E. G. R. Taylor, *Late Tudor and Early Stuart Geography*.

tion of North America has a curious history. The first mention of the Strait of Anían appeared in Gastaldi's *La Universale Discrittione del Mundo,* published in 1562.[3] Although this book disappeared from the Royal Library in Turin, we have a few extracts from Gastaldi that were reproduced in Stefano Grande's *Notizie Sulla Vita e Opere di Giacomo Gastaldi* (1902) to the effect that "Asia has its boundary toward the east the Strait called Anían . . . ."[4]

Bolognino Zaltieri seems to have been acquainted with the Gastaldi view, for in 1566 he published in Venice his *Il Disegno del Discaperto della Noua Franza.* Here he produced the first known map showing the strait between America and Asia as the "Streto di Anían."[5] Although the Strait of Anían was a sixteenth-century creation, the origin of the name dates back much farther, for it seems to step from the pages of Marco Polo where he discusses the Chinese Province of Anía.

Another strait was imagined on the northeast coast of America and was called Baccalaos. The name seems to have originated with the voyage of João Vaz Corte-Real, who with two Danish seamen, Pining and Pothhorst, sailed under the command of King Afonso in 1473. The actual course of the group is still unknown, but it is believed that they visited either Newfoundland, Labrador, or Greenland, to which they applied the name *Terra Noua dos Bacalhaus* or New Land of Codfish.[6] However, by 1576, when there was more information regarding this region, the name Baccalaos was still retained, but it was disassociated from Greenland proper and applied to a gulf to the south and west of Cape Farewell in 60 degrees north latitude and a coast running to the west in 67 degrees latitude.

With these two straits now existing in geographical thought, the argument developed for a northwest passage by a strait which had its mouth in 67–68 degrees north latitude at Baccalaos and its opposite

[3] The 1548 edition of Ptolemy's *Geography* was made by Giacomo Gastaldi and included for the first time a series of plates of the New World. Boies Penrose, *Travel and Discovery in the Renaissance,* 259–60.

[4] Henry Raup Wagner, "Some Imaginary California Geography," *Proceedings of the American Antiquarian Society,* XLI, 15.

[5] The Zaltieri map of 1566 is reproduced in Winsor, *Narrative and Critical History of America,* II, 451, and in George Parker Winship (ed.), *The Journey of Coronado, 1540–1542,* 368–69.

[6] H. P. Biggar (ed.), *The Voyages of the Cabots and of the Corte-Reals to North America and Greenland, 1497–1503.*

end near the Sierra Nevada, the area of the Strait of Anían. This conception was widely disseminated by the prominent English intellectual, John Dee, who had been a student of the five greatest geographical contemporaries: Pedro Núñez, Gemma Phrysius, Gerard Mercator, Abraham Ortelius, and Orontius Finaeus. Dee numbered among his students such famous explorers as Richard Chancellor, Stephen Borough, Martin Frobisher, Henry Gilbert, John Davis, Walter Raleigh, Richard Willes, and, it seems most likely, Francis Drake. In their geographical conceptions and reports is seen the influence of their instructor as well as the philosophies of Dee's able teachers.

The attention of England was largely turned to the theory of a northwest passage through the efforts of Sir Humphrey Gilbert, half-brother of Sir Walter Raleigh. In a treatise, *Discourse of a Discoverie for a New Passage to Cataia,* which he wrote in 1566 and circulated in manuscript form for almost a decade before it was published in 1576, Gilbert focused interest on a broad western passage between 62 and 72 degrees north latitude. English interest in the New World was again stimulated by several books appearing toward the close of the sixteenth century which discussed the records of British exploratory achievements and posited the existence of such a passage. These were Richard Hakluyt's volumes, *Voyages* and *Principal Navigations.* Two decades later Samuel Purchas published *Purchas His Pilgrimage,* a compilation of over seven hundred accounts of voyages and expeditions, that was to give added impetus to the existing passage theory.

As the exploration of North America continued and the various expeditions failed to discover the much desired "waterway to Cathay," the strait theory began to lose prestige in some quarters. However, the idea of a water passage to the East was not dispelled though it was changed in form. Now, instead of a broad water passage to the north of the continent, a river was envisioned that would traverse this great area. This view is quite interestingly shown in the note given to the Jamestown colonists in 1607 advising them to settle on a navigable river, "that which bendeth most towards the N.W., for that way you shall soonest find the other sea."[7]

This general belief that a river on the Atlantic Coast might per-

[7] From MS instructions for the voyage to Virginia, "Instructions by way of Advice," as quoted in Taylor, *Late Tudor and Early Stuart Geography,* 158.

21

haps lead to the Pacific Coast or that it would aid in reaching the other sea was widespread. Although by this time the coasts of both oceans had been explored to fairly high latitudes, little or no penetration had been made into the continent from either the east, west, or north; therefore, the exact width of the continent was still undetermined. In 1523, when the Florentine, Giovanni de Verrazano, sailed along the coast of the New World, he touched the Hatteras Sand Spit, prompting him to report that only a narrow neck of land separated the two oceans. The Verrazano conception seems to have met with little acceptance, for most of the sixteenth-century maps show America as a large continental land mass increasing its diameter considerably about 40 degrees north latitude.[8] However, the problem of the width of America was to confound explorers for centuries. Those who had some comprehension of the extent of this new terra firma were inclined to agree with the instructions given to the Virginia colonists. They pointed to the hydrography of Russia, showing that the sources of many of that country's rivers were in the interior of the continent close to each other, as is evidenced by the Volga River's emptying into the Caspian Sea while the Dvina deposits its waters to the north of the continent in the White Sea.

Thus the transformation of the "waterway to Cathay" continued from a strait to a river to several rivers, but the location of this elusive passage retreated before the approaching explorers. The last stage of this evolution is the trans-Rocky Mountain water passage envisioned by many cartographers of the eighteenth and early nineteenth centuries as a series of rivers with interlocking headwaters.[9] With the appearance of many fanciful streams on contemporary maps, expeditions were led into the last great unexplored area on the North American continent south of Arctic latitudes. Here in the Great Basin, the San Buenaventura, the most persistent of the mythical

[8] Examples of these are Ortelius' *Theatrum Orbis Terrarum* (1570), Mercator's *Western Hemisphere* (1587), and De Bry's *America Sive Nova Orbis* (1596).

[9] A few of the most representative maps showing the fictitious rivers are: John Melish, *Map of the United States with the Contiguous British and Spanish Possessions* (Philadelphia, 1816, 1820); John H. Robinson, *A Map of Mexico, and Louisiana, and the Missouri Territory* . . . (Philadelphia, 1819); James Wyld, *A Map of North America from 20 to 80 Degrees North Latitude* (London, 1823); and A. Finley, *Map of North America including All the Recent Geographical Discoveries* (Philadelphia, 1826).

rivers, wrote the last chapter to the fascinating history of the quest for the "waterway to Cathay." A paradoxical motivating force, indeed, for this was the land of interior drainage with no outlet to the sea!

It is a strange but undeniable fact that the mythical, the exotic, and the fabulous produce greater enthusiasm and interest than the realistic and the known. That this is so has already been illustrated in the search for a water passage, but the innate tendency soars to even greater heights in the quest of these legends or myths. Some were distinct forms in themselves; others were essentially alike, varying slightly from place to place and undergoing minor changes as they proceeded down through the centuries. These legends were prime motivating forces in the discovery of America and even persisted for four centuries after that eventful day, performing the service of unveiling the new continent and adding a new dimension to human knowledge.

One of the best-known myths, and thus one that prompted perhaps the most extensive exploration, was that of the Seven Cities. On late medieval maps, the Seven Cities are frequently placed upon the island of Antilia, as exemplified by the map of Graciosus Benincasa produced in 1482. He placed the island of Antilia about as far west of the Madeiras as those islands are distant from Spain.[10] Then when Marco Polo's book eventually won recognition as a valid description of the Far East, his account of Cipango or Japan was sometimes applied to the legendary Antilia, and the two tended to become almost synonymous in the geography of the Renaissance.[11]

With the discovery of America by Columbus and the subjugation of the Aztec civilization by Cortés, a new continent was waiting to be explored. The mythical Seven Cities firmly implanted themselves to the north of the Spaniards and thus motivated exploration in this direction from New Spain. Herbert E. Bolton says that Nuño de Guzmán was told of the Seven Cities by an Indian slave.[12] Carl Sauer more or less supports this story, presenting only a minor variation to the effect that Guzmán learned of the cities through an Indian whose father traded in the back country.[13] Nevertheless, the reactivation of

[10] E. G. Bourne, *Spain in America*, 6.
[11] J. A. Williamson, *The Ocean in English History*, 7.
[12] *The Spanish Borderlands*, 80.
[13] *The Road to Cibola*, 9.

23

this myth sent Diego de Guzmán north in 1533, and, although the desired end was not achieved, geographical knowledge was extended six hundred miles beyond the exploration of Cortés.

With the Narváez–Cabeza de Vaca expedition, fact was elaborated into fiction, and interest was stimulated in northern New Spain both in America and in Spain itself. After an eight-year Odyssey which resulted in the crossing of Texas, Coahuila, Chihuahua, and Sonora, Álvar Núñez Cabeza de Vaca arrived in 1536 in Culiacán, the northern outpost of New Spain. His reports of hearing of large cities to the north of his path reinforced the Seven Cities conception, and, consequently, in March of 1539, Father Marcos de Niza was sent out to reconnoiter. After reaching the border of the Zuñi pueblos in western New Mexico, Friar Marcos reported that the Seven Cities of Cíbola were larger and finer than Mexico.[14]

While the De Soto expedition was conducting its search for Cíbola from the east, Francisco Vásquez Coronado, the governor of Nueva Galicia, was setting out from Compostela. In order to discover Cíbola as well as the waterway through the continent, Alarcón was sent up the coast from Acapulco to co-operate with Coronado. Coronado pressed northward and finally came to Cíbola, the first of the Zuñi villages to be reached. Castañeda, the historian of the Coronado expedition, said: "When they saw the first village which was Cíbola, such were the curses that some hurled at Friar Marcos that I pray God may protect him from them. It is a little, crowded village, looking as if it had been crumpled all up together."[15]

Coronado's disappointment was soon converted into anticipation as the will-o'-the-wisp now disguised itself in the form of Gran Quivira, and Coronado in April, 1541, set out from Tiguex to find it. After crossing the mountains and traversing the area between the Grand Canyon of the Colorado and Kansas, he reached Quivira in eastern Kansas, probably a settlement of Wichita Indians. The land of Golden Quivira with its solid gold dishes and tinkling bells had

14 The Seven Cities of Cíbola supposedly merge from the union of an Indian folk tale of seven caves with the old geographical myth of the Seven Cities. However, the word "Cíbola," which is believed to be a Spanish form of the word "Shirvina," by which name the Zuñis referred to their tribal range, was not known to the Spaniards until Estevanico sent back his report to Father Marcos.

15 See Castañeda's narrative in *The Journey of Coronado, 1540–1542* (ed. by Winship), 23; also Herbert E. Bolton, *Coronado on the Turquoise Trail*, 118.

not been found. But the ill success of the Coronado expedition in its search for riches did not deter cartographers. Quivira was made an established point on contemporary maps. Although its position might vary from Kansas to California or appear in the southern part of the Great Basin, depending upon the whim of the cartographer, it remained on the maps and soon pushed the results of the Coronado expedition into virtual oblivion.

Rumors persisted of wealthy Indians living in great houses to the north whose civilization was in marked contrast to that of the Indians living in northern Mexico. The Spaniards thought that these reports undoubtedly described another Mexico or Peru, and, therefore, the rediscovery of New Mexico and adjacent regions began in 1580. Impetus was given to these beliefs when Antonio de Espejo returned in 1582 and elaborated on the great number and wealth of the people to the north. His report prompted the crown to authorize the settlement of New Mexico, and Juan de Oñate, of Zacatecas, was chosen to lead this colonizing expedition. He set out in 1598, crossed the Río Grande at the site of modern El Paso, Texas, and proceeded up that river.

The search for Quivira[16] again came to the fore when Jusepe, one of Oñate's guides, informed his leader of this fabulously wealthy country. In the summer of 1601, Oñate set out in quest of Quivira, as Coronado had done sixty years before. The results of the expedition were approximately the same: when Oñate reached the great bend of the Arkansas where it is joined by the Walnut River, he too, found a large population but one that was lacking in material wealth.

Interest now lagged in the northern portions of New Spain, and New Mexico became one of the most isolated Spanish colonies in North America. Although this area was remote from Mexico, its inhabitants continued to dream of riches long after the dissipation of the Quivira myth. Now a blue mountain made of silver was envisioned somewhere west of the Zuñi and Hopi villages in what is now New Mexico, Arizona, and southern Utah. The first reports of this topographical phenomenon occur in vague form in the early seventeenth century, but we first hear of Sierra Azul, as such, during the time of Peñalosa, when he conducted his fictitious expedition to

---

[16] George P. Hammond, "The Search for the Fabulous in the Settlement of the Southwest," *Utah Historical Quarterly*, Vol. XXIV (Jan., 1956); George P. Hammond and Agapito Rey, *Don Juan de Oñate, Colonizer of New Mexico.*

Gran Quivira in 1622. Sierra Azul was thought to be another Zacatecas or Potosí and Huancavelica combined. Perhaps it was considered to be even richer than the latter two, for there were reports that in the province of Moqui pure quicksilver was to be found in liquid form in the hollow of a certain rock or cave. It was reputed to drip down into a pool from the surrounding rocks, which were all of this same metallic substance.[17] These reports of quicksilver mines contiguous to Sierra Azul excited the most interest, particularly on the part of the crown, for a cheap source of quicksilver for working the mines of New Spain was greatly in demand at the moment.

In 1680, when the Pueblo Revolt occurred in New Mexico, the legend of Sierra Azul took on new significance. This insurrection forced the withdrawal of the Spaniards from northern New Mexico and left that area on a rather indefinite basis for the following twelve years until Diego de Vargas began the reconquest of the region. The importance of Sierra Azul in this connection lies in the part it played in hastening the pacification of the lost area. It is evident that the initiative in emphasizing the search for and verification of Sierra Azul came principally from Vargas as a means of furthering his own desire to reconquer New Mexico at an early date and to reap the reward. His interest is clearly shown in a letter he wrote to the Count of Galvé, in which he said: "I repeat, your Excellency, that I shall take the risk at any cost to find the mine, and dispose of the apprehension about these stories, all of which appear so wonderful."[18]

Others used the legend of Sierra Azul for personal motives, as is illustrated by the glowing reports by such people as Father Carlos Delgado and other missionaries who visited the Moqui villages between 1742 and 1745. These stories were primarily propaganda of the Franciscan missionaries devised to reawaken interest in this area because of their fear of being forced to surrender the Moqui villages to the Jesuits. However, after the rivalry of these two religious groups was settled in 1745, little attention was given to Moqui for the next thirty years.

Although interest in Sierra Azul now waned, a number of eight-

[17] José Manuel Espinosa, "The Legend of Sierra Azul," *New Mexico Historical Review*, Vol. IX (April, 1934), 133.

[18] Diego de Vargas to the Count of Galvé, El Paso, October 4, 1691, as quoted in Espinosa, "The Legend of Sierra Azul," *New Mexico Historical Review*, Vol. IX (April, 1934), 133.

eenth-century map makers paid homage to it. Father Kino's map of Lower California (1701) placed it in the northeastern corner of Lower California, just below the mouth of the Colorado, while Sánchez' map of 1757 and a late eighteenth-century map by Pfefferkorn placed it in the center of a range of mountains in central Arizona, not far from the southern boundary of the Great Basin. As the reader will notice, all of these maps placed Sierra Azul in the same vicinity, and in each case this mountain of silver was located in a region that was little known by contemporaries. Sierra Azul, like so many of the other mythical phenomena, had a great deal of buoyancy, for it even appears on a map as late as 1852, one that was drawn by Kiepert.

Another of the tales of riches concerned the elusive Copala and was first conceived about 1545, the date of the discovery of the Zacatecas mines. Francisco de Ibarra, nephew of the millionaire Diego de Ibarra, who made his fortune from the above mines, was commissioned to find Copala. In 1565 he explored a vast area to the north and west of Zacatecas but with little success.

In 1626 an account was written by Fray Gerónimo de Zárate Salmerón narrating a glowing story which he allegedly heard while he was a missionary among the Jémez Indians. Copala, he states was the original home of the Aztecs before their migration to the Valley of Mexico and was situated a fourteen days' journey to the westnorthwest.

Teguayo was a relatively late entrant into the myriad of legends and became entwined with Copala. It was first reported about the middle of the seventeenth century through the machinations of the rascally Peñalosa, former governor of New Mexico who had deserted to France. In 1678, Peñalosa proposed to the king of France that he lead a military expedition to conquer Quivira and Teguayo. In this proposition he appears to make the first usage of the word *teguayo,* which land he pictured lying east of the Rocky Mountains and which he claimed to have visited when he was governor in 1662. Interest in Teguayo led to the famous report of 1686 of Fray Alonso de Posadas, who had been a missionary in New Mexico for many years, that Teguayo was the same as Copala and lay beyond the lands of the Utahs. Thus Father Posadas implied that Copala-Teguayo lay in what is now known as the northern Great Basin. Although Father Posadas did not repeat the usual stories of the lake's being surrounded by cities rich in precious metals, whose inhabitants wore bracelets of gold, he urged the exploration of this area. In 1776 the Domínguez-Escalante party gave the Copala-Teguayo myths their final resting place—the Great Salt Lake deep within the Great Basin.

While the lands of legendary riches were of particular delight to the romantic Spanish mind, the French and British were searching for wealth in the form of the fur pelt. The American fur trade began with the first explorations of the North Atlantic Coast, but this early fur trade was primarily concerned with the entire pelt, which was valued for its beauty, luster, and warmth. This form of the fur trade was practiced in the first half of the sixteenth century and was of minor importance.

The interior exploration of North America began about the time Europe was seeking new materials for clothing, and thus fur took on a new significance. With the discovery of the many uses for the beaver pelt, the fur trade underwent a metamorphosis and became an important force in motivating exploration. The fur of the beaver may be divided into two categories: the guard hair, which is about two inches in length, and the underhair or fur, which measures about one inch. Examined under a microscope, this underhair contains numerous small barbs, and it was these barbs that made it especially suitable for the manufacture of felt and, more particularly, felt hats. Because the beaver is not a highly reproductive creature and is not a migrant, extermination of the animal in a given locality made it necessary for hunters to move into new areas, and thus explorers and trappers in their quest of beaver pelts penetrated into the heart of North America.

France, which had done little in regard to exploration in the New World in the fifteenth and sixteenth centuries, was led into the St. Lawrence basin by intrepid pioneers and fur trappers in the wake of their countryman, Jacques Cartier. From here the French pushed their frontier to the Great Lakes and spread their domain between the English on the Atlantic Coast and the Spaniards in the Southwest. One of the greatest names in the story of French empire building is that of Samuel de Champlain, who took an active part in the exploring of the lower course of the St. Lawrence and the Lake Nipissing and the Georgian Bay areas, and was the first white man to blaze the fur trader's trail into the interior. When Champlain heard of a great waterway to the west, he believed it to be the route to China, and sent Nicollet to make an investigation, which resulted in the exploration of the south shore of the Upper Peninsula of Michigan and the southern extremity of Green Bay. Although we do not have a complete record of the activities of Radisson and Groseilliers, we do know that a large extent of land at the western end of Lake Superior was added to French geographical knowledge by these two trappers.

The quest of a waterway to the west was still important, as evidenced by the fact that Champlain sent Nicollet to investigate. Such a river, had it existed, would have been of primary economic significance to the fur trade since it would have facilitated the sending of the fur pelts directly from the New World to the great fur mart in Canton, China.

In 1673 the religious element entered the field of exploration in the persons of Fathers Louis Jolliet and Jacques Marquette. In that year they reached Green Bay, followed the Fox and Wisconsin rivers to the Mississippi, and discovered the mouth of the Missouri River, which was to be the great highway to the West in the nineteenth century. The priests were astounded at the rapid flow of the water, and Father Marquette remarked: "There are many villages of savages along this river, and I hope by its means to discover the vermilion or California Sea."[19] Thus the fur trade and the search for the waterway drew the French inland, whether they were secular or clerical.

As the French were groping their way along the extensive water network of North America, the English were following their northern orientation into the high latitudes of 50 to 60 degrees. In 1668 two vessels, under command of Prince Rupert, cousin of Charles II, sailed from England to Hudson Bay, and their voyage led to the formation of the Hudson's Bay Company in 1670. The French now had competition in their quest for furs as well as in their quest of the water passage, as the charter which organized the company clearly shows: "Whereas our dear entirely beloved Cousin, Prince Rupert . . . , have at their own great cost, and charges, undertaken an expedition for Hudson's Bay in the north-west part of America, for the discovery of a new passage into the South Sea, and for the finding some trade for furs, minerals, and other considerable commodities . . . ."[20]

Although the Hudson's Bay Company, by the terms of its charter,

19 *Jesuit Relations and Allied Documents* (ed. by Edna Kenton), 357.
20 Beckles Willson, *The Great Company*, 515.

was obligated to take part in the search for a passage, it evinced little interest in this phenomenon when the search for furs became its most absorbing concern. In order to placate public opinion, however, several ships were sent to plod along the western shore of Hudson Bay, an area thought by some to contain the elusive passage because reports of the Button expedition, based on observations of the tide, had suggested the existence of a connection with the Pacific Ocean near the mouth of the Churchill River.[21] The prevailing attitude toward the company is clearly shown in a letter written by Charles Wager to Arthur Dobbs on March 4, 1737, in which he states:

> I believe you judge very right, that the Hudson's Bay Company do not desire to have any body to interfere with them in the Fur Trade in those Parts. They seem to be content with what they have, and make, I believe, more considerable Profit by it, than if it was further extended, which might be the case if a further Discovery was made; For, tho' they should not find a navigable passage thro' into the South, they might probably find Indian Nations from whom Furs might be bought cheaper than they can be bought in Hudson's Bay, which would be a Disadvantage to their Trade.[22]

Perhaps much of the criticism which arose over the Hudson's Bay Company's supposed neglect of its stipulated obligations was engendered by its prosperity, a condition which often incites envy. A number of Parliamentary sessions were devoted, in part, to this subject during the middle of the eighteenth century. In March of 1749 a Parliamentary committee was appointed "to enquire into the right of the Hudson's Bay Company to an exclusive trade, etc. in that bay."[23] In November of 1754 one of the objects which was considered worthy of Parliamentary interposition was the case of the Hudson's Bay Company.[24]

The concern shown in regard to the Hudson's Bay Company's carrying out the terms of its contract, especially the provision relating to the discovery of a water route to the Orient through North America, is indicative of the growing British desire for this coveted

21 Edward Heawood, *A History of Geographical Discovery in the Seventeenth and Eighteenth Centuries,* 30.
22 *Gentleman's Magazine,* Feb., 1744, p. 83.
23 *Ibid.,* March, 1749, p. 100.
24 *Ibid.,* Nov., 1754, pp. 503–504.

passage. During this period in England, interest in the waterway was great, and attention was turned to the possibility of a northwest passage particularly through the works of Arthur Dobbs, Daines Barrington, and the Royal Society. To give financial encouragement to this project, the act of 1745, which had provided for a reward of £ 20,000 to any British ship, barring naval vessels, which might pass from the Atlantic to the Pacific through Hudson Bay, was amended to include ships of the Royal Navy and substituted for Hudson Bay any region north of 52 degrees.

Perhaps this discussion seems very remote from the Great Basin, but such is not the case. The search for the "waterway to Cathay," the trapping of furs, and the quest of the legendary lands of riches almost purely economic forces, played significant roles in the discovery and exploration of the Great Basin. It was these motives, either singly or combined, that prompted the exploration of this land of interior drainage.

Spain, who was the first to colonize on the North American continent, was likewise the first to start exploring this new land. She had subdued the high culture areas of the Azetcs and Incas and was interested in discovering another Mexico or Peru; therefore, the stories of the mythical lands of riches were especially intriguing to the Spaniards. The legends of Cíbola, Quivira, Sierra Azul, Copala, and Teguayo, as well as others, secured for the Spanish crown, and later the Mexican nation, a vast extent of territory in the heart of North America, part of which lay in the Great Basin and was not relinquished until 1848.

The fur trade played a significant role in the exploration of North America, for intrepid trappers traced out the watercourses of the continent and penetrated almost every corner of north and north-western America. The Hudson's Bay Company and the North West Company dominated the scene after France suffered reverses in the Seven Years' War, ending in the Treaty of Paris in 1763. However, with the rise of the United States of America, a new group of trappers followed the river networks of the Mississippi basin, up the Missouri to the Columbia, and were quick to challenge British supremacy there. New, virgin trapping grounds were the order of the day, attracting partisans from both nations into the Great Basin, where Anglo-American rivalry continued, as exemplified by the episode which took place on the Weber River near present Mountain Green,

Utah, in 1825. Although a century and a half had passed and the places had changed from Hudson Bay, St. Lawrence, and the upper Mississippi regions to the Missouri, Columbia, Snake, and adjacent areas, and the names of Prince Rupert, Champlain, and Mackenzie had evolved into those of General Ashley, Peter Skene Ogden, and Jedediah Smith, the motivating force was still the same—the fur trade. Then, too, the same ostensible results were achieved: the economic enrichment of the parties concerned and, most important of all, the unveiling of the North American continent.

The search for the "waterway to Cathay" was an interesting phenomenon, for it engaged the resources of most of the nations of western Europe. It was not, like the search for the legendary lands, an almost purely Spanish endeavor or, like the fur trade, chiefly French and English and later American. The quest for the Strait of Anían brought into its service famous men and companies such as Francis Drake, Urdaneta, Frobisher, Henry Hudson, the Muscovy Company, and the Dutch West India Company, and was finally given substance by Vitus Bering, a Dane sailing in the service of Peter the Great. As time progressed, the strait theory was reduced to that of a river flowing through the continent and, later, to a series of rivers with interlocking headwaters. During the latter part of the eighteenth century and on to the middle of the nineteenth, the western appendage of this watercourse was sought most commonly in the form of the San Buenaventura River,[25] thought to exist in the last large unexplored area on the North American continent, the Great Basin. Finally, in 1844, Frémont came to the reluctant conclusion that the vast interior between the Wasatch and the Sierra Nevada was indeed a great basin, and so named it. The dream of a western road to Cathay, set in motion by Columbus, finally came to rest in this area when the last spike of a transcontinental railroad was driven at Promontory Point, Utah, in 1869.

[25] C. Gregory Crampton and Gloria G. Griffen (Cline), "The San Buenaventura, Mythical River of the West," *Pacific Historical Review*, Vol. XXV (May, 1956), 163–71.

3

THE FIRST ENTRANTS

THE SEARCH FOR THE WATER PASSAGE, for furs, and for the lands of legendary wealth was important in prompting exploration of North America; it was also an indirect motivating force for a second Spanish advance northward. With the converging of the various European nations upon this continent of the Western Hemisphere, Spain, who had not moved northward because the material inducement was not sufficient for her to battle the troublesome Apaches and Comanches, now realized that she must protect her territories, and this incentive aroused her from her lethargy.

The threat of foreign encroachment was keenly felt by the Spaniards. There is abundant evidence that an advance as far as the Colorado and Gila rivers was officially planned for at least three-quarters of a century before the Anza expedition of 1774. The Council of the Indies, after quoting the correspondence leading to the decree of December 4, 1747, and citing two royal decrees of August 19, 1606, with regard to making a settlement at Monterey, pointed out the dangers that would result from a French advance to that port by way of the Colorado and Carmelo rivers.[1] They believed that the French would then dominate the Pacific and threaten Spanish trade with the Philippines as well as curtail Spanish activities on the lower Colorado.

Northward expansion from New Spain may be said to have followed three principal lines: northwestward to Sonora and the Californias; up the central plateau through Nueva Vizcaya to New

---

[1] Father Sedelmayr had said that Indians had told him that the Colorado River flowed to the west, a little north of where he had traveled, which led to the conjecture that there might be a branch of the Colorado emptying into the Pacific, possibly the Carmelo.

33

Mexico; and up the central plateau but branching off to run through Coahuila into Texas. The northern advance up these corridors had been checked by the continual Indian wars. The Apaches had begun their raids into Sonora before the close of the seventeenth century; the Pimas in Pimería Alta were in serious revolt in 1695; the Indians of the eastern Sonoran missions as well as the Seris were in open rebellion at approximately the same time. These wars persisted particularly after the middle of the eighteenth century, when in 1751 the Seris and the Pimas revolted and gave almost continuous trouble from that time until 1771. The Apache campaigns also continued to occupy attention along the entire northern frontier from Sonora to Texas.[2]

With the establishment of order in Sonora by the *visitador,* José de Gálvez, a northward advance was made possible. During the same period, also because of Gálvez' efforts, the expulsion of the Jesuits in 1767 was consummated, engendering in the Franciscans a new zeal to make a good showing in Pimería Alta, the missionary field to which they fell heir in 1768. Thus began a renewal of the northward explorations and projects for converting the Indians of the Gila and those as far away as Moqui, which even led the followers of this mendicant order into the Great Basin and earned for them a prominent position in the realm of western exploration.

As late as 1769 the interior of Alta California was unknown. The California coast had not been charted by a recorded expedition since Vizcaíno, and the Utah and Nevada basins were untrod by white men. In this year, two land expeditions were sent up the peninsula of California and three ships were dispatched by sea. A junction was achieved at San Diego after the loss of one ship. From this point the commander-in-chief, Gaspar de Portolá, proceeded northward in search of Monterey, which he actually visited but failed to recognize from the description of the port given by González Cabrera Bueno and Vizcaíno. He then pushed on and discovered San Francisco Bay before returning to San Diego, where a mission and presidio were established.

With the erection of the mission at San Diego, other missions were quick to follow: Monterey in 1770 and San Antonio and San Gabriel in 1771. Now Spain was faced with the problem of supplying these new outposts which lay so far afield. The Indians of the region were

2 Jack D. Forbes, *Apache, Navaho, and Spaniard.*

on such a low cultural level that they had almost nothing which could serve the needs of white men. Not only were there no agricultural products capable of sustaining a white population, but also there were no domestic animals. Baja California, despite the fact that it had been established for three-quarters of a century through the efforts of the Jesuit fathers Salvatierra and Ugarte, could not supply the more northerly province since it could hardly raise enough for its own subsistence. Indeed, one of the most important factors in the preservation of the Alta California settlements was the annual visit of the supply ship from San Blas; however, this system was not satisfactory, and it became apparent that an overland route was essential if Spanish control were to continue on the California coast and Spanish domination were to endure over the Pacific Ocean.

Thus the important chord had been struck: an overland route to California in order to connect the Spanish settlements of New Mexico with those on the Pacific Coast. The search for this route through much arid country, the greater part of which was, of course, unknown, is actually the first chapter in the history of the Great Basin. For it was Fathers Garcés, Domínguez, and Escalante who found this trail on separate exploring expeditions; Garcés on the west and Domínguez and Escalante on the east, both parties, however, reaching Moqui. These friars are of particular significance because they were the first white men to penetrate the façade of the Great Basin. The results of their explorations provided a better understanding of this previously unknown region, yet they developed a great cartographical extravaganza which was to postdate them for better than half a century and to mold western exploration in a new form.

Foremost among the missionary fathers was the Franciscan Father Francisco Hermenegildo Garcés, who made more country known than any other of Spain's explorers in the Southwest. He ranged out from the Mission of San Xavier del Bac, made friends with the Yuma Indians, and then opened a trail between the Sonora and California frontiers in 1771. To find a better route, an expedition under the leadership of Juan Bautista de Anza was organized and Father Garcés was made a member. The party set out from Tubac on January 8, 1774, crossed through Papaguería to the junction of the Colorado and Gila rivers, and journeyed through the Colorado Desert to San Gabriel. Although this group proved the existence of a practicable route from Sonora to California, it was not thought to be a good one.

According to Father Garcés, the merits of the route to Alta California discovered by the first Anza expedition appeared to be meager: "Because of the extreme scarcity of water and pasturage and of the vast sand dunes, I consider it risky to make this new expedition by way of it."[3]

Of course, Garcés was referring to the second Anza expedition, of which he was a member and which left Tubac on October 23, 1775, for the purpose of leading colonists to California and ascertaining a better route to that region. Garcés had long hoped to find a more northern route than Anza's from the Colorado River to San Luis Obispo or Monterey and held the opinion that a direct road could be opened from Monterey to Santa Fé. Garcés left the Anza expedition in the vicinity of modern Yuma, Arizona, and traveled down the Colorado to the Gulf, then followed the Colorado northward to Mojave. He was probably the first white man to visit the Mojave tribe of Indians. In his journey to the north, Garcés passed the Needles and penetrated a short distance across the present boundary of the state of Nevada.

From a point on the Colorado River slightly south of the Needles, Garcés struck out to the west in hope of blazing a trail to the coast. This leg of the journey has particular significance, for it is at this time, March 7, 1776, that Father Garcés left the Colorado drainage system and entered the Great Basin. On March 9 he reached Soda Lake, the sink of the Mojave River.[4] These phenomena have typical Great Basin characteristics in that the lake has no outlet and varies in appearance with the seasons, on many occasions becoming dry and developing a white, flat surface from the alkali. The Mojave River, which follows a rather exotic course, was named by Garcés the *Arroyo de los Martires;* however, it appears on Font's map of 1777 as "R. de los Martires."[5] The Mojave River proved to be a considerable boon

3 Herbert E. Bolton, *Outpost of Empire,* 217.

4 Francisco Garcés, *On the Trail of a Spanish Pioneer: The Diary and Itinerary of Francisco Garcés in His Travels through Sonora, Arizona, and California* (trans. and ed. by Elliot Coues), I, 234–39; LeRoy R. Hafen and Ann W. Hafen, *The Old Spanish Trail.*

5 Father Font prepared two diaries of the second Anza expedition: one was translated and edited by Frederick J. Teggart in the Academy of Pacific Coast History *Publications,* III, 3–131; a longer version containing Font's geographical reflections and maps along with much additional matter was translated and edited by Herbert E. Bolton as *Font's Complete Diary: A Chronicle of the Founding of San Francisco.*

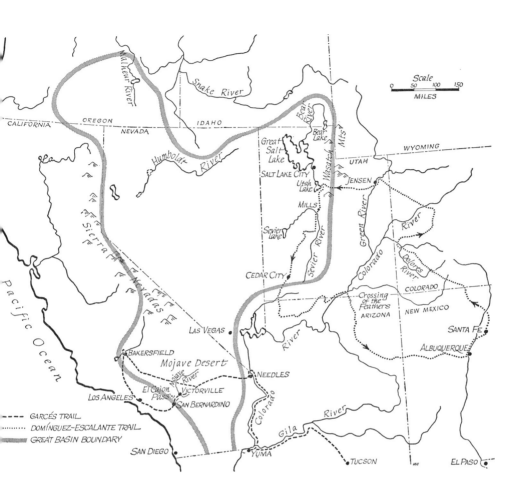

The Spanish Explorations (modern political features added)

37

to Garcés as it provided a southwestward course through this arid region which was only punctuated by small, dry lakes, a few springs, and potholes.

Garcés' course from the Colorado River was almost directly west, through the Providence Mountains to Soda Lake, which lies south of the site of present Baker, California, just a short distance from Highways 91 and 466. He followed the Mojave River up from its sink on a course virtually parallel to the above roads and to the well-known contemporary Highway 66. He passed through the site of present Barstow, California, and followed up the Mojave River to the vicinity of the modern town of Victorville, California. Although Coues and the Hafens seem to think that Garcés followed the Mojave River to its source, other historians believe that he did not, but struck out to the west and traveled through Cajon Pass in order to reach the coast.[6]

Passing over the mountains, Garcés now left the Great Basin on March 21, after having spent two weeks in the land of interior drainage. Upon reaching San Gabriel, he turned north, and after traversing the San Fernando Valley, crossed to the San Joaquin Valley by way of Tejon Pass. On May 1, Garcés came upon the Kern River, above modern Bakersfield, and named it the *Río de San Felipe*. He went on to the White River, which was his farthest point north, and from that place he reports that Indians "told me that northward seven days' journey there was a very great water that, according to their signs, was a river and ran from the northeast, uniting itself with the Río de San Felipe . . . one of the two branches into which it divides runs a course to the north; but they gave me to understand that the other river was three times larger than that of San Felipe."[7] No doubt they were referring to the San Joaquin–Sacramento River system.

At this time Garcés was close to the Sierra Nevada Mountains, which he called the *Sierra de San Marcos*. He turned back from the White River and left the San Joaquin Valley by way of Tehachapi Pass which brought him again into the Great Basin on the tenth or eleventh of May. On May 19, Garcés states: "I traveled four and a half

[6] Charles Edward Chapman, *The Founding of Spanish California*, 361; Bolton, *Outpost of Empire*, 449; Herbert E. Bolton, *The Early Explorations of Father Garcés on the Pacific Slope*, 318.

[7] Garcés, *Diary*, I, 289–90.

leagues in the same direction [southeastward] and fell upon the Río de los Martires near the position observed before in 34° 37'."[8] Garcés had crossed a large area of monotonous landscape, which can be appreciated only by those who are familiar with the region between this mountain pass and present Highway 66; yet Garcés was able to maneuver his way through this section and bisect his outgoing trail on the Mojave River in the vicinity of present Victorville, California. He now descended the Mojave River and reached Marl Springs, the principal watering place between Rock Springs and Soda Lake. From this position Garcés followed a trail slightly north of his previous one and left the Great Basin on May 25, 1776. Thus ended the first *entrada* into the Great Basin. Although he penetrated only a small portion of this vast region and, without a doubt, the most inhospitable section of it, Father Garcés had laid the basis for much conjectural geography which was to play a significant role in shaping the history of the exploration of the Great Basin.

Although Garcés was now somewhat familiar with the western part of North America, he did not have an accurate conception of the geography of the Great Basin north of the Mojave River. He suggested that the traveler proceeding west toward the Pacific Coast might "proceed through the Yutas and seek the Río de San Felipe, and down the banks of this will be my road."[9] The friar imagined that his Río de San Felipe (Kern River) originated far to the east of the Sierra Nevada Mountains (his Sierra de San Marcos). Garcés declared that the principal obstacle to be encountered between the "Yuta" (Ute) country and Monterey were the Tulares (of the San Joaquin Valley), which could be traversed by a small boat. Garcés remembered the "great water" which the Indians near present Bakersfield, California, had told him joined the Río de San Felipe. This, the San Joaquin River, he suggested might also be located by the west-bound traveler through the Ute country, and even though this trail would be longer than the one previously mentioned because it would be necessary to head the Tulares, it might prove to be an even better route to the coast. Garcés apparently imagined that the San Joaquin was a larger stream than the Kern and also that it had its source somewhere in the interior of the continent, probably in the area now encompassed by the state of Utah. He believed that this

8 *Ibid.*, 306.
9 *Ibid.*, 468.

stream flowed southwest, roughly parallel to the San Felipe, and emptied into the Tulares. Not satisfied with this idea, Garcés speculated that the stream might possibly be the Río Tizón of Oñate. He went on to say that were the Spaniards to possess this river, they might find it possible to reach the valley of the Tulares and then sail down the river to San Francisco. He now struck the basic theme: to possess this river would be to possess a route which, together with the Mississippi, would be of great advantage to the commerce between Spain and the Orient, as it would benefit New Mexico and the other interior provinces of New Spain. It is obvious that the idea of a Northwest Passage and the Straits of Anían had not died, but was only lying dormant waiting for one spark of hope which would again ignite it.

The geographical speculations of Garcés found expression outside of his diary in the words of his colleague, Father Pedro Font,[10] who was the chronicler on the second Anza expedition to California in 1775–76. Father Font had been with Juan Bautista de Anza when the site for the presidio of San Francisco was chosen in the last days of March, 1776. Before returning to Monterey, Anza explored the southern shore of San Francisco Bay to the mouths of the San Joaquin and the Sacramento rivers near the present California town of Antioch. Four years earlier, Pedro Fages and Father Juan Crespi had made an unsuccessful attempt to cross the bay and had gone over approximately the same route on the east side of the bay that Anza now followed. Fages and Crespi both agreed that their passage had been blocked by the waters of a large river, which Crespi chose to call the *Río Grande de San Francisco*. He drew a rather crude map of the bay showing the river flowing into it. Later in the same year, Fages crossed the southern end of the San Joaquin Valley in pursuit of some deserting soldiers and, in this way, formed an accurate opinion of its geographical character.[11] By rather devious reasoning, Font convinced himself and Anza that Crespi and Fages were in error and that their "Río Grande de San Francisco" was in fact not a river at all, but the mouth of a body of fresh water, surrounded by

[10] Carl I. Wheat, *Mapping the Trans-Mississippi West: The Spanish Entrada to the Louisiana Purchase, 1540–1804,* I, 92. The Font map illustrating Garcés findings is reproduced opposite page 92.

[11] *Fray Juan Crespi* (ed. by Herbert E. Bolton).

tules, which might extend through the Sierra Nevada.[12] Font visualized a great inland fresh-water sea in what is now southern Utah or Nevada, running west through the Sierra Nevada Mountains and connecting with the tulares of the southern San Joaquin Valley. On his map he terminates the Sierra Nevada at latitude 36 degrees, approximately east of the old Tulare Lake.

Garcés geographical conceptions are beautifully portrayed by a map drawn by D. Pedro Giraldo de Chares in 1803.[13] This map embraces the area between 23 and 33 degrees north latitude and 259 and 267 degrees east longitude and includes many of the place names used by Garcés. The most significant feature of this map is the elaborate river system which empties into San Francisco Bay. The "Río de S^n Felipe" and "Río de S^n Fran^{co}." are given prominence; however, the latter is shown to be of greater importance, flowing from an undetermined source east of the "Sierra de S^n Marcos."

In order to understand more fully the unveiling of this vast region which had hitherto been unexplored and to realize the full significance of Spain's efforts to connect her peninsulas of settlements, it is necessary to turn to the activities on the eastern periphery of the

[12] Font refers to a letter which had been written by Father Escalante on his journey from New Mexico to Moqui in 1775 and forwarded to him by the viceroy. "This father says that he reached Oraybe, the last pueblo of Moqui, and some fifty leagues west of the pueblo of Zuñi, which is in New Mexico; and that there a Cosnina Indian informed and told him that six days to the west of Oraybe, over a bad road, was the land inhabited by the Cosninas. He said that at nine days from Oraybe and more than a hundred leagues distant there is a high sierra which runs from northeast to southwest, inclining to the west; along its northern skirts the Río Grande de Misterios runs to the west." *Font's Complete Diary*, 398–99. Font continues: "In view of all this, I conclude that perhaps the Río Grande de los Misterios which the father tells about and of which they told him, must be some very large lake of fresh water lying in the direction of the tulares which we saw, or that they are these same tulares and water which extend through the immense plain which I have described. And this plain must run inland as far as the other side of the Sierra Nevada by some opening or openings, and it may have vast extent from east to west just as it has from north to south, unless it may be some matter of the Sea of the West as they call it." *Ibid.*, 402.

[13] D. Pedro Giraldo de Chares, *Mapa de la Nueva California al Excmo. Senor de la Paz* (1803), *Archivo de Servicio Histórico Militar*, Seville, Spain, which was made availalbe to the author by Donald C. Cutter of the University of Southern California. This map has been reproduced with a small portion deleted in *Cartografía del Ultramar*, II, No. 15, a publication of the *Servicios Geográfico e Histórico del Ejército*.

41

Great Basin. In 1765, by the order of the governor of New Mexico, Tomás Vélez Cachupín, the Rivera expedition was sent out from Santa Fé. The group followed a generally northwest course to the San Juan River and across to the La Plata Mountains; this range was given its present name because of some silver-like ore that was found there. Continuing northwest, the party descended probably the Dolores River and turned to the northeast, crossing the Uncompahgre Plateau, and then descended the Uncompahgre River to the Gunnison.[14]

No other official expeditions are known to have been made into this section for more than a decade. There is evidence, however, that private individuals, several of whom had been members of Rivera's group, began to look with interest upon the area that had been explored. The first definite reference that we have to any of these private enterprises is a statement made by Father Escalante concerning the expedition of Pedro Mora, Gregorio Sandoval, and Andrés Muñiz:

> There came to these two rivers[15] in the year 1765 Don Juan María de Rivera, crossing the same sierra de los Tabehuachis, on the summit of which is the place that he named El Purgatorio, according to the description that he gives in his journal. The plain on which he camped for the purpose of fording the river and on which he says he cut a cross in a young cottonwood, together with the initials of his name and the year of the expedition, are still found at the junction of these rivers on the southern bank, as we were informed by our interpreter Andrés Muñiz, who came with the said Don Juan María the year referred to, as far as the Tabehuachis Mountains, saying that although he had remained behind three days' journey before reaching the river, he had come the past year, 1775, along the bank of the river with Pedro Mora and Gregorio Sandoval who had accompanied Don Juan María through the whole expedition.[16]

14 The journal of the expedition has been lost, yet its contents are partly known for it has been established that it was used by Domínguez and Escalante, who seem to have followed it more or less closely as a guide on their expedition in 1776. Joseph J. Hill, "Spanish and Mexican Exploration and Trade Northwest from New Mexico into the Great Basin, 1765–1853," *Utah Historical Quarterly,* Vol. III (Jan., 1930), 4.

15 The Uncompahgre and the Gunnison.

16 *Doc. para la hist. de Mex.,* as reprinted in Hill, "Spanish and Mexican Exploration," *Utah Historical Quarterly,* Vol. III (Jan., 1930), p. 5, n. 5.

The Ute (Yuta) Indians had slowed the white advance, but when peace was made with them about 1750, Spanish trappers and traders, such as those previously mentioned, penetrated this area, remained there for two, three, or four months at a time for the purpose of obtaining pelts, and explored the major tributary streams and drainages on the left side of the upper Colorado from the San Juan to the Gunnison. By the time of the Domínguez expedition in 1776,[17] the region east of the Colorado and as far north as the Gunnison seems to have been fairly well known to the Spaniards of New Mexico since most of the more important physical features of the country were referred to in Escalante's diary by names which seemed to be common at the time.

Until the year 1776, the Great Basin had been untouched by white men; however, in this historic year, its façade was pricked by Father Garcés of San Xavier del Bac on March 7, and severely punctured six months later, on September 21, by the activities of Fathers Domínguez and Escalante, who ranged out from Santa Fe. This expedition was organized to explore the right bank of the Colorado River for the express purpose of finding a road to Monterey, which was also the ultimate aim of Father Garcés. Although Garcés had earned for himself a high place in the roster of western American explorers, Domínguez and Escalante are of greater significance in regard to the Great Basin.

On the 29th Day of July of the year 1776, under the patronage of the Virgin Mary, Our Lady of the Immaculate Conception, and of the most holy patriarch Joseph her most happy spouse, we, Fray Francisco Atanasio Domínguez, present commissary visitor of this Custodia of the Conversion of San Pablo of New Mexico, and Fray Francisco Silvestre Vélez de Escalante, minister and teacher of the Christian doctrine at the Mission of Nuestra Señora de Guadalupe de Zuní, accompanied voluntarily by Don Juan Pedro Cisneros,

17 The best edition of the Escalante diary is Herbert E. Bolton's *Pageant in the Wilderness: The Story of the Escalante Expedition to the Interior Basin, 1776, Including the Diary and Itinerary of Father Escalante*. This volume also contains a translation of the Miera report and a reproduction of the Miera 1778 Chihuahua map with some changes. The Escalante diary and related documents, with four versions of the Miera map, are also available in Herbert E. Auerbach, "Old Trails, Old Forts, Old Trappers and Traders," *Utah Historical Quarterly*, Vol. IX (Jan. and April, 1941), 13–63; and the same author's "Father Escalante's Route," *ibid.*, Vol. XI (Jan., April, July, and Oct., 1943), 1–132.

alcalde mayor of the said pueblo of Zuní; Don Bernardo Miera y Pacheco, retired militia captain and citizen of the town of Santa Fe; Don Joaquin Laín, citizen of the same town, Lorenzo Olivares, citizen of the town of El Paso; Lucrecio Muñiz; Andrez Muñiz;[18] Juan de Aguilar; and Simon Lucero; having implored the protection of our most holy patron and received the Holy Eucharist, we the persons named set out from the town of Santa Fe, capital of this Kingdom of New Mexico . . . .[19]

The little group departed, following the trappers' trail northwest past Mesa Verde, descending the Dolores River some distance, and then turning west to the Green River and the Colorado. From there it was Escalante's intention to strike out for Monterey, proceeding westward through the Sierras to the Pacific Coast. Bolton suggests that Escalante planned to negotiate the Sierra Nevada Mountains by a pass which Garcés thought he had seen when he was in the San Joaquin Valley; however, he tempers this statement by saying that "perhaps, on the other hand, Escalante's ideas on this last point were not so definite as this conjecture of mine."[20]

The party crossed the Uncompahgre Plateau, the Gunnison River, Grand Mesa, and Battlement Mesa, and reached the Colorado River in the vicinity of Grand Valley. Here they crossed the Colorado River, ascended the escarpments of the East Tavaputs Plateau, and at the divide passed over to the watershed of the Green River. They were now in new territory and began to give names of their choice to the prominent geographic features. After descending the long slope of the plateau, they crossed the White River and called it the *San Clemente*. Following the buffalo trails, they headed northwest and were deflected toward the west by the towering Yampa Plateau. Soon the explorers found themselves on the banks of a large stream which they chose to call the *San Buenaventura*.

In striking this river, the Spaniards had discovered the Green River, the main fork of the Colorado River. That the men of Spain were so long in reaching this river was due in part to the large canyons of the Colorado, which were even greater barriers to exploration than the ranges of mountains. However, Spanish and Mexican

18 The same Andrés Muñiz who was mentioned in connection with the Rivera expedition and the expedition of Mora and Sandoval.

19 Bolton, *Pageant in the Wilderness*, 133.

20 *Ibid.*, 14.

explorers eventually discovered all of the great tributaries of the Colorado River with the exception of Escalante River, which was discovered by the second Powell expedition and was named in honor of the Spanish diarist who never saw it. In the canyon country of the Colorado River, exploration usually proceeded on a horizontal plane. In most cases, the streams were first seen above their mouths, above the canyons, or at places between canyons. The courses of streams discovered could at first only be surmised, owing to the difficulty of lateral exploration. The routes of travel that developed on this trip and also from subsequent explorations generally followed this same horizontal plane. The general result was that the number of names for the same stream multiplied, and the exact geographical nature of the Colorado River system through the canyon areas was fragmentary and incomplete until John Wesley Powell carried through his vertical explorations beginning in 1869.[21] Most of the conjectural geography of the discoverers was quite sound; but, when they discovered the Green River,[22] they made the wrong guess, one that was to reach such proportions that it took more than half a century to dispel.

The Spaniards named their newly discovered river in honor of San Buenaventura, the thirteenth-century theologian, teacher, biographer of St. Francis, one-time minister-general of the Order of Friars Minor, cardinal, and saint. The Spaniards failed to realize that they had found the main tributary of the Colorado River; instead, they imagined that they were in another watershed. If there had been prior discoveries of the Green River below Tavaputs Plateau, where the relationship between the Colorado and the Green rivers could be surmised, the Spaniards probably would have recognized the river. Since the Green River is located deep in the center of Uinta Basin, which could easily be mistaken for a drainage pattern unrelated to the Colorado, they could only guess the course of the river above and below the discovery point. Escalante noted that they learned from the Indians that the San Clemente (White River) emptied into the San Buenaventura. Because the river was unknown before and since it was the longest stream that they had encountered since leav-

[21] John Wesley Powell, *Exploration of the Colorado River of the West and Its Tributaries.* See also Richard A. Bartlett, *Great Surveys of the American West.*

[22] C. Gregory Crampton, "The Discovery of the Green River," *Utah Historical Quarterly,* Vol. XX (Oct., 1952), 299–312.

ing Santa Fe, the San Buenaventura did not fit well into the drainage pattern of the Colorado as the Spaniards understood it. Therefore, they guessed that it was the main stream of an unrelated river system.

Escalante cited some evidence in support of this conclusion. He says that they thought it was the river which Fray Alonso de Posadas had mentioned in a report written in the seventeenth century. The report of this friar is probably a fair summary of what was known of the geography of the western part of the North American continent in the middle of the seventeenth century, and, as such, it is a valuable historical document; however, parts of it are imaginary and conjectural and are, therefore, confusing. The report indicates that the general nature of the Rocky Mountains was understood and states that some of the rivers flowed westward from these mountains to the Pacific, but Posadas named only the San Juan and the Grande (Colorado); conseqently, it is not clear exactly what part of the report Escalante had in mind when he cited Posadas in his diary. Although Escalante's San Buenaventura (Green River) is not located in the Great Basin but is an integral part of the Colorado River drainage system, it was nevertheless destined to figure prominently in Great Basin exploration.

The Escalante party forded the river a mile north of their camp and proceeded through the Uinta Basin. On September 21 the diary records: "We continued through the grove which became more dense the farther we went, and having traveled half a league west, we emerged from it, arriving at a high ridge from which the guide pointed out to us the direction of the Lake, and, to the southeast of it, another part of the sierra in which he said lived a great many people of the same language and character as the Lagunas." Thus the Domínguez-Escalante expedition had crossed over the divide near Diamond Creek and made the first entrance into the Great Basin above the latitude of the Mojave Desert. There is no indication whatsoever that the explorers had any idea that they were in an interior drainage basin.

Proceeding westward, the party descended into Utah Valley, where, Escalante states,

To the north of the Río de San Buenaventura, as we have said above, there is a sierra which in parts we saw runs from northeast to southwest more than seventy leagues, and its width or breadth

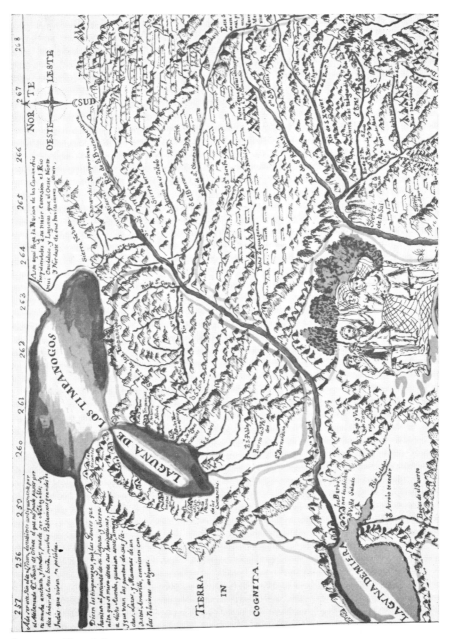

Lawrence Kinnaird

Miera y Pacheco map of the Domínguez-Escalante expedition, 1776.

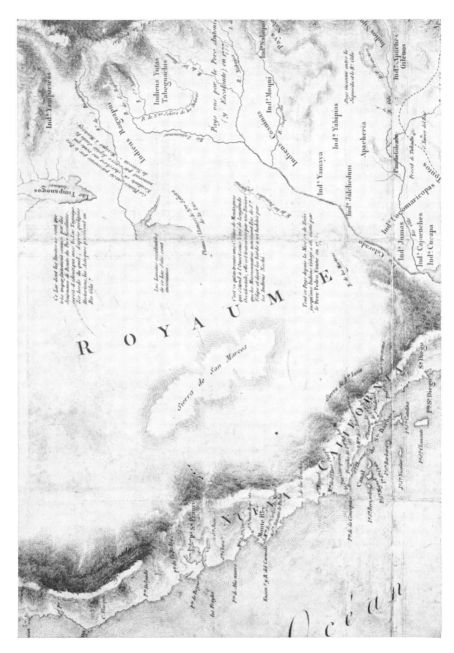

Baron von Humboldt's map of 1811.

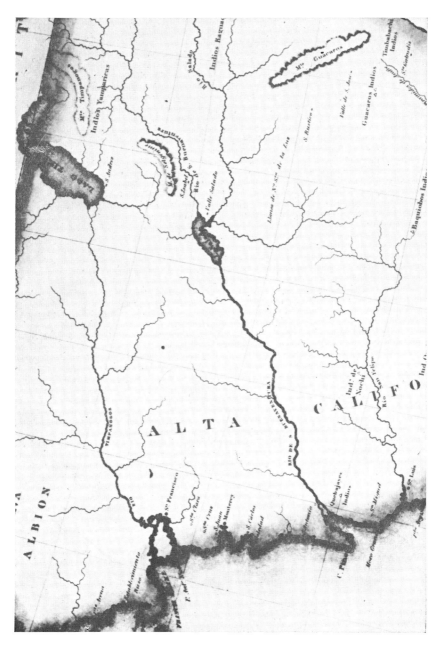

Las Mejores autoridades, 1828.

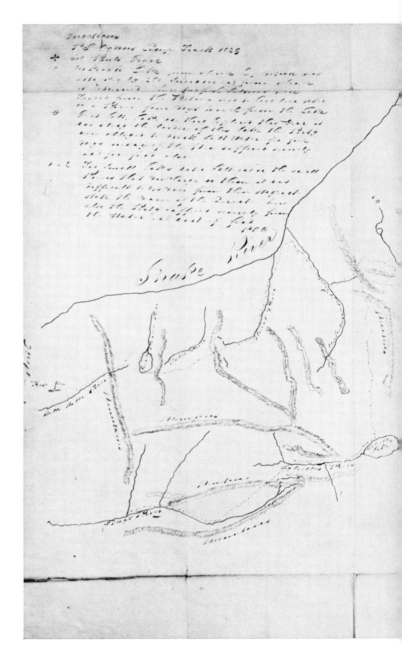

Hudson's Bay Company

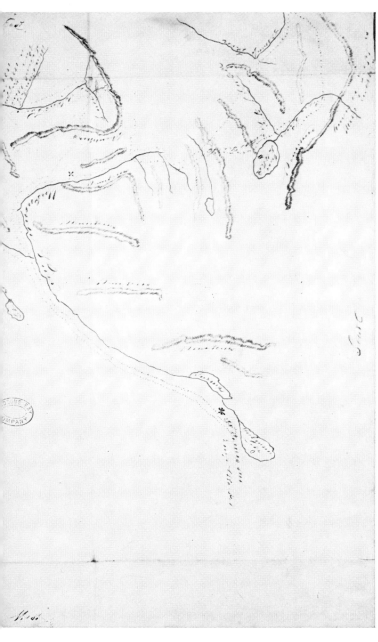

p of Peter Skene Ogden's 1828–29 Snake Country Expedition.

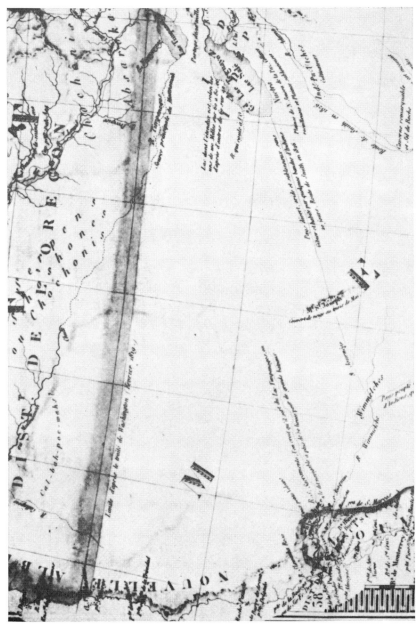

The Brué map of 1834.

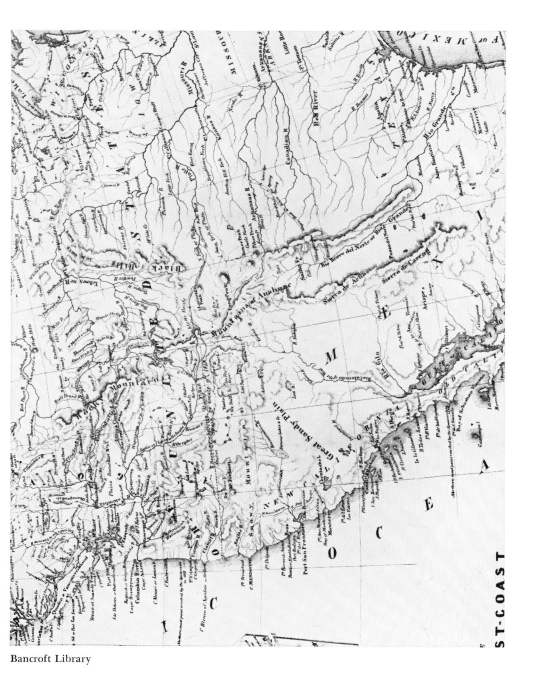

David H. Burr's map of 1840.

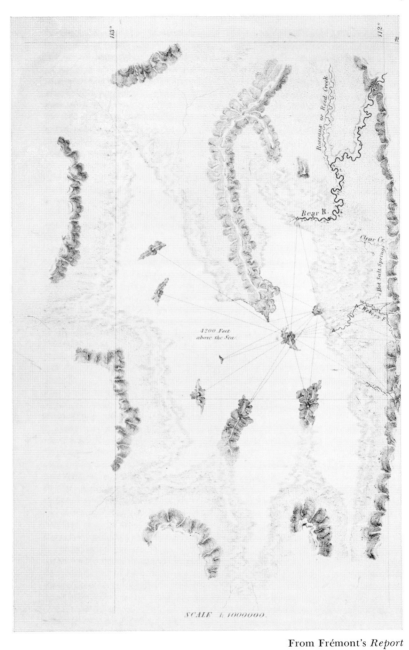

From Frémont's *Report*

Map of Great Salt Lake, made by Charles Preuss.

must be at forty leagues, and where we crossed it, thirty. In the western part of this sierra in latitude 40° 49′ and about northwest by north of the town of Santa Fe, is the valley of Nuestra Señora de la Merced de Timpanocutzis, surrounded by the peaks of the sierra, from which flow four fair-sized rivers which water it, running through the valley to the middle of it where they enter the lake. . . . Toward the south and southwest close by there are two other extensive valleys, also having abundant pasturage and sufficient water. The lake, which must be six leagues wide and fifteen leagues long, extends as far as one of these valleys. It runs northwest through a narrow passage, and according to what they told us, it communicates with others much larger.[23]

Of course, Escalante was now hearing about the Great Salt Lake, which lay to the north of the explorers' trail and which the party did not see, and about the Jordan River, which flows between the two bodies of water. He says further: "The other lake with which this one communicates, according to what they told us, covers many leagues, and its waters are noxious and extremely salty, for the Timpanois assure us that a person who moistens any part of his body with the water of the lake immediately feels much itching in the part that is wet."[24] When the expedition discovered Utah Lake and learned from the Indians that it was connected with a salt lake to the north, they conceived the idea that this was still another drainage system which had an outlet to the sea.

Upon leaving Utah Valley, the Spaniards turned to the south in order to reach the latitude of Monterey before turning west. On September 29, they reached the Sevier River near the present site of Mills, Utah, and there imagined themselves to be on the lower course of the San Buenaventura. Continuing southward, the party passed close to Clear Lake and proceeded through Beaver River Valley. It was now October, and the harsh physical conditions of the Great Basin began to make themselves felt, as is evidenced by diary entries: "We quickened our pace and found that what we had thought to be water was in places salt, in others saltpeter, and in others tequesquite." And, "Although we were greatly inconvenienced by lack of firewood and the excessive cold, we were unable to leave San Arteno-genes today either, because, with so much snow and water, the land

23 Bolton, *Pageant in the Wilderness*, 184–85.
24 *Ibid.*, 186.

47

which here is very soft, and was impassable."[25] On October 8 the party was forced to accept the reluctant conclusion that they should return to Santa Fe:

> Hitherto we had intended to go to the presidio and new establishments of Monterey, but thinking them still distant because, although we had to descend only 1° 23½' to this place of Santa Brigida, we had not advanced toward the west, according to the daily directions, more than 136½ leagues. According to the opinion which we had formed, partly on account of not having heard among all these last people any report of the Spaniards and fathers of Monterey, partly because of the great difference in longitude between this port and the town of Santa Fe as shown on the maps, there were still many more leagues to the west. Winter had already begun with great severity, for all the sierras which we were able to see in all directions were covered with snow. The weather was very unsettled and we feared that long before we arrived the passes would be closed and we would be delayed for two or three months in some sierra, where there might be no people nor any means of obtaining necessary sustenance, for our provisions were already very low, and so we would expose ourselves to death from hunger if not cold. . . . Therefore, we decided to continue to the south, if the terrain would permit it, as far as the Río Colorado, and from there proceed toward Cosnina, Moqui, and Zuñi.[26]

The group did continue south to the vicinity of the modern Cedar City, Utah, where they left the Great Basin and crossed to the Colorado River, negotiating it by what since has been known as the Crossing of the Fathers. They finally arrived at their home base, Santa Fe, on January 2, 1777.

Although the explorers were not able to achieve their desired goal of blazing a trail between Santa Fe and Monterey, they did make the first comprehensive traverse of the Colorado Plateau and of a considerable portion of the Great Basin. The diary kept by Escalante and the maps drawn by Bernardo Miera y Pacheco[27] are important items in western American historical literature, since they provided a basis for further exploration and additional conjectural geography which was to achieve world-wide fame.

[25] Entry for October 7, *ibid.*, 195. Letter from Herbert E. Bolton to Gloria Griffen (Cline), April 4, 1951.

[26] Bolton, *Pageant in the Wilderness*, 195–96.

[27] Wheat, *Mapping the Trans-Mississippi West*, I, 94–116.

The geographical contribution of the Domínguez-Escalante expedition is beautifully illustrated on the maps made by Bernardo Miera y Pacheco. The region north of Santa Fe and along the crest of the Rockies to about the forty-second parallel and west to about meridian 113 degrees, 30 minutes, is drawn with considerable accuracy. The region to the north and west of the Colorado is mapped here for the first time from the data obtained from the actual expedition. Miera's map depicting the travels of the Domínguez-Escalante expedition is known to exist today in at least six distinct manuscript copies, each exhibiting a few differences from the others. However, they represent three basic forms or types which Carl Wheat has designated for convenience (1) the undecorated type, (2) the Tree and Serpent type, and (3) the "Bearded Indian" type.[28] On all of the copies the basic topographical information is similar, the major difference being in the title and dedication and in the presence or absence of decorative material. The Miera maps contain enough geographical, historical, and anthropological data to make them the rival of Escalante's diary, but they contain two colossal errors which were perpetuated and elaborated by others and thus caused confusion to the explorers who came later.

One of the mistakes is found in Miera's description of Utah Lake and the Great Salt Lake. The Spaniards did not visit the latter, but heard about it from Indians, and thus conceived of the two lakes as being one body of water. Miera shows the two lakes as one and calls it *Laguna de Timpanogos,* the Indian name for Utah Lake. On one of the maps, Miera shows a large stream flowing into the part that corresponds to Great Salt Lake, named the *Río de las Yamparicas.* Although this river was given credence by several notable cartographers in the following decades, it had little durability in comparison with the concept of the Buenaventura River.

Miera's other mistake was in his delineation of the Green River. The river which the Spaniards had named the San Buenaventura is accurately shown in relation to the streams of the Uinta Basin, but instead of connecting it with the Colorado River, Miera lifts it out over the Wasatch Mountains and identifies it with Sevier Lake, the salty sink of the Sevier River in the Great Basin. He called Sevier Lake *Laguna de Miera,* the western limits of which are not shown. It is not easy to see how Miera could have identified the Green and

[28] *Ibid.*

Sevier rivers, although it seems that the suggestion was made by Indians. The San Buenaventura seems to have been mainly Miera's creation and was not concurred in by his companions on the expedition. In his report to the king of Spain on October 26, 1777, Miera elaborates about this river: "The river which the inhabitants say flows from the lake, and whose current runs toward the west, they say is very large and navigable. And if it is as they say, I conjecture that it is the Río del Tizón discovered long ago by Don Juan de Oñate, first colonizer of New Mexico."[29]

When Miera drew his maps, in addition to using information supplied by his Indian informants, he undoubtedly consulted some of the documentary sources which were available to him in Chihuahua, at that time the capital of Spain's internal provinces in North America. He also possibly made use of the works of Posadas, Zárate Salmerón, and others, and it appears quite certain that he had access to Venegas' works on California and was thus familiar with the current geographical ideas pertaining to the unexplored portions of North America.

Miera places no faith in the Sea of the West fantasy which was in vogue during the second half of the eighteenth century. On one version of his map, he states that he believes the Sea of the West as it had appeared on "recent maps" to be a mistake.[30] Instead, Bernardo Miera y Pacheco asserts that the area which is said to be covered by the inland sea in fact is "Tierra Firme" and is inhabited by many natives. However, Miera did not delineate the western bounds of his Laguna de Miera, which fact seems to hint that this body could be of considerable magnitude. With such a portrayal of the heretofore unexplored areas, it appears certain that Miera was familiar with the works of Miguel Venegas as published by Andrés Marcos Burriel in 1757, in which he undertook a most extensive as well as a most critical study of the Sea of the West fantasy.

29 Bolton, *Pageant in the Wilderness*, 243–50.

30 The Sea of the West or *Mer de l'ouest* appeared as early as 1705 and was portrayed as a gulf extending inland to the foot of the Rocky Mountains. Thus what was to become known as the Great Basin was at this time conceived of by many to be the floor of the sea. The conception of the Sea of the West developed greater magnitude during the middle of the eighteenth century through the works of Joseph Nicolas Delisle, who in 1752 produced the standard representation of the Sea of the West. A reproduction of this map may be seen in Wheat, *Mapping the Trans-Mississippi West*, I, opposite p. 141.

In describing Lake Timpanogos, Miera may have had in mind the Lahontan geography.[31] The description of Lahontan's salt lake and the Indians' vivid description of the saline qualities of Lake Timpanogos would be quite a temptation for conjecture. Miera seemed quite certain that the river system in the Great Salt Lake region did have a connection with the sea, and was disgruntled when the expedition was forced to return to Santa Fe and he was cheated of verifying his elaborate conclusions.

Miera was also familiar with the map of the Viceroyalty of New Spain made by Joseph Antonio Alzate y Ramirez and published in 1768.[32] Although this map was constructed by one of Mexico's most learned men, it is, according to Wagner, one of the poorest in the delineation of the northwest coast of America. About latitude 41 degrees, Alzate shows the Tizón River flowing into the bay of the Puerto de la Conversión de San Pablo, both said to have been discovered by Oñate. This was the only map showing the Tizón discharging on the northwest coast, and inasmuch as Miera has the Tizón flowing out of Great Salt Lake just under latitude 42 degrees, it seems safe to assume that Alzate was his model.

Alzate's portrayal of the interior between the California coast and New Mexico is nearly blank except for his version of Lake Teguayo. This is placed in approximately the right location for Great Salt Lake, and he has it surrounded by the mythical "Quivira Fabulosa" and "Sierra Azul." Alzate noted on his map that from the environs of

31 Louis Armand de Lom d'Arce, baron de Lahontan, was an imaginative Frenchman who in 1688 traveled from the French post at Michilimackinac to the Mississippi River via the Fox and Wisconsin rivers, and there he discovered a stream which he called the "Long River," which flowed to the west. He supposedly ascended this stream to its headwaters, where he learned from the Gnacsitares Indians that the *Rivière Longue* rose in the same ridge as another river flowing toward the west. This stream was said eventually to empty into a salt lake which in turn drained into the ocean through a large mouth two leagues in breadth. Although there has been much discussion in regard to the validity of some of Lahontan's travels, his name has become intimately known in the Great Basin, for it has been perpetuated in Lahontan Basin, the depression created by one of the ancient Great Basin lakes, Lake Lahontan, and is widely known today in the form of Lahontan Reservoir near Fallon, Nevada. See Lahontan's "Memoirs of North America," in John Pinketon (ed.), *A General Collection of Voyages and Travels*, I.

32 D. Josef Antonio de Alzate y Ramírez, "*Nuevo Mapa Geográfico de la América Septentrional, perteneciente al Virreynato de México . . . ,*" *Cartografia de Ultramar*, II, No. 5.

this lake the Aztecs went forth to the Valley of Mexico. Miera makes this statement on several of his maps, his source no doubt being the Alzate map.

Data for the later elaboration of the San Buenaventura myth were developed by the contemporaries of Miera and Escalante in California, most notably Father Garcés and Father Font. The geographical works of Miera and Font were brought together by Manuel Agustín Mascaro, who made a general map of Spanish North America in 1782 which is considered the best produced to that date. Mascaro was an engineer and was better acquainted with New Mexico than California and consequently drew heavily upon the maps of Miguel Costanso[33] and Pedro Font for the coastal regions.[34] In his portrayal of the New Mexican area, Mascaro incorporates bodily the data from Miera's map of 1778 with little change. He accepts the Río de San Buenaventura with no change except that Miera's name is deleted from Laguna de Miera or Sevier Lake, into which the Buenaventura supposedly flowed. Later cartographers appear to have made use of Miera's work indirectly through that of Mascaro, and as a result he has received little credit for his geographical contributions.

In the space between the area mapped by Miera and the coast, Mascaro gives a prominent place to the stream which Garcés heard of in the San Joaquin Valley and which Coues identifies as the San Joaquin River. This is shown as a large river covering three degrees of longitude and is separated from Sevier Lake by only two degrees and from San Francisco Bay by one degree. Although these bodies of water are not connected, there are no mountain barriers indicated as an obstacle to such a connection. Looking at Mascaro's map, it would have been easy to join mentally all three and thus have the San Buenaventura empty into San Francisco Bay by the River of

[33] Costanso was also an engineer and something of a map maker, and had sufficient nautical knowledge to be able to make fairly accurate observations of latitude. He had been a member of the Portolá expedition and was thus familiar with the Pacific Coast.

[34] *Mapa geográfico de una gran parte de la América Septentrional comprendido entre los veinte y quarenta y dos grados de latitud norte y los dos cientos quarenta y nueve y dos cientos ochenta y nueve de longitud oriental de Tenerife . . .* , drawn by Mascaro in 1782 and by Mascaro and Costanso in 1784. Neither of the two maps, discussed by Henry R. Wagner in *The Cartography of the Northwest Coast of America to the Year 1800*, I, 181–82; II, 347–49, was ever published.

San Francisco. Mascaro apparently did not accept Font's interpretation of the tulare region, but he did give prominence to Garcés' San Felipe, which flows from a point in the interior south around the Sierra de San Marcos and turns northwest as Font shows it on his map. It is evident from the study of Mascaro's maps that there was yet no accurate understanding of the Great Basin–Sierra Nevada geography; instead, Mascaro clearly sets forth the prevailing opinion that the streams north of the Colorado River which rise on the western slopes of the Rocky Mountains flow to the west and eventually into the Pacific Ocean. This erroneous conception was retained until the end of the Spanish period, until the end of the Mexican period, and even into the American period, despite the findings of many of the explorers, and was to shape significantly the history of the Great Basin.

Miera's report to the king of Spain was written on October 26, 1777, and firmly demonstrates Miera's belief that in order to hold the Pacific Coast the hinterland must be subdued and colonized in strategic places:

> With three presidios, together with three settlements of Spaniards, the door will be open to a New Empire which may be explored and colonized. The chief one, and the one that should be the first objective, should be on the shores of the lake of the Timpanogos, or one of the rivers that flow into it, for this is the most pleasing, beautiful, and fertile site in all New Spain . . . .[35] The second presidio and the settlement of families attached to it also are very desirable, and should be founded at the junction of the river of Nabajoo[36] with that of Los Animas . . . .[37] The third presidio is likewise very desirable, and it is most necessary that it also be built strong enough, and provided with both soldiers and settlers. And if it were placed at the junction of the Jila River with the Colorado, or in that vicinity, which offers conveniences for its firm establishment, it would be useful in many ways. It would serve as a way station on the road from Sonora; for communication with the above-mentioned establishments; to protect and aid the converted tribes in its vicinity; and to check the ravages of the hostile Jila Apaches who live toward the east.[38]

35 Bolton, *Pageant in the Wilderness*, 244.
36 San Juan River.
37 Near present Farmington, New Mexico.
38 Bolton, *Pageant in the Wilderness*, 245–47.

In 1780, at the viceroy's order, two missions were founded near the Yuma junction on the west bank of the Colorado River; but the two other mission and presidio sites referred to by Miera were neglected. Ten Spanish families were settled at each mission to serve as protection to the Franciscan friars and as an example to the neophytes. In July of 1781 trouble broke out in the form of the well-known Yuma Massacre, which was led by a Yuma chief who had been baptized Salvador Palma by the Spaniards. The mission was destroyed, and Father Garcés, the first Great Basin explorer, was killed, along with a number of Spanish colonists who were passing through Yuma on their way to found Los Angeles.

With the Yuma Massacre, the project for a mission in the Great Salt Lake region was forgotten and little attention was focused upon this region for at least half a century. The reason for this apparent lack of interest is not difficult to understand when the activities of Spain as a whole are considered. The Nootka Sound Controversy took place in 1789 and resulted in the lands of the Pacific Coast of North America north of the Spanish settlements being thrown open to England; it also marked the beginning of a spiritless defensive on the part of Spain which led to the inevitable disintegration of her colonial empire. To make matters worse, the French Revolution occurred a little later in the same year, and the vacillating policies of Spain, as set forth by Floridablanca, Aranda, and Manuel Godoy, resulted in the Treaty of Basel in 1795. An alliance between France and Spain was formed in 1796, and a declaration of war against England followed. With the rise of Napoleon, Spain proved to be even more of an instrument in the hands of the French, and consequently her colonial empire was neglected.

Thus the Garcés and Domínguez-Escalante explorations of 1776 were the last official Spanish expeditions to penetrate the Great Basin. However, a few documents have come to light which indicate that there was almost continual contact between the Spaniards of New Mexico and the Ute Indians. These parties seem to have followed the Rivera and Domínguez-Escalante course from Santa Fe northward and, in some cases, extended their travels as far north as Utah Lake.

From a letter written on September 1, 1805 by Joaquín de Real Alencaster, the governor of New Mexico, to Commandant-General Salcedo of Chihuahua, we learn of the merits of a Ute interpreter who had apparently made a number of trips into the Great Basin for the purpose of recovering horses. This letter seems to indicate that there had been almost continual contact between the Spaniards of Santa Fe and the Indians of the "Lake Timpanogos" region from a time even prior to the Rivera expedition of 1765, for Alencaster says, "Manuel Mestas, a Genizaro of seventy years old, who for approximately fifty years has served as Yuta interpreter, was the one, who reduced them to peace."[39] Very little information is available in regard to the later activities of Manuel Mestas and the parties that he accompanied.

However, a little light has been focused upon the Great Basin for the year 1813 by a document which was discovered by Mr. J. J. Hill in the Spanish Archives in Santa Fe, New Mexico.[40] This document tells of a previously unknown trading expedition which was made into the Great Basin under the leadership of Mauricio Arze and Lagos García. The party of seven men left Abiquiu on March 16, 1813, and returned four months later, on July 12. It seems that the governor of New Mexico received information concerning the expedition and on September 1, 1813, ordered the members of the party to appear before Manuel García, the *alcalde* of Villa de Santa Cruz de la Cañada, and make a report of their activities. We have the sworn testimony of five of the seven members of the expedition: Miguel Tenorio, Felipe Gómez, Josef Santiago Vejil, Gabriel Quintana, and Josef Velásques.[41] In the main, these affidavits are very similar and vary only in minute detail. None of the accounts of these traders give information regarding the route between Abiquiu and the Utah Lake region. This, no doubt, is because the trail northward into this area was so well known that they felt no necessity to expound upon it. If there had been intercourse between the Spanish settlements of New Mexico and the Utah Lake region for the past half-

39 Letter from Governor Alencaster to Commandant-General Salcedo, September 1, 1805, MS in Spanish Archives of New Mexico. Photostatic copy in *New Mexico Archives Documents*, Vol. 65, photostats 26–28, Bancroft Library.

40 "Spanish and Mexican Exploration," *Utah Historical Quarterly*, Vol. III (Jan., 1930), 17.

41 *New Mexico Archives Documents*, Vol. 73. See testimony of the following traders: Miguel Tenorio, photostats 268–71; Felipe Gómez, photostats 271–73; Josef Santiago Vejil, photostats 273–75; Gabriel Quintana, photostats 275–77; and Josef Velásques, photostats 277–80. This testimony has no title but is listed by Ralph Emerson Twitchell, *The Spanish Archives of New Mexico*, as No. 2511, in II, 577.

century, as seems likely from the Alencaster-Salcedo correspondence, the Arze expedition was justified in not detailing its course.

Although these documents are not complete, we do learn that the party proceeded as far north as Utah Lake, where they remained for three days trading with the Indians. Difficulty arose between the traders and the Indians because the former did not wish to buy slaves, and the expedition was forced to leave the immediate area. Now the group moved into a section which seems to have been unknown to them. They state that through the aid of a Ute Indian of the Sanpete Nation they traveled for three days until they were led to a tribe of Utes with whom they were unfamiliar. These Indians were of considerable interest to them, for they were clearly the "Bearded Utes" whom Domínguez and Escalante had encountered near the Sevier River and whom Miera had pictured on his map of 1778. From these documents it seems most likely that the Great Basin was not unknown to the traders of New Mexico. The trail which they followed was no doubt similar to the one used by Domínguez and Escalante in 1776, and although they were familiar with this segment of the Great Basin, they had no geographical understanding of the region and its relationship to adjacent areas.

While Spanish traders were pushing northward from Santa Fe into the Great Basin, Spaniards in California were showing interest and concern about the area east of the Sierra Nevada Mountains. Although the Spanish settlements in Alta California were materially unable to sponsor expeditions into the Great Basin itself, the findings of several Spanish expeditions ranging out from this quarter did have a bearing upon this region. Undoubtedly the most famous explorer and Indian fighter in California during the first few decades of the nineteenth century was Gabriel Moraga, who at the head of a number of expeditions explored the area immediately to the west of the Great Basin, and on two occasions crossed over the rim and into the land of interior drainage.

One of the most significant expeditions took place in 1806 when Gabriel Moraga led a party into the San Joaquin Valley, making the first transit of this area.[42] In the report of his peregrinations in this

42 Undoubtedly, Moraga knew many of the explorers and cartographers of California personally, for he came to California at an early date in 1781 to join his father, José Joaquín Moraga, who had been second in command of Anza's colonizing expedition of 1776. Young Moraga and his mother were members of

region, one can see that Moraga was influenced by some of the early geographers and explorers of the area, for he believed that the San Joaquin River flowed from the east. When Moraga was encamped in the vicinity of the present town of Merced, California, he seems to have developed this idea and continued to hold it until his death.[43] While engaged in this expedition, Moraga and his party continued down the San Joaquin Valley and reached the southwestern rim of the Great Basin, when they traveled up what is now the Grapevine Grade on U. S. Highway 99 and continued through Tejon Pass to reach the *rancho* of Mission San Fernando. The next day, November 3, 1806, the expedition ended when the group marched southward and reached Mission San Fernando.

Although Moraga made the initial reconnaissance of the northern half of the Great Valley of California in 1808, exploring the Sacramento and Feather River valleys, little was done in penetrating the Sierra Nevada Mountains from which these streams flow. However, there was much speculation in the next decade concerning what lay to the east of this mountain range, and it points up the Spanish apprehension of foreign intrusion into unoccupied Spanish lands. This concern was eloquently expressed by Father Durán in 1817 when he was speaking about the desire for an examination of the Sierra Nevada Mountains: ". . . we would be able to ascertain the truth of what the Indians have told us for some years past, that on the other side of the Sierra Nevada there are people like our soldiers. We have never been able to clear up the matter and learn if they are the Spaniards of New Mexico, the English of the Columbia,[44] or the Russians of Bodega."[45]

the Rivera expedition to California in 1781, some of whom were slain along with Father Garcés at Yuma during the Yuma Massacre, which cut the Spanish land route from Sonora to California.

[43] Fr. Mariano Payeras, *"Noticia de un Viaje a San Rafael"* (MS); Donald C. Cutter, "Moraga of the Military: His California Service, 1784–1810" (unpublished Master's thesis, University of California, 1947); *The Diary of Ensign Gabriel Moraga's Expedition of Discovery in the Sacramento Valley, 1808,* (trans. and ed. by Donald C. Cutter).

[44] This is a most interesting comment, for the earliest record of a British expedition's reaching an area east of California is when the Mackenzie Snake River Brigade visited the Bear River in the eastern portion of the Great Basin in 1818, one year after the Durán report. There is no record of Russians from the Bodega Bay penetrating the Great Basin or the region east of the Sierra Nevada Mountains.

[45] Entry for May 20, 1817, in Narciso Durán, *"Diario de reconocimiento hecha*

Within the next decade there were no significant Spanish expeditions in the California–Great Basin region, and it was not until the unfortunate disaster at Mission San Buenaventura in early 1819 that the first and only Spanish penetration from California into the Great Basin took place.[46] When twenty-two Mojave Indians visited the mission for trading purposes, a misunderstanding developed which led to a conflict in which ten of the twenty-two Mojaves were killed. As a result, the Spanish inhabitants of Southern California were alarmed for fear of retaliation by these desert people. Thus three expeditions were organized: the first expedition under the command of Sergeant José Sánchez set out from San Francisco and reached the lower San Joaquin Valley via San Jose; the second, under the command of Lieutenant José María Estudillo, left Monterey for the Tulare region; while the third expedition, led by Gabriel Moraga, had instructions to march to the Colorado River and to the Mojave villages and thus into the heart of the southern Great Basin. Moraga in command of thirty-five cavalrymen, Lieutenant Narciso Fabregat with members of the Mazatlán cavalry, four artillerymen with a small cannon, and a large number of native allies left Mission San Gabriel on November 22, 1819, and marched eastward. The group traveled about 225 miles into the desert before their horses and mules began to play out from lack of water and forage. Then Moraga decided to retrace his steps to San Gabriel, which was reached on December 14.

The Moraga expedition of 1819, like the Arze-García expedition of 1813, is of little importance to the history of the Great Basin, for this punitive expedition into the western Great Basin, like the trading expedition into the eastern Great Basin, developed no geographical understanding of the land of interior drainage. Although these expeditions, which were the last Spanish movements into the Great Basin, added little to existing geographical knowledge, Spain must be remembered for her explorers—such as Garcés, Domínguez, and Escalante—who in the preceeding half-century entered the Great Basin, gave literary as well as cartographic expression to their activities in that area, and thereby set the course of subsequent explora-

---

en el mes de Mayo de 1817 por el Senor Comandante del real presidio de Nuestra Padre San Francisco, Teniente Don Luis Arguello," MS, p. 4.

[46] Hubert Howe Bancroft, *History of California*, II, 331–37.

tion; they also established the eastern and western approaches to the Old Spanish Trail, which was to be inaugurated by William Wolfskill and George C. Yount during the winter of 1830–31.

4

INFLUENCE OF THE PACIFIC
UPON GREAT BASIN EXPLORATION

THE FIRST AND LAST OFFICIAL SPANISH EXPEDITIONS into the Great Basin took place in 1776, but Spain, in spite of her international handicaps, continued to search for the entrance of a strait along the Pacific Coast until 1793. Spaniards from Louisiana, in hope of reaching the western sea, followed up the Missouri to the mouth of the Yellowstone and beyond, opening a trail which was still fresh when the Lewis and Clark Expedition ventured that way.[1] However, with the European scene becoming more clouded, particularly from the standpoint of Spain, she was able to do little with the findings and recommendations of her explorers. Ironically, it was these Spanish expeditions which were to serve as motivating forces for British exploration on the northwest coast of America.

England, who had become a major force on the European scene following the Treaty of Paris in 1763, now became interested in lands beyond the continent of Europe. With the concept of useful knowledge, or the "Enlightenment," permeating British society, the cause of exploration was, quite naturally, espoused by the Royal Society and even by the monarch, George III. In 1774 the Royal Society wrote to the Admiralty submitting a novel plan for the search for the Northwest Passage, proposing the reverse of the usual line of travel. The recommendation called for an attempt to discover the passage by sailing from the Pacific Ocean to the Atlantic and suggested that a ship should be victualed in Canton and thence sail across the Pacific to the northern part of New Albion.[2] This opera-

---

[1] A. P. Nasatir (ed.), *Before Lewis and Clark;* Pierre-Antoine Tabeau, *Tabeau's Narrative of Loisel's Expedition to the Upper Missouri* (trans. and ed. by Annie Heloise Abel).

[2] Charles Richard Weld, *History of the Royal Society.*

tion was so new, so extensive, and so various that it was felt that the skill and experience of Captain Cook was requisite to conduct it. Therefore, Lord Sandwich invited Cook to dinner and presented the whole scheme to him, with the result that he was commissioned on February 10, 1776.

The supposed secret instructions for Captain Cook which were signed on July 6, 1776, by C. Spencer, H. Palliser, and Lord Sandwich explain clearly the course of action that Captain Cook was to follow on the northwest coast:

> Upon your arrival on the coast of New Albion, you are to put into the first convenient port to recruit your wood and water, and procure refreshments, and then proceed Northward along the coast, as far as the latitude of 65°, or farther, if you are not obstructed by lands or ice; taking care not to lose any time in exploring rivers or inlets, or upon any other account, until you get into the beforementioned latitude of 65°, where we could wish you to arrive in the month of June next. When you get that length you are very carefully to search for, and to explore for, such rivers or inlets as may appear to be of considerable extent, and pointing towards Hudson's or Baffin's Bays; and if, from any information you may receive from the natives . . . there shall appear to be a certainty, or even a probability, of a water passage into the aforementioned bays, or either of them, you are, in such case, to use your utmost endeavors to pass through with one or both of the sloops, unless you shall be of the opinion that the passage may be effected with more certainty, or with greater probability, by smaller vessels.[3]

In March, 1778, the Cook expedition sighted the northwestern coast of America. The entry in Cook's Journal for Wednesday, March 11, gives a description of the coastal areas, as does the entry for Sunday, March 29. Captain Cook wrote: "That part of the land, which we were so near when we tacked, is of moderate height, though, in some places, it rises higher within";[4] and, "The appearance of the country differed much from that of the parts which we had before seen; being full of high mountains, whose summits were covered with snow."[5] These two statements seem to express quite adequately the findings of the Cook expedition, which are well illustrated on

[3] Captain James Cook, *A Voyage to the Pacific Ocean*, I, xxxiii.
[4] *Ibid.*, 260.
[5] *Ibid.*, 264.

Cook's maps[6]—that the northwest coast is bordered by mountains, which implies, as portrayed on his maps, that there is little likelihood that a river could break through this mountainous mass.

Besides its geographical contributions, the Cook expedition seems to have inadvertently played an important role in the mercantile world. The vivid descriptions of the animal life on the northwest coast of America which appear frequently throughout the pages of the Cook Journal, as well as the tremendous prices obtained for the few otter skins which Cook had carried to China with him, developed a vigorous British interest in this region. The lure of wealth, in the form of pelts, no doubt helped to accelerate the movement of the North West Company and the Hudson's Bay Company westward, and thus again the fur-bearing animals proved to be an important motivating force in western exploration.

George Vancouver, who had been with Captain Cook on his second and third expeditions, was commissioned in 1791 to carry the Nootka Treaty into effect and to examine the northwest coast from 30 to 60 degrees north latitude in order to search for the elusive passage to the Atlantic Ocean. On April 17, 1792, Vancouver sighted the northwest coast at about 39 degrees, 27 minutes north latitude and proceeded to examine the coast carefully. The findings of this expedition are beautifully portrayed by several maps drawn by Lieutenant Joseph Baker, which corroborate the Cook geography but add considerably more information. Vancouver depicts the coast from 30 degrees north latitude to Cook's Inlet, showing a continuous range of mountains parallel to the coast. He shows the Columbia River—the only river that appears—as penetrating this mountainous barrier; however, even it is shown to be more or less hemmed in by spur ranges from Mount St. Helens to Mt. Hood.[7]

Although the Cook and Vancouver expeditions came no closer

6 "Chart of the N.W. Coast of America and N.E. Coast of Asia Explored by Capt. Cook and Capt. Clarke, in the Years 1778 and 1779." However, no mountain range is portrayed in the area between latitudes 49½ and 56 degrees as the ship was too far off the coast to determine topography.

7 "A Chart shewing part of the Coast of N.W. America, with the tracks of His Majesty's Sloop Discovery and armed tender Chatham," which shows the coast from 38° 15′ to 45° 46′ north latitude, and "A Chart shewing part of the Coast of N.W. America, with the tracks of His Majesty's Sloop Discovery and armed tender Chatham. Continental Shore has been correctly Traced and Determined," which pictures the coast from 30° north latitude to Kodiak Island.

than 250 miles to the Great Basin, they were to play an important part in ascertaining the geography of that area. If a coastal range existed along the Pacific, was it great enough to keep all streams from the interior from reaching the ocean? The Domínguez-Escalante expedition had visited the Great Basin and had discovered the San Buenaventura River, which Miera so eloquently argued deposited its waters in the sea. Now the question arose whether this river was of great enough magnitude to break through the coastal range and whether it had some connection with the Columbia River.

The results of the Vancouver expedition caught the eye of Alexander Mackenzie, whose explorations, together with those of Hearne, had burst the bubble of a sea-level route connecting the two oceans south of Arctic latitudes. When he published his journal in 1802, he envisioned the Columbia, which he mistook for the Peace-Frazer River system that he had discovered in 1793, as the future western appendage of the main route between the Atlantic and the Pacific.[8]

The Vancouver reports also caught the attention of Thomas Jefferson, who identified the Columbia with the Oregon, or River of the West, a vestige of the Sea of the West. Whereas Mackenzie believed that the rivers Nelson, Saskatchewan, and Columbia would provide the best route to India, Jefferson believed that the Missouri and the Columbia would do so, and sent Lewis and Clark out to prove it. The United States now had the opportunity to explore the Mississippi and Missouri basins since a vast new area of land, the Louisiana territory, had been bought from France in 1803. This purchase gave a new incentive to American exploration, and trappers, traders, and explorers entered the area and helped to lift the shroud of mystery that had for so long enveloped this and the far western regions. The ill-defined boundaries of the Louisiana Purchase were stretched farther and farther as interest developed, and eventually these adventurers pushed to the Pacific Ocean under the pretext of exploration.

In order to learn more about the new acquisition, President Jefferson chose Meriwether Lewis, his private secretary and a fellow Virginian, to lead an expedition into the territory and sent him to Phila-

---

[8] Mackenzie's account appears in his *Voyages from Montreal, on the River St. Lawrence, through the Continent of North America, to the Frozen and Pacific Oceans; in the Years 1789 and 1793* . . . , which contains three large maps illustrating his discoveries.

delphia for several weeks to study botany and astronomy in preparation for the trip. Lewis, in turn, invited William Clark to be co-leader of the enterprise. Fourteen soldiers and nine Kentucky hunters were also selected to make the journey. The civilians were enlisted in the army as privates since the venture was to be a military expedition.

Jefferson gave orders to the explorers to observe and to make a record of soils, minerals, plant and animal life, climate, and all noteworthy facts regarding the sources and courses of rivers and the latitude and longitude of important points. He also told them to ascertain the routes of Canadian traders and to find out whether furs could be advantageously collected at the head of the Missouri and transported to the States by that stream.

Lewis left Washington in July of 1803 and was joined by Clark and his party on the Ohio River. Winter overtook the group, and they made camp on the Dubois River, nearly opposite the mouth of the Missouri. On May 14, 1804, the expedition set out from this winter camp. The party traveled up the Missouri River, passed through the Arikara and Mandan villages, and in April, 1805, reached the mouth of the Yellowstone. On August 12 they reached the source of the Missouri, crossed the Continental Divide, and came upon the Lemhi River, a tributary of the Columbia. They reached the banks of the Clearwater River and on October 7 started downriver in their canoes. On November 7 they reached the Pacific Ocean and made their winter quarters at Young's Bay;[9] after spending a few months here at their quarters called Fort Clatsop, they started for home on March 23, 1806. They proceeded up the Columbia and reached the Clearwater; then the party divided on the Bitter Root River to explore possible new routes. Lewis explored the area around the Great Falls of the Missouri and the Marias River, while Clark followed in part the old route to the Three Forks and continued eastward. Thereafter the parties reunited and passed through the Mandan villages and reached St. Louis on September 23, 1806.[10]

In describing the Pacific Northwest, the Lewis and Clark Journal pays particular attention to the Multnomah River (Willamette),

[9] Near the present Oregon resort of Seaside.

[10] The standard editions of the Lewis and Clark journals are those edited by Elliott Coues (4 vols., N.Y., 1893), which will be referred to here; and by Reuben Gold Thwaites (8 vols., N.Y., 1904–1905). Bernard De Voto's edition of *The Journals of Lewis and Clark* is a convenient condensation.

saying: "The current of this latter river is as gentle as that of the Columbia, its surface is smooth and even, and it appears to possess water enough for the largest ship, since sounding with a line of five fathoms, he could find no bottom for at least one-third of the stream."[11] The Journal continues the discussion of the river, stating that the Multnomah "appears to be washing away its banks, and has more sandbars and willow points than the Columbia. Its regular gentle current, the depth and smoothness, and uniformity with which it rolls its vast body of water, prove that its supplies are at once distant and regular; nor, judging from its appearance and courses, is it rash to believe that the Multnomah and its tributary streams water the vast extent of country between the western mountains and those of the seacoast, as far perhaps as the waters of the gulf of California."[12]

These statements reiterate the great hope on the part of explorers, traders, merchants, and others for more than two centuries to discover a passage through the North American continent.

It is apparent that Lewis and Clark were familiar with the geography of the West as developed by Domínguez and Escalante in 1776. On the map drawn by William Clark the Multnomah was depicted as extending in a southwesterly direction from about 45.5 degrees to 38 degrees north latitude. The Domínguez-Escalante geographical conceptions are reflected in a river drawn by Clark which he calls the *Río de San Clementi* and which is the tributary of an unnamed river which empties into the Multnomah. According to Escalante, the "Río de San Clemente" (White River) emptied into the San Buenaventura. The similarity of the two names appears to be too close to be coincidental, and it seems safe to assume that the unnamed tributary of the Multnomah as drawn by Clark is the San Buenaventura. It is also interesting to note that Clark depicts several unnamed rivers branching off to the north of the Multnomah; however, across this region is written "Indians Yamparicas," which no doubt stems from Miera's "Río de las Yamparicas."[13]

Lewis and Clark were also well acquainted with the Garcés geo-

11 Lewis and Clark *Journals*, III, 33.

12 *Ibid.*, 34.

13 William Clark, "A Map of part of the Continent of North America . . . shewing Lewis and Clark's route over the Rocky Mountains in 1805 on their route to the Pacific from the United States."

graphical conceptions, for Clark's map reproduces a unique form of Garcés' findings. The "Río de los Martires" which was discovered by Garcés in 1776 and which is today the Mojave River, is pictured by Clark as a tributary of an unnamed stream emptying into San Francisco Bay. Thus it seems that Clark condensed Garcés' geographical speculations concerning the San Felipe, the tulares, and the river which he had heard about to the north and gave them concrete expression in 1811. This is most ironic since the Mojave River or "Río de los Martires" is in reality a meager, exotic stream which passes through such barren country that it is forced to take an underground course in places.

The Americans Lewis and Clark also made use of the Cook and Vancouver geography. Their geographical conceptions are depicted by Clark's drawing of a range of mountains along the coast, and he even portrays a mountain range parallel to the unnamed river depositing its waters in San Francisco Bay.

Manuscript field maps were made by William Clark at various times during the course of the two-year expedition,[14] and these illustrate in detail the entire route of the journey with indications of camp-sites and Indian villages. They also contain Clark's comments on the country that the expedition visited and the natives who were encountered along the way. Clark's final and complete map was based upon his original field maps and information that he obtained from other explorers and travelers. This project, which was begun in 1806, was not completed until 1811. The Clark map shows the Lewis and Clark trail and adjacent regions quite accurately but falls into error south of it, most likely on account of Clark's reliance upon two maps which were produced at this time by Baron Alexander von Humboldt and Zebulon Montgomery Pike which were considered the most authoritative and the most definitive to date.[15]

It is not surprising that Clark would be influenced by the maps of Alexander von Humboldt for an area with which he was unfamiliar

14 Clark's field maps are of various sizes and shapes, many of them pieced together from several sheets of paper. It is interesting to note that many of them were drawn on the backs of treaties that Jefferson had had printed for the explorers to use in their negotiations with the Indians, which seems to indicate that the party was running short of paper.

15 Alexander von Humboldt, *Carte du Mexique des Pays Limitrophes Situés au Nord et a l'Est* (Paris, 1811); Zebulon Pike, *A Map of the Internal Provinces of New Spain* (Philadelphia, 1810).

since Humboldt had one of the greatest scientific minds of the day and, perhaps with the exception of Napoleon Bonaparte, was the most famous man in Europe. He was greeted with applause from everyone; and academies, both domestic and foreign, tried to add his name to their roster of members. Humboldt was in the New World from 1799 until 1804, at which time he prepared his maps showing the western part of North America. He made a general map to accompany his political essay on New Spain and used, among other sources, the large manuscript Mascaro-Costanso map of 1784.[16] Humboldt thus became the first person to publish the results of the Domínguez-Escalante expedition. In using this source, Humboldt, of course, relied upon the expedition cartographer, Bernardo Miera y Pacheco, and accordingly incorporated into his maps Miera's two great errors, Lake Timpanogos and the San Buenaventura River. Humboldt's use of this source was to have a profound effect upon the course of western American cartography, particularly in the Great Basin area, for his map of New Spain was celebrated and soon became the model for European cartography dealing with this area.

Baron von Humboldt completed his map of New Spain in 1804, and on his return trip to Europe stopped in Washington for a visit with President Jefferson and gave him a copy. This copy was destined to form the basis for the maps of New Spain published in Zebulon M. Pike's account of his western travels which appeared in 1810.[17]

Pike, too, had never seen the Great Basin or some of its adjacent areas, and therefore he was more than willing to draw his information regarding this region from such a respectable source as Alexander von Humboldt. Pike had been ordered in 1806 to restore fifty Osages to their homes and to explore the country. This assignment

16 Humboldt's essay was written in French and published in Paris in 1811. It was translated by John Black and was published in four volumes in London in 1811 under the title *Political Essay on the Kingdom of New Spain*. The atlas which accompanied the French edition contains two general maps of New Spain which very clearly reflect the Miera conceptions of the Great Basin. This is natural since Humboldt, in his long introduction, acknowledges the use of Mascaro and Costanso, who had appropriated the Miera geography. For additional information, see C. Gregory Crampton, "Humboldt's Utah, 1811," *Utah Historical Quarterly*, Vol. XXVI (July, 1958), 268–81.

17 The standard scholarly edition of the journals of the Pike expedition is that edited by Elliott Coues. In volume II, pp. *xlii–xliii*, Coues points out Pike's indebtedness to Humboldt's map of New Spain.

took him through what is now Kansas and southern Nebraska into the present state of Colorado; there, on November 23, 1806, he saw the mountain which now bears his name. He then passed to the south, where he struck the South Platte and explored much of this country until he was taken as a Spanish prisoner to Chihuahua; his travels, however, did not take him far enough west for him to gain an accurate picture of the Pacific Slope or the Great Basin.

Pike's map, *A Map of the Internal Provinces of New Spain,* was published in 1810. It is very similar to the Humboldt map and incorporates the Miera and Font geography as it had been passed down through Mascaro-Costanso and Humboldt. The Pike map covers an area to 41 degrees north latitude, while the Humboldt map portrays the region to 42 degrees north latitude, and thus the northern part of Lake Timpanogos is reduced on the former; however, in other respects the two maps depicting the Great Basin are almost identical.

The narrative of the Pike journey attained virtually world-wide fame. Pike's *Account of an Expedition to the Sources of the Mississippi and through the Western Parts of Louisiana . . . and a Tour through the Interior Parts of New Spain* was published in Philadelphia in 1810, and in the following year was reprinted in London. In 1812 a French version was published in Paris, and in 1812–13 a Dutch version was published in Amsterdam.

The works of Pike, Humboldt, and Lewis and Clark, all of which were published in the years between 1810 and 1812, had a marked effect upon the Great Basin. Prior to this time, there had been only two well-documented expeditions into this area, but the journals and the reports of these expeditions had been deposited in archives where they became virtually unknown to the contemporary world. Thus it was through the efforts of these men that suddenly light was focused upon the area, and the Great Basin, which had been labeled *"Unbekante Gegenden Quivira"*[18] as late as 1807, now became a region of interest. The San Buenaventura River which Miera had created now provoked much speculation. The works of Pike, Humboldt, and Lewis and Clark, which were widely read and copied, sparked a cartographic extravaganza which lasted for thirty years and was focused in the latitudes of the Great Basin.

Lewis and Clark were of particular aid to the mythical cartogra-

18 Johann Walch, *Charte von Nordamerica* (Augsburg, Germany, 1807), as reproduced in the *Alaskan Boundary Tribunal Atlas*, I.

68

phers, for Clark depicted the Columbia breaking through the Cascades as well as another river emptying into San Francisco Bay. If it were true that two rivers heading in the vicinity of the Rockies could run directly through the mountain ranges to the sea, the cartographers felt that this would be true elsewhere. They therefore went to work, disregarding Vancouver's coast range, and emptied half a dozen Rocky Mountain rivers into the Pacific south of the Multnomah (Willamette). Of these, the San Buenaventura, which was carried from Sevier Lake, where Miera had left it, to San Francisco Bay, was the most promising possibility for the water route through the continent. It proved to be the last to fall, partially because of the stature of its first endorsers, Pike, Humboldt, and Lewis and Clark.

In 1810, John Jacob Astor, who had become extremely enthusiastic over the commercial possibilities revealed by Lewis and Clark, decided to enter aggressively the far western fur trade. On July 23 of that year, Astor completed the final articles of arrangement for the establishment of a company that was to be known as the Pacific Fur Company and that was to take part in the commerce and the fur trade on the Pacific Coast. In order to prosecute this scheme, Astor devised two expeditions, one to go by sea and the other to go by land. The former was to carry the stores, ammunition, and merchandise for establishing a trading post at the mouth of the Columbia River. The overland expedition, which was to be conducted by Wilson Price Hunt, was to proceed up the Missouri and across the Rocky Mountains. It was the purpose of this expedition to explore a line of communication across the continent and to note the places where interior trading posts might be established.[19]

Lewis and Clark had proved in 1804–1806 that the far northwestern territory of the United States could be reached by transcontinental travel within her own domain, but their line of march, though the logical one for an initial exploration, lacked the directness which prospective commerce would need. Thus in 1811–12 Wilson Price Hunt and his companions who were Astoria-bound took a more southerly route and thereby avoided the Lewis and Clark trail except for its eastern and western ends. In broad outline, Hunt's trail followed the main watercourses, such as the Wind and Snake rivers, which provided a rather devious track; however, he did

[19] *The Discovery of the Oregon Trail: Robert Stuart's Narratives* (ed. by Philip Ashton Rollins).

shorten his route by taking a more direct course from the Snake River to the Columbia by way of the Burnt, Powder, Grande Ronde, and Umatilla rivers, a route which was later to become dominant in the annals of the Snake River Brigade of the Hudson's Bay Company.

The Hunt expedition itself did not enter the Great Basin and is, therefore, not of primary interest to us in this context. However, an incident occurred on October 8, 1811, which does figure prominently in the history of exploration of this area. On this date, Joseph Miller announced at Henry's Fort[20] his intention of throwing in his lot with Jacob Reznor, Edward Robinson, John Hoback, and Martin Gass, four trappers whom Hunt had just detached from the expedition so that they might do local trapping. They were instructed to deliver their pelts to the nearest of the fur company's prospective posts. On October 10, Miller and his four companions began their extensive wanderings, which took them into the northeastern corner of the Great Basin, an area not previously seen by white men.

On June 9, 1812, a party under the leadership of Robert Stuart left Astoria to make a trip east to deliver dispatches to Astor. Stuart's companions were six men, all of whom were veterans of Hunt's westbound caravan: Benjamin Jones, John Day, André Valle, Francis LeClairc, Robert McClellan, and Ramsay Crooks. The group left the mouth of the Columbia and pushed to St. Louis by way of the westernmost fragment of the trail which had been used both by Lewis and Clark and by Hunt and his party. They then followed a westerly section of the independent trail of Hunt and traversed a previously unknown area before they utilized the second bit of Hunt's path. Now they plunged across an area which was unfamiliar to white men and traveled into the South Pass region and into the Sweetwater country, where they struck the Platte River and returned by way of it to St. Louis.[21]

It is of note than on Thursday, August 20, 1812, while the Stuart party was proceeding eastward, they met Miller and his companions who had detached themselves from the Hunt expedition at Henry's Fort the previous year. A good description of this reunion is given in Stuart's Journal for this day and seems to be the only record of the meeting and the course followed by the trappers:

20 Henry's Fort was built in the autumn of 1810 on the north fork of the Snake River in the vicinity of the present St. Anthony, Idaho.
21 *Robert Stuart's Narrative,* lxvi–lxvii.

. . . went East by South 12 Miles across two Bends[22] where going to drink we found John Hobough fishing and in an instant Mr. Miller, Edward Robinson, and Jacob Reznor who had been similarly employed came out of the Willows and joined us. They had on leaving the Party at Henry's Fort last Fall, gone 200 Miles South, where they made that season's Hunt on a River which must discharge itself into the Ocean to the Southward of the Columbia. From thence they steered 200 more due East where they found about Sixty lodges of Arapahays [who are an out law'd band of the Arapahoes], who robbed them [of several horses as well as the greater part of their clothing etc.] they then left them & continued their journey 50 miles, where they wintered, and early in the Spring were overtaken by the same Rascals, [who then] robbed [them] of all their Horses & almost every thing else. They [with half of the ammunition left] purchased of them two of their own Horses and after travelling 950 miles in which they suffered greatly by Hunger, thirst & fatigue, met us (almost in a state of nature) without even a single animal to carry their Baggage—Cass one of their party, having villainously left them with one of the Horses [while] on [the head waters of] the Big Horn, and the other was stolen by some Indians on this side of the Rocky Mountains.[23]

It seems quite likely that Miller and his party traveled into the extreme southern portion of what is now Idaho and a northerly section of the present state of Utah since Stuart refers to their having "gone 200 Miles South." The river on which they made their fall hunt was undoubtedly the Bear River, an important Great Basin stream. The Bear River follows a curvaceous course, entering the southeasterly corner of the present state of Idaho and thence flowing north and northwesterly to the northern end of Bear River Range, where it makes a hairpin turn before running south to discharge its waters in Great Salt Lake. Rollins feels that Miller and his companions had their fall hunt on this stretch of the Bear River just below the turn, and is confident for the following reasons that they were not on the Green River: (1) the men's mention of their travel having been south and not southeasterly to the stream where they trapped; (2) their implication of this river's flow as southward; (3) Miller's recognition of Bear River when he later encountered it with Stuart; and

22 Stuart cut across the bases of the bend containing Castle Buttes and the bend lying three miles southeast of it. *Ibid.*, 103, n. 173.

23 *Ibid.*, 85–86.

(4) Miller's futile attempt, after leaving Bear River, to find a stream flowing to the south.[24]

Miller joined Robert Stuart and his party, and the group proceeded on their way to St. Louis. They passed along Marsh Creek to the Portneuf River, and on Wednesday, September 9, entered the Great Basin. The entry in Stuart's journal for that day says:

> Here ascending, we passed through a Gap in the mountains on the left; which soon brought us to the opposite decent [*sic*] and discovered an extensive Plain lying before us—through this we steered due East and in 18 Miles struck a River running through an apparently level country in about a South direction, which Mr. Miller at once pronounced the Stream where he had made his last Falls hunt,—This River is 100 yards wide, and is here confined between a high Rocky bank and a [high] Hill partially covered with Trees of the Pine species.[25]

The group thus left the floor of the basin in which Fish Creek flows, crossed the hills which form the watershed between the valleys of Fish Creek and Bear River, and entered the Great Basin in the vicinity of the present town of Alexander, Idaho. This route is quite similar to that used by Peter Skene Ogden when he and his Snake Country Expedition entered the Great Basin in the spring of 1825. The Stuart-Miller party followed a southeast course, and on the second night within the Great Basin camped on the right bank of the Bear River about one mile northwest of the mouth of Ninemile Creek. On Saturday, the twelfth, Stuart made this entry in his Journal: "Immediately on leaving our last nights station the country opened very much to the South, the mountains receded to a great distance and a beautiful low Plain occupied the intervening space— 8 Miles E.S.E. and 6 S.E. brought us to the Forks of the River, where the banks were well supplied with a middling growth of Cottonwood."[26] This entry no doubt refers to the confluence of the present Bear Lake outlet with that of Bear River near the modern town of Dingle, Idaho. The next day, Sunday the thirteenth, the party came upon Thomas Fork of the Bear River, as this entry demonstrates: "Going 10 Miles East over hills to where a large Fork came in from

24 *Ibid.*, 104, n. 176.
25 *Ibid.*, 129.

the North . . . ."[27] They crossed the border into what is now the state of Wyoming and proceeded northward almost parallel to this political boundary.

Upon the following day, September 14, Stuart and his companions left the Great Basin after their very brief sojourn in that area as indicated by his entry for that day: "We unexpectedly passed the night in quietness and soon after sunrise continued up the Fork 3 miles, then ascending the Mountains on our right steered a little to the W. of N. for 18 more, when we found a considerable Branch running due north on which we stopped for the night."[28] It seems most likely from this entry that the party passed up the right fork of Thomas Fork and encountered the southern end of Gannett Hills, which rise to an elevation of about eight hundred feet at the entrance to Thomas Fork Canyon. They then struck Spring Creek, a northwardly flowing tributary of Crow Creek, which is a confluent of Salt River, so they had now left the Great Basin and entered the Snake River drainage system.

It has often been speculated whether, in their trek across the northeastern corner of the Great Basin and into the present southern Wyoming region, the Stuart party in the fall of 1812 encountered South Pass, the superb corridor through the Rocky Mountains. Phillips suggests that South Pass might have been visited some months earlier, in the spring of 1812, by a group of Manuel Lisa's men.[29] An article which appeared in the *Missouri Gazette* on May 15, 1813, seems to indicate that South Pass had been visited by Caucasians, for this account is strangely reminiscent of a report made by General Ashley describing this same phenomenon more than a decade later. The article says:

> . . . it appears that a journey across the continent of N. America, might be performed with a waggon, there being no obstruction in the whole route that any person would dare to call a mountain in addition to its being much the most direct and short one to go from this place to the mouth of the Columbia river. Any future party who may undertake this journey, and are tolerably acquainted with the different places, where it would be necessary to lay up a

26 *Ibid.,* 130–31.
27 *Ibid.,* 131.
28 *Ibid.,* 132; 145–46, n. 61–64.
29 Paul C. Phillips, *The Fur Trade,* 266–67.

small stock of provisions would not be impeded, as in all probability they would not meet with an Indian to interrupt their progress; altho on the other route more north there are almost insurmountable barriers.[30]

However, if the discovery were made, the geographical findings of these expeditions were ephemeral, for it was not until 1824 that Jedediah Smith "rediscovered" South Pass and led the vanguard of the American fur men south into the untrapped beaver country of the Green River Valley and Great Basin.

Although the geographical knowledge gained by the Stuart party had little impact upon contemporary scientific circles, it is interesting to note the geographical conceptions of Miller and Stuart, because they with their companions were the first white men to visit the Bear River and this portion of the Great Basin. Miller's information concerning the river on which they hunted is of particular note in regard to the geography of this area, for as it was reported in Stuart's Journal, ". . . they made that season's Hunt on a River which must discharge itself into the Ocean to the Southward of the Columbia."[31]

Was Miller speaking of the Green River, which actually discharges its waters into the ocean by way of the Colorado River system? It seems unlikely, since it is strongly suspected that Miller and his party were on the Bear River, as indicated above. In support of this conclusion, Washington Irving in *Astoria* states:

> After leaving Mr. Hunt's party, they had made their way about two hundred miles to the southward, where they trapped beaver on a river which, according to their account, discharged itself into the ocean south of the Columbia, but which we apprehend to be the Bear River, a stream emptying itself into Lake Bonneville, an immense body of salt water, west of the Rocky Mountains.[32]

It appears, therefore, that Miller's interpretation of the geography of the West was a correlation of the Domínguez-Escalante and Garcés conceptions, for he suggests that this river which is in the vicinity of the San Buenaventura flows to the ocean. We do know that these men were familiar with the findings of Lewis and Clark, and it is interesting that they dissociated the streams of the area from the Multnomah,

30 *Robert Stuart's Narrative,* lxvii.
31 *Ibid.,* 86.
32 III, 32.

contrary to the Lewis and Clark geography, and thus helped to perpetuate the idea that a stream rising in this region had an outlet on the western coast south of the Columbia.

This composite geography is probably a result of their own findings and information taken from contemporary maps. No doubt, the Astorians were aware of the Humboldt and Pike geography even though Pike's map was only published in 1810, one year before they made their departure, and Humboldt's maps, as well as the map of Lewis and Clark, were not published until after the Astorians had passed to the Pacific Coast. Nevertheless, John Jacob Astor, who was a man of influence, probably obtained information concerning this area from his friend President Jefferson, the Astorians in turn gaining their information from Astor.

The explorations of the Astorians and of those who were to follow them were a direct result of the enthusiasm that was engendered by the foresight of John Jacob Astor and men like him. The British scientific expeditions had revealed the commercial possibilities of the North Pacific Coast and had established the fur trade in western North America. Within half a century of the Cook voyage, British and American fur trade rivalry in the Columbia and Missouri basins led the partisans of these nations into virgin territory—the last great area under Arctic latitudes to be explored, the Great Basin.

Although Cook and Vancouver coasted the shores of the Pacific Ocean some distance from the landlocked Great Basin, and Lewis and Clark, seeking the shores of the Pacific overland, passed several hundred miles to the north of this land of interior drainage, their geographical findings had a direct bearing upon the Great Basin. The coastal ranges portrayed cartographically by the British scientific expeditions were in part torn down by Lewis and Clark, who argued for a waterway from the interior of the continent to the Pacific Coast. Using Spanish sources, principally Miera, Clark tied the British coastal explorations to the Spanish interior expeditions and attempted to develop an understanding of the area that lay between, the Great Basin. Clark had substantial aid in disseminating this conclusion of a water passage, for through the works of Alexander von Humboldt and Zebulon Pike, published in many editions and numerous languages, a wide audience was informed of scientific and geographical developments. The Great Basin, with the exception of a small portion of its eastern flank, and a small corner of its southwestern rim, still lay unknown, but now this unexplored region in the heart of the Trans–Rocky Mountain West became the center of a cartographic extravaganza. Because of the turbulent world conditions—marked by the French Revolution, the Napoleonic wars, the War of 1812, and the struggles for independence in Latin America—national governments were unable at this time to take an active part in the expansion in western North America. However, with attention directed to the Great Basin area, other individuals besides John Jacob Astor began to recognize the commercial potentialities revealed by Cook, Vancouver, and Lewis and Clark. Thus it came about that it was the fur trappers and traders who were destined to explore the interior-drainage basin, although it was the leader of another scientific expedition, John Charles Frémont, who was to achieve a geographical understanding of the Great Basin and so name it.

5

THE LURE OF FUR

THE FUR TRADE FOR MORE THAN TWO CENTURIES was the principal business, if not the only one, transacted upon the American frontier. This commercial enterprise, which was so well suited to the North American continent, was pioneered by the French and British, who had abandoned their visionary dreams of wealth derived from precious metals for more substantial goals. With the Peace of Paris of 1763, Britain replaced France as the supreme power in North America, and with the culmination of the American Revolution in 1783 the United States became the competitor of John Bull. Thus while the first explorers and cartographers were focusing attention upon the Trans-Mississippi West, British and American competition in the Columbia and Missouri basins stimulated interest in the southern drainage area and led fur trappers into the Great Basin.

Although the Astorians were the first significant group to cross the continent to the Pacific after Lewis and Clark, their expedition was similar to the Spanish expeditions, for from a historical and geographical standpoint only a small amount of information was acquired and disseminated by them, and therefore they did little to mold the pattern of future exploration of the Great Basin. However, the route used by the returning members of the Pacific Fur Company in the fall of 1812 would undoubtedly have led to exploration south and west of South Pass almost at once had it not been for the War of 1812, which disrupted the fur trade and prevented the use of this avenue of travel for more than a decade. Although the War of 1812 was one of a number of minor incendiary conditions in the world at the time, it had important consequences in North America. Indeed, it was this same war which postponed Anglo-American rivalry on the Pacific Slope and made the Great Basin rather than the Columbia

77

River Valley the field of battle for British and American fur companies.

The War of 1812 affected the Trans-Mississippi fur trade considerably, particularly on the Columbia and upper Missouri rivers, by diminishing the territory in which the trade was carried on and by causing the price of pelts to fall on account of uncertainty regarding the outcome. This is most clearly illustrated by a letter written by Charles Gratiot to John Jacob Astor in 1813, in which he states: "Since the Declaration of War the traders will not receive any [skins] from the Indians, that article having fallen in price."[1]

The second and most serious effect of the war was the general unrest incited among the Indian tribes within the reach of border influence and the imminent danger that the frontier settlements of Missouri would suffer from an Indian war. British influence among the various tribes of Indians was strong, and it was certain that now that the two countries were at war, no effort would be spared to utilize this influence to the utmost. Trade was virtually suspended on the river, and reports came in substantiating the supposed conditions, such as this one which appeared in the *Missouri Gazette* on June 5, 1813:

> Arrived here a few days ago from the Mandan villages [Upper Missouri], Mr. M. Lisa, acting partner of the Missouri Fur Co. From Mr. Lisa we learn that the Arapahoes, Cheyennes, Aricaras, Gros Ventres, and Crows are, or may be, considered at war with the Americans. The British Northwest Company having a number of trading houses within a short distance of the Missouri, are enabled to embroil our people with the savages, who are constantly urged to cut them off.[2]

The North West Company was indeed a formidable opponent and was firmly entrenched within the area whose name it bore. It had had its beginnings in an agreement made by a number of Montreal merchants in 1779 to pool traffic and had passed through a series of subsequent agreements until, in 1787, all the important merchants were brought together into a partnership. This company had two classes of shareholders: the eastern partners, who were merchants of substance in Montreal and Quebec who supplied the capital for the

1 Hiram Martin Chittenden, *The American Fur Trade of the Far West*, II, 555.
2 *Ibid.,* II, 557–58.

venture, and the so-called "wintering partners," who contributed
the skill and leadership needed in the field. The North West Company reached great proportions, employing almost two thousand men
at its height, and at Montreal and at Fort William on the western
shore of Lake Superior, the company had large warehouses which
assured to the interior posts regularity of supply.

The formation of the North West Company forced the Hudson's
Bay Company to expand westward for fear of losing the trade with
the western Indians which she had gained after the expulsion of the
French. As a result, both these British companies began to push operations westward and to establish posts farther and farther from their
home base, so that, by the end of the eighteenth century, each company had traders on the upper Missouri.

In 1804 the North West Company made a resolute attempt to gain
control of this trade and sent out François Antoine Larocque to win
over the Sioux and Crow Indians. Larocque's party spent the winter
in the Mandan villages near which Lewis and Clark had made their
camp. In 1805, Larocque passed through the Mandan villages to
the Little Horn, the Big Horn, and finally the Yellowstone, striking
it near Pryor's Fork.[3] The United States refused to allow this trade
within its borders, and the North West Company had to continue
its western expansion to the north.

The work of carrying the trade of the North West Company to
the Pacific Coast was entrusted to a group of able men, the most
notable of whom was David Thompson. In 1807, Thompson actually
crossed the Rockies and reached the headwaters of the Columbia.
In 1809 he again crossed the mountains and built Kullyspell House
on the east shore of Lake Pend Oreille. From this point, he moved
to Clarks Fork of the Columbia and in November built the first
Salish House, which was located near the site of present Thompson
Falls, Montana. Shortly thereafter, Thompson or one of his companions built Spokane House, which definitely entrenched the North
West Company in the Columbia Basin. After carrying his explora-
tions down the Columbia to below the mouth of the Snake River,
Thompson claimed this whole area in the name of Great Britain.[4]

Ironically, ahead of Thompson at the mouth of the Columbia

---

[3] *Journal de Larocque de la rivière Assiniboine jûsqu' à la rivière "Aux Roche
Jaunes"* (ed. by L. J. Burpee), 16–42.

[4] Gordon Charles Davidson, *The Northwest Company.*

River was the first party of Astor's Pacific Fur Company under the command of Duncan McDougal and three other men, all former Nor'westers. The promising outlook for the Pacific Fur Company, however, was abruptly changed by the War of 1812, and, conversely, the position of the North West Company strengthened. When news of the outbreak of war was brought to Astor's men and a British warship was reported sailing for Astoria, Astor's partners in the Oregon country—probably influenced by their British citizenship and previous connections—decided it would be useless to attempt to hold their ground. Thus in October, 1813, they sold Astoria and all of the Pacific Fur Company's interest in the region to the North West Company.[5] With the arrival of the British war vessel, Astoria was renamed Fort George and began a colorful career as the major British entrepôt on the Pacific Coast until 1825, when it was superseded by Fort Vancouver.

With these negotiations, the North West Company was firmly implanted on the Pacific Coast of North America, and the bitter rivalry between this company and the Hudson's Bay Company continued and increased in its fierceness. For the next eight years, rival posts fought each other at close range; there was undercutting and overbidding, and the Indians were competitively plied with liquor while each side attempted to seize and confiscate the other's supplies and furs. The result was the complete disorganization of the northern fur trade. Prices that were paid to the Indians for furs rose to such levels that profits became out of the question. By 1820 this struggle had brought the two belligerents to the verge of bankruptcy.

Finally, in 1821, peace between the two companies came when the North West Company merged with the Hudson's Bay Company, with the latter retaining its own identity and keeping its charter and ancient privileges undisturbed. As a reward for the peace and to insure against any further outbreak of such competition, the British government conferred upon the reorganized company, under an act of Parliament of 1821, exclusive trading rights for twenty-one years in the part of British North America lying between Rupert's Land and the Rocky Mountains, in addition to sole trading rights in the Oregon country. The whole area which is now the Dominion of Canada, with the exception of the St. Lawrence Valley and the Maritime Provinces, together with what is now the Pacific North-

[5] For the Bill of Sale, see *ibid.*, Appendix M, 293–96.

west of the United States, was under the control of the Hudson's Bay Company after 1821. This was a great advance for the company, which had been limited previously to the area east of the Rockies, the area drained by Hudson Bay. Now it was the Hudson's Bay Company that fell heir to John Jacob Astor's fort at the mouth of the Columbia and was to compete with the companies of the United States and Russia.[6]

The American fur trade, with its headquarters at St. Louis, began before the close of the eighteenth century, with such prominent traders as Manuel Lisa and Auguste and Pierre Chouteau. As a result of the Lewis and Clark Expedition, which revealed the economic potentialities of the Pacific Northwest, Lisa led a party up the Missouri to the mouth of the Yellowstone, thence up that river to the mouth of the Big Horn, where he established a trading post. Lisa was so impressed with the possibilities of the fur trade on the upper Missouri that he decided to form a company of the leading fur traders of St. Louis. This was the Missouri Fur Company, organized in 1808 with Pierre and Auguste Chouteau, William Clark, and five others. The first expedition under Lisa's command started up the Missouri in the summer of 1809 and built a post where the three forks of the Missouri unite. However, the Blackfeet, who had long traded with the British and who were apparently incited by them, now began open hostility which was characterized by a series of attacks. With the War of 1812 as well as the Indian depredations, the company continually declined, although it went through several reorganizations. One by one the partners dropped out, some of them forming competing companies.

After the fur trade had remained almost inactive during the War of 1812, interest was revived at the close of the war, and by 1820 a four-way competition was shaping up for the wealth of the upper Missouri. Another company joined those interested in the beaver country of the north—the Rocky Mountain Fur Company, founded by General William Ashley and Major Andrew Henry in 1822, which contained the most impressive roster of names connected with exploration of the Great Basin.

Indian depredations continued to limit operations on the upper Missouri. In October, 1822, Michael Immell and Robert Jones of the

[6] John S. Galbraith, *The Hudson's Bay Company as an Imperial Factor, 1821–1869.*

Missouri Fur Company, after wintering at the mouth of the Big Horn, lost four of their men to Blackfeet, and then they themselves, along with five others, were killed by a group of Bloods.

In the spring of 1823 a party belonging to the Rocky Mountain Fur Company was trapping above the Great Falls of the Missouri when it was attacked by Blackfeet. With the death of four of the eleven members of the party, operations in the high Missouri ceased for at least six years.

Then in 1823 occurred the greatest disaster in the history of the American fur trade. When General Ashley and his party were passing through the Arikara villages on their way to the Yellowstone to rejoin the detached group who had wintered there, they were attacked by the Arikaras. Ashley lost thirteen men, and eleven more were wounded, two of whom later died; the number of dead alone comprised one-sixth of Ashley's force.

Conditions seemed to be growing worse and no respite was in sight, as is attested by this letter written by Colonel Leavenworth from Fort Atkinson to army headquarters in which he refers to Major Henry's party and Indian conditions: "They received information from the Crow Indians, that the Blackfoot Indians were determined to hunt continually for the trapping parties and destroy them, whenever it was possible to do so. This was also the expectation of the whole party."[7]

After further skirmishes with the Indians which resulted in a great loss of men as well as traps and supplies, the trapping grounds of the upper Missouri were losing their appeal. On July 9, 1824, Major O'Fallon wrote a letter to William Clark in which he very aptly described the state of affairs: "Mr. Vandenburg & Co. have returned (that is, Fort Recovery itself has been abandoned)—The surrounding trappers and hunters are descending from the mountains and are going out of the Indian country, leaving the upper Country stained with the innocent blood of the most daring and enterprising portion of our people."[8] Now Fort Kiowa was the sole bastion of the fur trade above Council Bluffs.

The difficulties on the upper Missouri had a definite effect upon the history of the Great Basin, for, after a series of attacks which practically crippled the already financially precarious companies,

7 Dale L. Morgan, *Jedediah Smith and the Opening of the West*, 103.
8 *Ibid.*, 113.

operations had to be halted in that region, and the Blackfoot country of Montana had to be avoided. As a result, American fur operations shifted gradually to the south to take advantage of the trade with friendly tribes of Indians, and this led to the exploration of the Great Basin by the mountain men.

The activities of Jedediah Strong Smith of the Rocky Mountain Fur Company played a dominant part in bringing about this southern shift and the selection of the Great Basin as the field of trial in a test of strength between the British and American fur companies. After General Ashley and his party had met their fate at the hands of the Arikaras in 1823, Smith was ordered to take a route which had been hitherto unused for trapping incursions. He proposed to strike out for the Black Hills by a route as direct as possible. He struck the winter camp of the Crows high up on the Wind River, and when spring came, planned to cross the mountains via Union Pass, the route the outbound Astorians had used in September, 1811. The Crows, however, made a most important recommendation—that Smith and his party should negotiate the mountains to the south of Union Pass, by way of what was to be known as the famous South Pass.[9] Adopting this advice, the detached band of the Rocky Mountain Fur Company trappers followed up the Sweetwater River, and in the early spring of 1824 made the effective discovery of the mountain gateway which brought this superb natural phenomenon from obscurity and established an eastern entrance into the Great Basin. This afforded a southwestern orientation from the Wind River area of Wyoming and led trappers, traders, explorers, and emigrants into the labyrinth of basins and ranges which characterize the region of interior drainage.

When Jedediah Smith and the vanguard of the Rocky Mountain Fur Company entered the Great Basin in 1824, they brought into this region the American trapping techniques which became so much a part of the Great Basin during the second and third decades of the nineteenth century and were characterized by some of the most picturesque practices in American history. The most notable was that of the rendezvous, a system of predetermined meetings which began in July of 1825 and were held yearly until approximately 1839, the year in which the annual rendezvous was abandoned by the American Fur Company. Each year a valley was chosen as the site of the ren-

9 *Ibid.,* 89–90.

dezvous for the coming year, and it was arranged that the various mountain parties should meet there on a particular date. To the rendezvous came the caravans from the East, generally from Independence, Missouri, which were laden with equipment to supply the trappers for the next year's hunt. From other directions came the company hunters who would turn over their furs to the eastern caravan in return for their wages and new equipment; there also came the free trappers and Indians who sold their furs on the best obtainable terms and purchased their equipment for the ensuing year. While business was being transacted and the cargoes of furs were being stowed for the homeward journey, this heterogeneous assemblage indulged in a good time. Of the approximately fifteen meetings of this fur trade institution, a number were held in the Great Basin and had the effect of drawing trappers as well as Indians from every possible direction to take part in the proceedings.

With the initiation of the rendezvous by the Rocky Mountain Fur Company and its firm adoption as the standard procedure in the mountain country, trappers were allowed the freedom of traveling widely within this new area without having to report their operations to a fort or post or losing much of their hunting time in retracing their steps to their source of supply. Thus Ashley's Rocky Mountain Fur Company and its successor, the firm of Smith, Jackson and Sublette, were able to move out from their rendezvous in the Great Salt Lake or Green River area to almost every part of the Great Basin and were, therefore, the discoverers and explorers of many of the most important physical features of the land of interior drainage, including the Great Salt Lake.

The British companies employed quite different means of securing furs, which did not prove to be advantageous at all times. In eastern Canada the practice had been to establish a post and then wait for the local Indian tribes to bring furs into the fort to trade. This system, which was traditional with the North West Company, had never proved successful on the Pacific Slope, and the company was in the end forced to adapt, at least partially, to the new conditions and to the methods employed by the Americans. For, as Governor Simpson of the Hudson's Bay Company observed in 1824, "They [the western Indians] are very independent of us requiring but few of our supplies and it is not until absolutely in need of an essential article or an

84

article of finery such as Guns and Beads that they will take the trouble of hunting."[10]

Upon the appointment in 1822 of George Simpson as the Hudson's Bay Company's governor of the Northern Department and the territory west of the Rockies, a swift and thorough reorganization of the old North West Company properties and practices took place. Posts that were found to be no longer useful were abandoned, and those that were thought to be poorly located were shifted. By 1824 there remained only one great area now belonging to the Hudson's Bay Company to be rehabilitated, the area lying west of the Rocky Mountains—the Columbia Department. No solid foundation for authority existed here, as its sovereignty was still undetermined. Russia, Great Britain, and the United States all laid claim to it. By 1824, however, the Russians were on the verge of withdrawing to the parallel of 54 degrees, 40 minutes. After the failure of Great Britain and the United States to agree to the partition of this area, a treaty had been concluded in 1818 which provided for joint occupation and gave to the nationals of each country the right to trade in all of the region for a period of ten years.

To make the Columbia Department more profitable, Governor Simpson made a trip to the Pacific Coast in 1824. His findings are most enlightening and divulge a great deal of information pertaining to the current methods and practices. In an entry in his diary for Tuesday, November 2, 1824, in connection with Fort Nez Percés, which had been built under the direction of Donald Mackenzie in 1818, he comments on the old North West Company's system of establishing a post and waiting for trade:

There is an Establishment of Eleven in all attached to it which will admit of reduction and by lopping off the superfluities in the outfit I am in hopes that the next year it will shew a very material amendment. Its returns this season are estimated at 2000 Beaver got principally from a branch of the Nez Perces tribe called the Caiuses and it does not appear to me that there is a prospect of any considerable increase unless trappers are introduced as the Indians cannot be prevailed on to exert themselves in hunting.[11]

10 Entry in George Simpson's diary for November 2, 1824, *Fur Trade and Empire: The Journal of Sir George Simpson* (ed. by Frederick Merk), 54–57.
11 *Ibid.*

Many expeditions with these posts as their bases were combing the western watercourses for furs. One of the most important and one that was to play a significant role in the exploration of the Great Basin was the Snake Country Expedition. This expedition, which was known as "the most hazardous and disagreeable office in the Indian Country," was to become one of the largest sources of furs for the Columbia Department. Donald Mackenzie, who had established this brigade in 1818, led the expedition himself on three successive occasions. Since no one on the Columbia felt it was either his interest or his duty to take Mackenzie's place, no quasi-permanent appointments were made until 1823, when Alexander Ross took the post. Ross's leadership of this group was short lived, for in 1824, when Governor Simpson was making his rounds of inspection he stated:

> This important duty should not in my opinion be left to a self-sufficient empty headed man like Ross who feels no further interest therein than in as far as it secures to him a Sal^y of L 120 p.Annun and whose reports are so full of bombast and marvellous nonsense that it is impossible to get any information that can be depended on from him. . . . A charge of such consequence I therefore conceived should be in the hands of a commissioned Gentleman and knowing no one in the country better qualified to do it justice than Mr. Ogden I propose that he should undertake it and it affords me much pleasure to say that he did so with the utmost readiness.[12]

With this appointment, Peter Skene Ogden, one of the most important mountain men to enter the Great Basin, became the leader of the Snake Country Expedition, which post he was to hold until 1830. During this period, he led large fur brigades over more territory than any other man, with the possible exception of Jedediah Smith, the spark of the Rocky Mountain Fur Company. In 1825 his was the first party to enter Ogden Valley, and his explorations in this area have been remembered and perpetuated through the attachment of his name to such features as Ogden City, North Ogden,[13] Ogden Valley, and Ogden River.[14]

12 Entry for Thursday, October 28, 1824, *ibid.,* 44–47.
13 However, Ogden never visited the sites of the present Ogden City and North Ogden.
14 David E. Miller, "Peter Skene Ogden's Exploration of the Great Salt Lake Region: A Restudy Based on Newly Published Journals," *The Western Humanities Review,* Vol. VIII (Spring, 1954), 139–50.

The fact that Ross was leader of the Snake Country Brigade was not the only fault that Governor Simpson found with this body for he says:

It has hitherto been usual for the Snake Country Expedition to start from the Flat Head Post in the month of February, and then return in the month of November laying idle at that place all Winter; but several objections presented themselves in my mind to this arrangement:—viz., By laying idle at the Flat Head Post from the month of Nov. till Feby. the best hunting season when Fur bearing animals are in their prime is lost their hunts are consequently of little value the Furs being out of Season; a great deal of time is also lost in going to and returning from their hunting Grounds, say half the year unprofitably consumed and the very season when they could be most usefully and industriously occupied as then there is little danger comparatively speaking to be apprehended from roving War parties it being well known that Summer is the favorite time for these excursions and that the plain Tribes of the East side of the Mountain are following the Buffalo about the North and South branches of the Saskatchewan all Winter. In the next place by laying at the Flat Head Post such a length of time the Freemen consume in the course of the Winter their ammuntion and other supplies which they receive in the Fall and will not start in the Spring until they have a second outfit which they cannot afford to pay for. Moreover if there is a scarcity of Provisions at the Flat Head Post in the Winter their Horses are consumed and the company must supply them anew which is at times a difficult matter each hunter requiring three Horses to do his duty well; and lastly when such a worthless and motley crew are collected together laying idle for Four Months on end they are forming plots and plans quarrelling with the natives and exposing themselves and us to much trouble and danger.[15]

This method of combing the fur-bearing areas was the direct antithesis of the rendezvous system employed by the Americans. It was the latter system, I believe, which accounts for the exploration of such vast areas in a relatively short period by the Americans and which brought about the contest for the "Oregon country" at an earlier date than might otherwise have been the case.

In the United States no great companies arose until late in the

[15] Entry in Simpson's diary for October 28, 1824, *The Journal of Sir George Simpson*, 44-47.

first decade of the nineteenth century, and, as a result, the American fur trade did not follow any elaborate scheme of organization such as that of the Hudson's Bay Company. Circumstances in the United States had been unfavorable to the building of such a trade. The Revolutionary War had absorbed the energies and attention of the people, and at its end they were little prepared to enter at once upon great commercial undertakings. When American fur operations did begin, its partisans, accustomed to acting individually, felt no need to wait upon a weak government for aid which it could not have given in any event. Therefore, the American trade followed in good part a principle of free trade as opposed to the mercantile practice of the British companies, and thus the concept of individualism met the onslaught of social organization in the barren arena of the Great Basin.

Governor Simpson had already pointed out his objections to many of the British methods, and in 1826, Peter Skene Ogden reiterated the same point most strongly. In a letter written from Burnt River, Ogden said:

> In all the different expeditions to the Snake Country two thirds of the time is lost in travelling to and from headquarters, far different is the mode the Americans conduct their trapping expedition, their trappers remain five and six years in their hunting grounds and their equippers meet them annually secure their furs and give them their supplies and although great expense and danger they have to encounter to reach the Missouri,[16] still they find it to their advantage to conduct their business in this way.[17]

Governor Simpson devoted much time in his recommendations to the improvement of the Snake Country Expedition since he saw in it an instrument to combat the Americans who were beginning to penetrate across the Rocky Mountains and well onto the Pacific Slope. The governor and committee of the Hudson's Bay Company were most apprehensive in regard to the western movement of the Americans, and in a letter written as early as 1822, they expressed their concern in regard to a certain article from an American news-

[16] Ogden seems to have been somewhat confused about where the rendezvous was held.

[17] Letter, P. S. Ogden to Governor Simpson, July 1, 1826 as quoted in *The Journal of Sir George Simpson,* Appendix A, 276–77.

paper which stated that 150 Americans had left the Missouri on an expedition across the Rockies toward the Columbia. The governor and committee also stated that they had learned of the intention of the United States government to form a settlement on the Columbia and requested information concerning these developments.[18]

The replacement of Ross by Peter Skene Ogden in 1824 seems to have had far greater significance than the mere changing of the leadership of an interior brigade. Ogden, the old Nor'wester who had been passed over during the merger of the two companies because of his intense feeling against the Hudson's Bay Company during the competitive period, now was thought to be of considerable service in combating the American threat; as Simpson put it, "he does not now want for ability."[19]

In replacing Ross, Simpson struck the chord that was to initiate a new Hudson's Bay Company policy. This action was to give to the heretofore motley Snake Brigade political overtones which were to have international ramifications. In referring to the Snake Country Expedition, Governor Simpson said: "If properly managed no question exists that it would yield handsome profits as we have convincing proof that the country is a rich preserve of Beaver and which for political reasons we should endeavor to destroy as fast as possible."[20] Thus began the famous "scorched earth" policy, a familiar Hudson's Bay Company weapon which was employed fairly effectively, although it did not in the end produce the desired results. And, of course, it was made obsolete by the international decisions of the United States and Great Britain in 1845–46 when the British with their Hudson's Bay Company retreated into the area of present Canada.

It is apparent that at least two important considerations were the motivating forces in promulgating this so-called "scorched earth"

18 The Governor and Committee to John Haldane and John D. Cameron, September 4, 1822, *ibid.*, 187–88.

19 Governor Simpson to A. Colville, September 8, 1823, *ibid.*, 203. For further information concerning Ogden's appointment, see Gloria Griffen Cline, "Peter Skene Ogden's Nevada Explorations," *Nevada Historical Quarterly*, Vol. III (July–Sept., 1960); Gloria Griffen Cline, "Jedediah Smith: Leading Contender in the Anglo-American Fur Rivalry," *The Pacific Historian*, Vol. V (August, 1961), 95–103.

20 Entry in Simpson's diary for October 28, 1824, *The Journal of Sir George Simpson*, 44–47.

policy. First, and what seems by far the more important cause, the British were anxious to trap out the interior parts of North America, namely the Great Basin and the Snake and Green (Colorado) drainage areas, to discourage economically the American trappers in their thrust westward and to retain for the British their hold on the rich areas of the Columbia Basin and New Caledonia. Second, when it became apparent that Great Britain could no longer hope for a boundary which would include the Oregon country, the Hudson's Bay Company wanted to obtain as many pelts from that area as possible.

The diaries and correspondence of this period contain many undertones which allude to these motives. As early as 1822, when the Hudson's Bay Company had just taken possession of the North West Company's lands, a letter was written by the Governor and committee to Governor Simpson stating:

> We understand that hitherto the trade of the Columbia has not been profitable, and from all that we have learnt on the subject we are not sanguine in our expectations of being able to make it so in future. But if by any improved arrangement the loss can be reduced to a small sum, it is worth a serious consideration, whether it may not be good policy to hold possession of that country, with the view of protecting the more valuable districts to the North of it.[21]

In order to lessen the inducements for the American trappers, the various interior posts were improved and the brigades were made larger. Fort Nez Percés on the Walla Walla River, which became one of the most important headquarters for the Snake Country Expedition, was ordered in 1824 to "be made as respectable as possible, as well as any others on the North side of the River, and as we cannot expect to have a more Southern boundary than the Columbia in any Treaty with the Americans (altho' we are entitled to it from occupancy) it will be very desirable that the hunters should get as much out of the Snake Country as possible for the next few years."[22]

After Ogden's first expedition into the Snake country, the gov-

[21] Letter, the Governor and Committee to George Simpson, February 27, 1822, *ibid.*, Appendix A, 175.

[22] Letter, the Governor and Committee to J. D. Cameron, July 22, 1824, *ibid.*, Appendix A, 241-42.

ernor and committee wrote a letter to the chief factors of the Columbia Department in which they said: "We also notice Mr. Ogdens observations respecting the Trade of the interior, and as you are already in possession of our views as far as regards the Americans, we have merely to observe that it will be advisable to work the southern portion of the Country as hard as possible, while it continues free to the subjects of both Nations."[23]

These words were repeated over and over and were decidedly heeded, as is shown by actions in the field as well as by correspondence such as this excerpt from a letter complimenting Dr. McLoughlin on his work in the Columbia Department: "We are desirous that those Parties should be kept in constant and active employment, should they even do no more than clear expenses, as the impoverishment of the country situated to the Southward of the Columbia, we consider the most effectual protection against opposition from the Americans."[24]

This "scorched earth" policy proved economically profitable, for in 1828, when Jedediah Smith spent the winter at Fort Vancouver, he reported that the post was flourishing. Supply ships came regularly from London to this depot on the Columbia to stock the large warehouses and to sail away with the valuable furs. Smith reported that thirty thousand beaver skins, valued at $250,000, in addition to large quantities of other furs, had been brought to that fort during the preceding year.[25]

The British settlements on the Pacific Coast went virtually unchallenged until the forties. Overland migration of actual American settlers did not begin until 1841; prior to that time the only Americans in the Oregon country were either retired trappers or persons connected with one of the missions. By the year 1843, however, the methods of overland travel had been fairly well worked out, and the number of emigrants increased annually. By 1844 the political parties took up the question of the Oregon boundary, and, in the national presidential campaign of that year, the Democrats adopted the slogan

23 Letter, the Governor and Committee to the Chief Factors of the Columbia Department, July 27, 1825, *ibid.*, Appendix A, 252–53.

24 Letter, the Governor and Committee to John McLoughlin, October 28, 1829, *ibid.*, Appendix A, 318.

25 LeRoy R. Hafen and Carl Coke Rister, *Western America*, 234–35; J. A. Hussey, *The History of Fort Vancouver*, 50–51.

of "Fifty-four forty or fight." Upon the victory of that party and the inauguration of President Polk, American title to the whole of Oregon was asserted to be "clear and unquestionable." The net result was the stimulation of emigration, which reached three thousand in 1845 and made the Americans predominant in Oregon.

With American ascendancy in that quarter, President Polk asked Congress in December of 1845 to serve notice on England of the termination of the joint-occupation agreement pertaining to the Oregon country. With this request acceded to and the required one year's notice given for the abrogation, the two countries attempted to decide upon a boundary. Inasmuch as the United States was engaged in a war with Mexico in 1846, she was hardly in a position to fight for 54 degrees, 40 minutes, so when England proposed a continuation of the forty-ninth parallel across the Rocky Mountains to the Pacific Coast, the United States accepted. Thus ended one of the most colorful periods in American history, and the Hudson's Bay Company and the British government retreated into the Northland, where their latitudinal orientation had originally led them, and left behind only a few place names to serve as a reminder that the members of this truly "Great Company" had added a great deal of knowledge to the geographical understanding of the Great Basin as well as of the vast areas of the Pacific Northwest.

6

BRITISH BRIGADES
IN THE GREAT BASIN

IN THE THREE DECADES before the British were forced to retreat into northern North America, they played a significant role in the exploration of the Great Basin. It was the Snake River Brigade, inaugurated by the North West Company in 1818 and adopted by the Hudson's Bay Company in 1821, that discovered and explored many of the most important features of the land of interior drainage. The members of the Snake Country Expedition proceeded southward from their posts in what is now the northwestern United States and pushed into the Great Basin as early as 1818, at least six years before American penetration. Although the British brigades did not discover the Great Salt Lake, perhaps the most important topographical feature in the Great Basin, they are credited with the discovery and exploration of a large part of the northern Great Basin, particularly those sections lying within the present political boundaries of northern Utah and Nevada, southwestern Idaho, and southeastern Oregon. For this reason, no history of the Great Basin would be complete that did not include the activities of the North West and Hudson's Bay companies and their vital organ, the Snake Country Expedition.

In the second decade of the nineteenth century, the trapping brigade became an effective device in the procuring of beaver pelts. The character of the fur trade was beginning to change under the pressure of necessity; consequently, the trader was becoming also a trapper. It was now apparent that white hunters in small groups, usually two or three to a group, could trap streams more efficiently than the Indians. Activities on the American side of the divide had taken this turn but for naught. The Missouri Fur Company attempted such an experiment on the Yellowstone and Upper Mis-

93

souri, but the participants were routed by the Blackfeet, while the southern experiment on the Arkansas and South Platte, led by Auguste Chouteau and Jules De Mun, was thwarted by the Spanish authorities in Santa Fe.

Donald Mackenzie, the former Astorian and famous Nor'wester, was quick to perceive the change the fur trade was undergoing and shrewd enough to grasp its possibilities in the struggle between the North West Company and the Hudson's Bay Company. In 1816, when the former company took action to reorganize the Columbia District, Mackenzie was given full control over the interior while James Keith was given full sway over the coast and its trade. The result was antagonism between Keith and Mackenzie, and the former delayed Mackenzie's plans by refusing to grant him men and material with which to develop the interior. By 1818, however, both were forthcoming, and Mackenzie made a momentous innovation in the conduct of the western fur trade by the organization of the Snake Country Expedition, which was to distinguish itself in exploration of the Great Basin.[1]

With the acquisition of men and supplies, Mackenzie set out for the interior to establish headquarters for this region. He felt that Spokane House, which had served this purpose, was a "useless and expensive drawback," and proposed to establish a new fort on the east bank of the Columbia River, about half a mile from the mouth of the Walla Walla River. Alexander Ross gives a vivid picture of the site selected:

The place selected was commanding. On the west is a spacious view of our noble stream in all its grandeur, resembling a lake rather than a river, and confined on the opposite shore by verdant hills of moderate height. On the north and east the sight is fatigued by the uniformity and wide expanse of boundless plains. On the south the prospect is romantic, being abruptly checked by a striking contrast of wild hills and rugged bluffs on either side of the water, and rendered more picturesque by two singular towering rocks, similar in color, shape and height, called by the natives "The

[1] Alexander Ross, *The Fur Hunters of the Far West,* (2 vols., 1855). A more recent edition of Ross's 1855 account was edited by Kenneth A. Spaulding and published in one volume by the University of Oklahoma Press in 1956. References here are to the 1855 edition.

Twins," situated on the east side; these are skirted in the distance by a chain of the Blue Mountains, lying in the direction of east and west.[2]

This establishment, which was built by Mackenzie in 1818, came to be known as Fort Nez Percés and was to be a point of rendezvous for the trade of the interior. From this post many of the Snake Country Expeditions set out in their treks to the unknown areas to the south. It became the center for a great expanse of country, for the Snake Country Brigade combed an extensive area: "1st the Snake Country is bounded on the North by the Columbia Waters On the South by the Missourie, On the West by the Spanish Territo[ries] and the east by the Saskatchewan Tribes. 2nd The Principal Stream is the South Branch of the Columbia which takes its rise from a range of Mountains having nearly a South West Course and discharges into the Columbia three miles above Fort Nez Perces Establishment and 380 miles from Cape Disappointment."[3]

In the latter part of September, 1818, Mackenzie was ready to leave Fort Nez Percés on his first Snake Country Expedition. As Ross aptly puts it, "The principal cause which led to the establishing of this post was the extension of trade; consequently the next step was to pave the way for discoveries."[4] And this Mackenzie surely did. He and his men roamed as far south as the Bear River in the Great Basin and as far east as the Green River Valley, trapping these productive streams at least five years before Jedediah Smith penetrated across South Pass. They trapped the Snake River from near its source to its mouth and gave to its tributaries names which endure today. Mackenzie's bold and imaginative use of his men for trapping rather than for manning the trading posts, plus his system of supply and transportation of furs which involved the use of horses rather than boats, laid the groundwork for the change which General Ashley and his associates were about to effect in the conduct of the American fur trade,[5] and which produced significant effects upon exploration of the Great Basin.

2 *Ibid.*, I, 175–76.
3 "Snake Country Report 1825/26," *Ogden's Snake Country Journals, 1824–25 and 1825–26, Publications* of the Hudson's Bay Company Record Society, Appendix B, 262.
4 Ross, *Fur Hunters*, I, 179.
5 Morgan, *Jedediah Smith*, 117–18.

The first Snake Country Expedition "was composed of fifty-five men of all denominations, one hundred and ninety-five horses, and three hundred beaver traps, besides a considerable stock of merchandise; but depending on the chances of the chase, they set out without provisions or stores of any kind."[6]

Mackenzie and his party crossed the Blue Mountains and continued into the Snake country. By October the group reached the Boise River, which they knew as the Skam-naugh River, and here they proceeded to trap. Unfortunately, Mackenzie never kept a diary, and thus information regarding the area he traversed is meager and it is practically impossible to follow his exact trail. Ross said that Mackenzie "detested spending five minutes scribbling in a journal. His travelling notes were often kept on a beaver skin written hieroglyphically with a pencil or a piece of coal; and he would often complain of the drudgery of keeping accounts."[7]

There is, however, an account of this expedition in Mackenzie's own words which was quoted in Alexander Ross's book. From this report, it appears that Mackenzie had difficulty with a group of Iroquois in his party and left them to trap on the Boise River. "From this place," said Mackenzie, "we advanced, suffering occasionally from alarms for twenty-five days, and then found ourselves in a rich field of beaver in the country lying between the great south branch and the Spanish waters."[8] It is apparent, then, that these members of the North West Company were in the area between the Snake River and the Colorado River and were quite probably on the Bear River. This conclusion is substantiated by a letter written by Peter Skene Ogden on July 10, 1825, in which he said, ". . . the 5th May we reach'd Bear River supposed by Mr. Bourdon[9] who visited it 1818 and subsequently Mr. Finan McDonald who were at its Sources to be the Spanish River or Rio Collorado, but it is not."[10] Thus Mackenzie and his brigade had entered the Great Basin and were the first trappers of a British company to penetrate across its borders.

[6] Ross, *Fur Hunters,* I, 184.

[7] *Ibid.,* 283.

[8] *Ibid.,* 200–201.

[9] A member of Mackenzie's first Snake Country Expedition.

[10] Letter, P. S. Ogden to the Governor, Chief Factors, and Chief Traders, East Fork, Missouri, July 10, 1825 as printed in "Snake Country Expedition, 1824–1825 (ed. by Frederick Merk)," *Oregon Historical Quarterly,* Vol. XXXV (June, 1934), 108.

Mackenzie seems to have left his men in the Great Basin to trap this newly discovered section, for he states:

> After disposing of my people to the best advantage, trading with the natives, and securing the different chiefs to our interest, I left my people at the end of four months. Then taking a circuitous route along the foot of the Rocky Mountains, a country extremely dreary during a winter voyage, I reached the head waters of the great south branch. . . . Thence I steered my course for the river Skam-naugh, where I had left my Iroquois to hunt beaver in October last.[11]

Mackenzie returned to Fort Nez Percés and from there started out a second time with a small party. On May 15, 1819, a westbound North West Company brigade reached Fort Nez Percés, bringing a party of fifteen men who were to join Mackenzie in the Snake country and give him aid. Alexander Ross, who was in charge of Fort Nez Percés, added eleven men to augment Mackenzie's forces and sent them out under William Kittson, who was then an apprentice clerk and novice in the country, but who was to become known later as the author of a superb journal of one of Ogden's Snake Country Expeditions. Kittson reached Mackenzie on the Skam-naugh (Boise) River after much difficulty and delivered to him the horses, men, and goods for the subsequent hunt.[12] From this point, Mackenzie went south with approximately seventy-five men, and did not return to Fort Nez Percés until June 22, 1820. This year's hunt was most successful, the expedition returning with 154 horses laden with beaver.[13]

Mackenzie took only twelve days to rest his horses and men, and then on July 4, 1820, started back to the Snake country with a party of seventy men. This time the brigade was absent a little over a year and returned to Fort Nez Percés on July 10, 1821, with even more pelts than in the preceding year and without the loss of a single man. No exact estimate has been given of Mackenzie's returns during his three years in the Snake country, but Morgan believes that perhaps

---

11 Ross, *Fur Hunters*, I, 201.

12 Little is known concerning Kittson's activities on this expedition, but in a letter written to Peter Skene Ogden from the head of the Salmon River on October 14, 1824, Ross mentions Reid's River, "on which an establishment was Commenced by Mr. Kittson in 1819." B. 202/a/1, H.B.C.A.

13 *Ogden's Snake Country Journals, 1824–26, xxxiii.*

they amounted to one-quarter of the complete returns of the Columbia Department.[14]

It is almost impossible to plot Mackenzie's courses on his second and third Snake Country Expeditions, but it seems probable that he followed much the same route that he had taken on his first expedition in 1818. He seems to have left Fort Nez Percés, crossed the Blue Mountains, and then pushed on to the Boise River. From there he trapped the many tributaries of the Snake River and, no doubt, crossed over to the upper course of the Bear River as he did in 1818. On his second expedition it seems that Mackenzie and his party pushed eastward from the upper courses of the Bear River into what is now the western portion of the state of Wyoming, trapping in the vicinity of the Three Tetons and the sources of the Green River. A letter written by Alexander Ross to Peter Skene Ogden in 1824 gives some information to support this hypothesis: "We then visited Mr. McKenzies Wintering ground of 1819/20 and the grand river beyond the trois butes."[15] Very little is known regarding Mackenzie's route during the course of his third expedition, but it seems quite likely that he visited much of the same country which he had traversed in the previous three years. With the developments of 1821, Mackenzie's Snake Country Expeditions came to a close, but the institution that he had founded continued, growing in importance and even becoming a significant instrument in the conduct of international relations.

In the history of the British fur trade, 1821 was a fateful year, for it was at this time that the merger of the North West Company and the Hudson's Bay Company took place. However, the consequences were not as drastic as they might at first appear since the Hudson's Bay Company continued many of the practices initiated by the North West Company. It adopted the Snake Country Expedition, which, however, functioned with rather dubious results until Peter Skene Ogden took command of it in 1824.

The first Snake Country Expedition under the direction of the Hudson's Bay Company set out in the spring of 1823 under Finan McDonald and Michel Bourdon. The journey was rough, and in one engagement Bourdon and five other men were killed. Apparently this expedition followed almost exactly the same route used by Mac-

14 Morgan, *Jedediah Smith,* 118.
15 Letter, Ross to Ogden, Oct. 14, 1824, B. 202/a/1, H.B.C.A.

kenzie's brigades and penetrated as far south as the Great Basin. This hypothesis seems logical, for several of the members of the expedition had been with Mackenzie, the most notable being Michel Bourdon, who lost his life on this fourth Snake Country Expedition. This supposition is further substantiated by the letter which Peter Skene Ogden wrote on July 10, 1825, in which he mentions "Bear River supposed by Mr. Bourdon who visited it in 1818 and subsequently Mr. Finan McDonald . . . ."[16] This was McDonald's first and only visit to the Great Basin. Neither it nor the adjacent area which the party traversed appealed to him. Upon his return, he wrote, "I got Safe home from the Snake Cuntre than . . . and when that Cuntre will see me agane the Beaver will have Gould Skin."[17] In some respects McDonald's dislike of the Snake Country was justified, for service with this brigade was considered, as has been pointed out, "the most hazardous and disagreeable office in the Indian country." Peter Skene Ogden makes a similar comment in January of 1829 when he refers to the death of Joseph Paul, who died along the banks of the Humboldt River in the Great Basin: "There remains now only one man living of all the Snake men of 1820, and rather extraordinary all have been killed with the exception of two who died a natural death and are scattered over the Snake Country, indeed for a country so lately discovered it is almost incredible the numbers that have fallen in it."[18]

Although assignment to the Snake Country expedition was considered an unpleasant duty, the returns were quite good and accounted in large part for the over-all returns of the interior trade. The financial report of 1823–24 points out that the total profit from the interior trade was £2264.8.7, of which £985.3.0 was contributed by the Snake Country Expedition, while Flathead Post added £367.5.6 to the total gains and the Kootenais and Spokane House contributed £363.19.7 and £538.0.6 respectively.[19]

With McDonald unwilling to return to the Snake country, Governor Simpson turned to Alexander Ross, the factor at Fort Nez

[16] "Snake Country Expedition, 1824–1825," *Oregon Historical Quarterly*, Vol. XXV (June, 1934), 108.

[17] Letter, Finan McDonald to J. G. McTavish, April 5, 1824, B. 239/c/1, H.B.C.A., as quoted in Galbraith, *The Hudson's Bay Company*, 84.

[18] Entry for Jan. 1, 1829 in "Ogden's Snake Country Journals, 1828–1829," B. 202/a/8, p. 19, H.B.C.A.

[19] "Report of Snake District, 1823–1824," B. 202/e/1, H.B.C.A.

Percés. Ross left Flathead Post on February 10, 1824, with a party of 54 men and lads, 20 lodges, 62 guns, 206 traps, and 231 horses. In an entry in his journal for February 10, the day of his departure, Ross showed some apprehension in regard to this trip: "There are many of these people too old for a long Voyage. . . . The Iroquois tho' in general good trappers, are very unfit people for a Snake Voyage being always at variance with the whites . . . too fond of Indians and of trafficking away their property with the Natives."[20] The Snake Country Expedition of 1824 is of little or no significance in the actual exploration of the Great Basin since it did not penetrate that far south, having become plagued with troubles which will be discussed later. Despite that fact, the expedition of 1824 does have some importance in regard to the history of the Great Basin, for it was Ross's return to Flathead Post with Jedediah Smith and his party of Americans that caused Governor Simpson to replace Ross with the able Peter Skene Ogden and to forge the Snake Country Expedition into a mighty instrument to counteract the American thrust in the direction of the Pacific Coast.

The expedition of 1824–25 was a powerful one. It comprised 58 men, and was equipped with 61 guns, 268 horses, and 352 traps in anticipation of a hunt of one year's duration.[21] In the words of Alexander Ross, "This is the most formidable party that has ever set out for the Snakes."[22] To supply food for such a large group was a major task, especially since it was Governor Simpson's policy that expeditions should live "off the land" rather than rely upon European goods. Consequently, it was one of Ogden's chief responsibilities to discover a route that would produce the necessities of life, for if the supply of game failed, horses would have to be slaughtered for food. And, of course, the chief duty of the brigade leader was to find streams with rich preserves of beaver where the party could make a successful hunt. This was not always easy, as Ross pointed out: "It is indeed Shameful that no Correct Journal of the Snake Country has ever yet appeared to point out where Beaver are and where beaver are not. Much time is lost in Wandering through these parts on that account."[23]

20 "Alexander Ross' Country Journal, 1824," B. 202/a/1, H.B.C.A.

21 *Ogden's Snake Country Journals, 1824–1826*, 2–3.

22 "Journal of Alexander Ross" (ed. by T. C. Elliott), *Oregon Historical Quarterly*. Vol. XIV (December, 1913), 388.

23 Letter, Ross to Ogden, Oct. 14, 1824, B. 202/a/1, H.B.C.A.

Ogden was instructed to proceed "direct for the heart of the Snake Country towards the Banks of the Spanish River or Rio Colorado pass the Winter & Spring there and hunt their way out by the Umpqua and the Wilhamet Rivers to Fort George next summer sufficiently early to send the returns home by the Ship."[24] The initial instructions to hunt toward the banks of the Río Colorado were based upon an incorrect conjecture by earlier Snake country leaders that the Colorado was an extension of the Bear River, which had been explored only in its upper courses; that Ogden also accepted this premise is substantiated by entries in his diary. The instructions for the homeward journey were based upon the assumption that the Umpqua and Willamette rivers had their sources not far to the west of Bear River Valley. This geographical conception is clearly depicted on the Kittson map which was drawn during the course of the Ogden 1824–25 Snake Country Expedition and on which Kittson states: "Bear River with all its branches enters the Pacific about 1 mile of Fort George, South side. The lower part of the above river was never visited either by us or Americans, although the latter said it was known to be rich. Their informers are the Utaws."[25] Kittson's conception seems reminiscent of the geography laid down by Lewis and Clark.

It also seems quite clear that Dr. McLoughlin and other officials of the Hudson's Bay Company entertained many of the geographical ideas that were current at the time, for there are frequent references to a river or rivers flowing from the interior into the Pacific Ocean in the region that is now embraced by southern Oregon and northern California. An excerpt from a letter addressed to Alexander McLeod, leader of the Umpqua Brigade, by Dr. McLoughlin is typical of the allusions made to the interior river: "After our conversations we have had on the subject of your Expedition I can only say I consider it of the utmost importance to us that if possible you should have a personal communication with the natives of the Large River South of the Umpqua."[26]

On Monday, December 20, 1824, Peter Skene Ogden and his party

[24] "Snake Country Expedition, 1824–1825," *Oregon Historical Quarterly*, Vol. XXV (June, 1934), 99.

[25] The Kittson map, B. 202/a/3b, H.B.C.A., which has been reprinted in *Ogden's Snake Country Journals, 1824–1826*.

[26] Letter, John McLoughlin to Alexander McLeod, Fort Vancouver, September 20, 1826. B. 223/b/2, H.B.C.A.

started on the sixth expedition into the Snake country. "Having finally equipped the Freemen, and all being in readiness," relates Ogden, "I gave orders for all to Start for the Horse Plains & in the afternoon I bade adieu to the Flat Head Post, leaving the Same in charge of Mr. Ross."[27] Accompanying Ogden's party were Jedediah Smith and his men, who had returned to Flathead Post with Alexander Ross the preceding fall. The Americans made much of the journey with the British brigade and did not take their leave from the latter until April 8, when Ogden recorded the following in his diary: "Weather very Warm the Freemen off to their traps the seven Americans who joined Mr. Ross last Summer & accompanied him to the Flat Heads & have since with us intend separating tomorrow requested to trade & tho' they found the prices high say the Freemens Tariff but being in Want they were obliged to Comply & traded 100 Lr. & Sm. Beaver this Same recompence for the Beaver they traded with our party last Summer."[28]

The British and American parties, although now separated, camped close together and took much the same course to and into the Great Basin. On April 17, Ogden wrote in his journal: "The Americans followed us this day & have encamped three Miles a head but this will avail them naught as independent of our party we have traps 12 Miles a head."[29] This entry gives some insight into American-British intercourse in this region and helps to explain, in part, the vociferous culmination of this rivalry which took place in the vicinity of the present town of Mountain Green, Utah, on May 22, 1825.

Until recently, only fragments of information concerning the activities of Ogden and his first Snake Country Expedition were available, but with the publication of two important diaries in 1950 by the Record Society of the Hudson's Bay Company much information has been revealed concerning this expedition. These diaries, kept by Peter Skene Ogden and by his chief clerk, William Kittson, supply the earliest written descriptions of the area traversed. They are to the history of northern Utah what the Escalante Journal is to the history of the central and southern portions of the state.

Ogden and his first Snake Country Expedition followed approximately the route that was later to be a segment of the Old Oregon

27 *Ogden's Snake Country Journals, 1824–26*, 5.
28 *Ibid.*, 33.
29 *Ibid.*, 41.

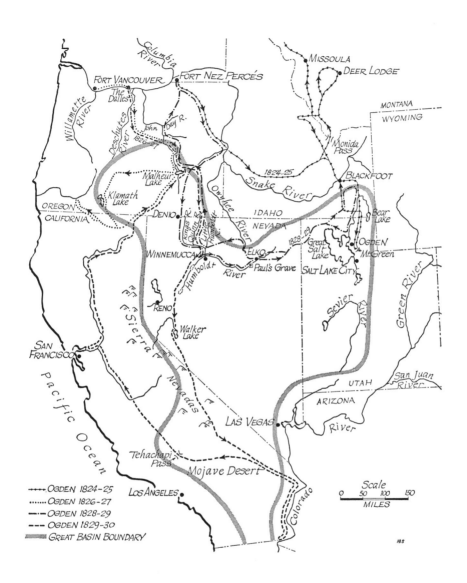

Legend:

········ OGDEN 1824–25
•••••••• OGDEN 1826–27
—·—·— OGDEN 1828–29
— — — OGDEN 1829–30
▨▨▨▨ GREAT BASIN BOUNDARY

Peter Skene Ogden's Great Basin Activities, 1824–30

Trail between the upper waters of the Portneuf and the big bend of the Bear River; and thus they entered the Great Basin in the vicinity of the present Alexander, Utah. They reached the Bear River just below where the town now stands, after having crossed two miles of rough lava beds which form the precipitous banks of this stream.[30] Ogden thus describes this prominent Great Basin stream:

> Raise Camp & proceeded over a fine plain for 15 miles when we reached Bear River a fine large Stream of Water about the 1/8 of a mile in width this River was discovered in 1819 by Michel Bourdon & the upper part has been trapped twice but the lower part never has been it takes its rise due east & was supposed to be the Rio Colorado & even now Said to be a Fork of the same.[31]

The party continued down the Bear River through Cache Valley until on April 30 they "had an indifferent road & were obliged to leave the River owing to the high rocks but by Crossing a Small mountain we shall again fall on it tomorrow we encamped on the banks of a Small river."[32] The river was no doubt Cottonwood Creek, which is a western tributary of Bear River. On the following day, the expedition passed around the Oneida Narrows of Bear River and made a steep climb out of Cottonwood Canyon. The trail left the stream bed somewhat below the present bridge and followed a route which has been utilized to a degree by U. S. Highway 34. After crossing the divide, Ogden struck the headwaters of Battle Creek, which led him back to the Bear River.[33]

On May 2, Ogden made an interesting entry in his diary: "Our hunt this day amounts to 74 Beavers & a Pelican also taken in the traps it was rather a Strange Sight to us all to see one of the latter in thees remote quarters."[34] This remarkable catch took place in

30 "Ogden's Journal of his Expedition to Utah, 1825," *Utah Historical Quarterly,* Vol. XX (April, 1952), 166, n. 14.

31 *Ogden's Snake Country Journals, 1824–26,* 40. From this entry in Ogden's diary, we can see that he had no accurate conception of the Great Basin; however, he did not completely believe, as did earlier Snake Country Brigade leaders, that the Bear River was an extension of the Colorado River.

32 *Ibid.,* 41.

33 "Ogden's Journal of His Expedition to Utah, 1825," *Utah Historical Quarterly,* Vol. XX (April, 1952), 169, n. 27.

34 *Ogden's Snake Country Journals, 1824–26,* 42.

the vicinity of present Preston, Utah, and, according to Professor William H. Behle of the Department of Biology at the University of Utah, constitutes the earliest known reference to a pelican in that region.[35]

By the fifth of May, the Ogden party was in the Cub River region and was speculating on the presence of a large lake in this vicinity, as shown by Ogden's entry:

> Weather cloudy & altho it appears we shall have rain Still we raised Camp as this Small river has been Well trapped by the Americans this Spring we shall now return to Bear River our Course this day was west over a fine Plain Covered with Buffaloes & thousands of Small Gulls the latter was a Strange Sight to us I presume some large body of Water near at hand at present unknown to us all.[36]

It was probably from this region that Jim Bridger made his voyage by bullboat down the Bear River to discover the Great Salt Lake.

Ogden and his men did not follow Bear River all the way down to Great Salt Lake as has been formerly believed, but left the main stream to trap along Logan River and Blacksmith Fork. From there they turned southwest through the location of present Hyrum to Little Bear River, which they ascended, passing through what is now Paradise to a point just below modern Avon. The Ogden party continued up to the divide and over it into Ogden Valley, probably quite close to the road which connects these two locations today.[37] Several days were spent in trapping the upper waters of Ogden River, and campsites were selected near the present towns of Liberty, Eden, and Huntsville in Ogden Valley.

Ogden and his party were the first Caucasians to enter Ogden Valley, which they recognized as a "hole," and so named it. William Kittson gives an apt description of the area: "We are now in a hole as I may say; as the place is surrounded by lofty hills. . . . This hole is but small not being above 50 miles in circumference, of an oblong shape, through the middle of which runs New River coming from

[35] "Ogden's Journal of His Expedition to Utah, 1825," *Utah Historical Quarterly*, Vol. XX (April, 1952), 169, n. 30.

[36] *Ogden's Snake Country Journals, 1824–26*, 44.

[37] "Ogden's Journal of His Expedition to Utah, 1825," *Utah Historical Quarterly*, Vol. XX (April, 1952), 175–77.

N.W. and taking a S.W. course near this place."[38] "New Hole" eventually became known as Ogden's Hole, and "New River" likewise assumed the name of its discoverer. A further description is given by Charles F. Middleton:

> Ogden hole or as some used to call it "Mr. Ogden's hole" is a low divide about 7 miles north of center of Ogden City. It used to be the only route over which the trappers and Indians traveled into and out of Ogden Valley which lyes directly east and north of Ogden City, this valley is about 10 or 12 Miles long North and south and 4 or 5 m. wide. The waters of this valley passes out through the famous Ogden Kanyon.[39]

The Kittson map reveals a remarkable amount of accurate detail in regard to the streams and mountains of this region. The Weber River and its junction with Ogden River and the mountains that separate the two streams are surprisingly well portrayed. This is most curious, as neither the Ogden nor the Kittson journal makes any mention of either author's having personally seen the Great Salt Lake or having explored the lower courses of any of the streams that drain into it.

From the vicinity of present Huntsville, Utah, the expedition continued southward, passing over the divide into Weber Valley and striking the Weber River near the site of present Mountain Green, Utah, where the unfortunate episode in Anglo-American relations took place. This was the most southerly point in the Great Basin that Ogden and his party reached on their first Snake Country Expedition. Now the group retraced its steps and traveled north over virtually the same route they had taken on the southward journey. On May 30 the expedition left the Great Basin in the vicinity of the present Preston, Idaho, when they struck Marsh Creek, one of the main tributaries of the Portneuf River. They subsequently struck the Snake River and, after lengthy peregrinations in this region, set out for home. On October 30, Ogden states in his diary: "As I am now

[38] William Kittson's Journal, as quoted in *Ogden's Snake Country Journals, 1824–26.*

[39] Letter, Charles F. Middleton to T. C. Elliott, May 7, 1909, T. C. Elliott Collection, Oregon Historical Society, Portland, Oregon. Mr. Middleton was well versed in the topography of the area, for he settled in Ogden, Utah, in 1850 and was a member of a party sent out by Governor Brigham Young to explore for a road through this region.

three days from Fort Nez Percés I purpose Starting tomorrow with two men."[40] Thus Ogden's first expedition into the Snake Country came to an end.

When Ogden returned from this expedition early in November, 1825, Dr. McLoughlin, according to plan, sent him to join Finan McDonald, who was trapping in the Klamath Lake region in what is now the southern part of Oregon.[41] Ogden found McDonald on the Deschutes River on December 9. The latter was without a guide who knew the country; accordingly, Ogden, not wanting to risk going on without a competent Indian guide, set his course across what is now the state of Oregon toward the Snake country. He thus followed the Crooked River, the south fork of John Day's River, and then passed on to Burnt and Snake rivers after having crossed a portion of the Oregon country which had never been trapped before. Following up the Snake, Ogden and his party proceeded as far east as the Portneuf River. Upon their return, they trapped several of the tributaries of the Snake and even penetrated a short distance across the present boundary of the state of Nevada. On this expedition, the members of the party did not enter the Great Basin, and consequently their trip plays no significant role in this narrative.

From Ogden's report of the 1825–26 expedition, however, we do gain information concerning trade on the periphery of the Great Basin, for Ogden wrote: "In regard to Trade little is carried on by us with the Snakes. On our goods with the exception of Knives they set little or no value."[42] Ogden continued to report that the Indians killed few beaver, a point which Alexander Ross made in 1824 when he stated, "On Beaver Skins they set no Value."[43] However, Ogden was optimistic in regard to future trade with the Snakes, saying, "I am of Opinion however it will increase."[44]

Financially the Snake Country Expedition of 1825–26 was quite successful, for the party brought out 2,180 beaver weighing 2,817

[40] *Ogden's Snake Country Journals, 1824–26,* 93.

[41] Letter, John McLoughlin to Finan McDonald, Fort Vancouver, August 17, 1825, in which he states: "When you are on the East side of the Mountains of the Willamette you will proceed in the direction you think will enable you to make the best Hunt Keeping in view if there is any possibility of your making a good Hunt in the Vicinity of the Lake so much talked." B. 223/b/1, H.B.C.A.

[42] "Ogden's Report of 1825–26," B. 202/e/2, H.B.C.A.

[43] Letter, Ross to Ogden, Oct. 14, 1824, B. 202/a/1, H.B.C.A.

[44] "Ogden's Report of 1825–26," B. 202/e/2, H.B.C.A.

pounds and 79 pounds of otter. The cost of procuring these furs, including the wages of the officers and men, the reduction of debts and gratuities, and the like, amounted to approximately £1,515.9.5. In a letter to the governor, the chief factors, and the chief traders, Dr. McLoughlin pointed out that if the beaver could be sold for 20.5/ per pound, the Snake Country Expedition "would Clear a 100 P.Cent."[45]

Because Ogden had had only twelve days' rest the previous year, he now took two months' vacation and was ready to start on his third expedition on September 18, 1826. With him at The Dalles were Thomas McKay and a party of thirty-five which was later increased to forty-three; the necessary horses numbered over one hundred.

This expedition was to lead Ogden into a very remote section of the Great Basin, one that is even today sparsely populated. He was instructed to achieve a double objective in his explorations of this year, for he was to trap Silvies River and to complete the work of exploration which the Umpqua Brigade under Finan McDonald had left undone. Silvies River is a stream in central Oregon, on the northern periphery of the Great Basin, which was discovered by Antoine Sylvaille in February of 1826 when Ogden sent Sylvaille and a party to the sources of the Owyhee and Malheur rivers with instructions to rejoin the main party upon its return. However, Sylvaille returned to Fort Vancouver independently and reported finding a stream which was very rich in beaver.[46] Thus, Silvies River on the

[45] Letter, John McLoughlin to the Governor, Chief Factors and Chief Traders, Fort Vancouver, August 8, 1826. B. 223/b/1, H.B.C.A. In a letter, John McLoughlin to John Dease, Fort Vancouver, August 8, 1826, Dr. McLoughlin gives further information concerning the financial returns of Ogden's 1825–26 Snake Country Expedition: "By the Included Account you will see Mr. Ogden has cleared £ 2500 on the new System and certainly in proportion to the Capital required this is the Best trade we have on this side of the Mountains, the Snake furs this year are the finest furs in the Columbia and will bear a Comparison with most of those on the other side." B. 223/b/2, H.B.C.A.

[46] Letter, John McLoughlin to the Governor, Chief Factors, and Chief Traders, Fort Vancouver, July 4, 1826, B. 223/b/1 H.B.C.A., in which he states: "On their way to this place they discovered a Country abounding in Beaver—Silvaille who has been these several years hunting on this side of the Rocky Mountains says the place discovered abounds more in Beaver than any he ever saw before. But they could not Remain to Hunt and Explore the Country as their Horses were Loaded

northern periphery of the Great Basin was to be one of the objectives of Ogden's third Snake Country Expedition.

The course followed by this expedition deviated somewhat from that taken the previous year, for now Ogden went south into parts of what is now Oregon that had been unknown to Caucasians prior to this time. Subsequently the members of the party crossed to the Crooked River and followed up it for some distance in order to reach the headwaters of Silvies River. Thus Ogden made his second entrance into the land of interior drainage, but on this occasion the physical environment was not nearly so hospitable as the section he had encountered in the Great Salt Lake region in the spring of 1825. On November 3, while encamped in the Harney Lake region, Ogden recorded in his diary the plight of his brigade and the physical and psychological effects of the Great Basin upon his men:

> We rais'd Camp taking nearly a West Course and soon reached the end of Salt Lake,[47] not near so long as I expected on first seeing it, it is however in some parts nearly five miles in width and appears deep . . . . Late in the evening Mr. McKay and party arrived with the following accounts, since yesterday we followed the same course but found no river nor appearance of any for some distance. . . . when these tidings were announced in the Camp it onely added to the general discontent already prevailing and this with all in a starving state tends greatly also to increase it, so much so that plots and plans are forming amongst the Freemen to separate.[48]

According to plan, Ogden should have moved his party from the Malheur-Harney Lakes region eastward into the valley of the Great Salt Lake, where buffalo were known to be plentiful. However, for several reasons, which Ogden implies in his journal to be scarcity of food and discontent among his men, the group turned westward, proceeding to the Little Deschutes River and thence southward, passing just to the east of Crater Lake before visiting the Klamath Lake area. Undoubtedly the harsh physical conditions were instrumental in forcing Ogden to lead his men out of the Great Basin and into a

with what they had taken out of River Mallin say about Eight hundred Skins between five Canadians and Iroquois and an Indian."

47 Harney Lake.

48 *Peter Skene Ogden's Snake Country Journal, 1826–27, Publications* of the Hudson's Bay Record Society, XXIII, 21–22. Notice the excellent introduction by D. O. Johansen.

more hospitable area where game might be found. Again the natural aspects of the land of interior drainage turned explorers away, so that only the fringes were visited and the heartland still remained a region of mystery as it had in the days of Domínguez and Escalante a century and a half before.

Ogden and his men trapped in the vicinity of Upper and Lower Klamath Lake and the Applegate, Rogue, and Klamath rivers during the winter of 1826–27, at which time Ogden saw Mount Shasta, one of the principal topographical features in what is today northern California. It was not until the latter part of April that the group began to push eastward, reaching the Pit River near the site of present Canby, California. During the next month Ogden and his men trapped this river system before proceeding northward across the southwestern rim of the Great Basin, skirting Goose Lake and passing to the west of the Hart Mountains before reaching Harney Lake on June 7. While making the trek through this inhospitable region, Ogden recorded in his diary on June 3rd, "I may say without exaggeration Man in this Country is deprived of every comfort that can tend to make existance desirable if I can escape this year I trust I shall not be doomed to endure another."[49]

Ogden's desire was not realized. He followed much the same course from the Pit River to Malheur Lake through this Great Basin terrain in the late spring of 1830. In a letter addressed to the governor and committee, Dr. McLoughlin stated in 1830, when referring to Ogden's return trip from the Gulf of California, that Ogden "ascended the North branch of the Bonaventura[50] till he came to the head of it, where he hunted winter 1826 & 7 and from thence to Walla Walla."[51]

In June of 1827, Ogden had hoped to take a southerly course from the Harney-Malheur Lakes region and proceed to the Snake Country and to the Great Salt Lake, but as he viewed the waters of this area, he wrote in his journal: "I had intentions of proceding in a South Course but find from the Country being overflowed it will be impossible for us to travel . . . for some distance and make the attempt in

49 *Ibid.*, 123.
50 Sacramento River.
51 Letter, John McLoughlin to the Governor and Committee, Oct. 11, 1830, *The Letters of John McLoughlin*, (ed. by E. E. Rich), *Publications* of the Hudson's Bay Record Society, IV, 85–86.

an other direction."[52] Thus Ogden and his party trapped in the Harney-Malheur Lakes region of the Great Basin for the next few weeks, forsaking it on June 26 because of the paradoxical presence of high water. By early July the group was trapping the Malheur River and its tributaries; from this part of the Snake River drainage, Ogden, after an unpleasant illness, left his main party under Mr. McKay and with two men started for Fort Vancouver, which they reached on August 5.[53]

The 1827–28 expedition is quite easily traced since it follows somewhat the same course as that of the previous expeditions. Ogden and his party crossed the Blue Mountains to the Grande Ronde Valley and then traveled along the Powder and Burnt rivers. The brigade kept to the north of the route that was later utilized by the Oregon Short Line Railroad. It went up the Boise River to its source and then crossed Big Camas Prairie to Lost River. Because the winter of 1827–28 was long and severe, the detached party under the leadership of Thomas McKay which was trapping on the Salmon River could not rejoin Ogden until May. This expedition, which reached Fort Nez Percés on July 19, 1828, was quite successful, returning with a catch of beaver which amounted to three thousand skins.[54]

The expeditions that have been described set the stage for Ogden's fifth Snake Country Expedition, which was destined to be one of his most important. As has been previously mentioned, Ogden had trapped along the major streams and their tributaries in what are now the present states of Montana, Oregon, Idaho, and Utah in the preceding four years, but as yet had not entered the largest area of the Great Basin, that region which lies chiefly within the boundaries of the modern state of Nevada.

Nevada remained almost untouched, probably because of its harsh physical characteristics. With the exception of one, all of the streams of this area of any importance are fed from the high mountains on the west. The Humboldt River alone derives its waters from the interior basin ranges, largely from the Ruby and East Humboldt Mountains. It was the Humboldt River that was one of the most important discoveries of Ogden's 1828–29 expedition. This river set

[52] *Ogden's Journal, 1826–27*, 125.
[53] *Ibid.*, 126–28.
[54] "Peter Skene Ogden's Snake Country Journals, 1827–1828" (ed. by T. C. Elliott), *Oregon Historical Quarterly*, Vol. XI (December, 1910), 355.

the course of the Overland Trail, providing water for the emigrants who followed its banks and water and forage for their animals. Its importance is shown by the entries in many of the emigrant diaries describing the unbearable conditions and misfortunes that beset travelers in their trek across the Forty Mile Desert after leaving the Humboldt River where it disappears into the Humboldt Sink near present Lovelock, Nevada. The Humboldt River was cursed by many of the forty-niners for the comparatively barren region through which it flows and for its brackish waters, but they failed to realize that this river established an artery across the western part of the Great Basin; had it not been for the Humboldt, they would have become lost among the various basins and ranges or been forced to follow routes through the present states of Oregon or Arizona in order to reach California. Even today the Humboldt River plays an important role: two transcontinental railroads and U.S. Highway 40 follow its course, and its waters irrigate the crops which are grown along its banks.

In 1828, Peter Skene Ogden knew little or nothing of the area that lay south of the Klamath and Snake rivers. The only person who had penetrated the central portion of the Great Basin prior to this time was Jedediah Smith, who had crossed what became the state of Nevada almost exactly at its center in 1827. Yet he did little exploring in the hurried trip which he made from the Pacific Coast to the Great Salt Lake region, and little geographical knowledge was gained in comparison with his daring exploits.

Little information has been available concerning the movements and activities of the 1828–29 Ogden Snake Country Expedition, which may be considered the most significant exploratory group to enter the northern Great Basin. Until now, historians have had to depend upon the inadequate transcriptions of the journal of this expedition made by Miss Agnes Laut shortly after the turn of the twentieth century and subsequently edited by T. C. Elliott as "Journals of the Snake Expeditions, 1827–28; 1828–29," and published in the *Oregon Historical Quarterly* in 1910. However, through the generosity and kindness of the governor and committee of the Hudson's Bay Company, the author was granted permission to examine the original journal. The excellent day-by-day entries clarify the route followed by Ogden and his men, which had been difficult to trace heretofore because of gaps of several weeks at a time in the Laut transcriptions.

The course that Ogden and the members of the fifth Snake Country Expedition took from Fort Nez Percés is easy to follow. Upon leaving the fort on September 22, 1828, they pursued the same route that they had taken the previous year, crossing to the Grande Ronde Valley and trapping along the Powder and Burnt rivers. However, when Ogden reached the Malheur River, he changed his course. The Ogden trail south from what is now central Oregon is the portion of the route that has caused much difficulty, for it is here that the Laut-Elliott transcriptions are silent for lengthy periods of time. Furthermore, this expedition took Ogden and his party into regions that were not known to them or to any other traders, either American or English, and thus they did not have a good geographical understanding of the region they were traversing.

Mr. T. C. Elliott, the author of many articles pertaining to Peter Skene Ogden and the editor of a number of Ogden's diaries, remarked that "By anyone not personally conversant with the local topography it is mere speculation to attempt to identify in detail the journey."[55] But much speculation about the route has taken place, and historians have generally agreed that Ogden passed southward into the Great Basin by way of the Owyhee River. Even those familiar with the local topography—for example, Mr. James Scrugham and Mr. F. N. Fletcher[56]—state that Ogden and his party trapped along the west branch of the Owyhee River and entered the present state of Nevada in the vicinity of the modern town of McDermitt located on the Nevada-Oregon boundary. Their assumption is based primarily on an entry in Ogden's journal for October 17, 1828, in which Ogden says, "I shall proceed to Sandwich Island River."[57]

Ogden's original journal, however, discloses that he and his party did not visit the Owyhee River at this time. Instead, the party trapped on the Malheur River from October 6 to 17, at which time they visited some of the country which they had trapped two years

[55] *Ibid.*, 357.

[56] James G. Scrugham, *Nevada*, I, 40; F. N. Fletcher, *Early Nevada*, 57.

[57] "Peter Skene Ogden's Snake Country Journal, 1828–1829," B. 202/a/8, H.B.C.A., p. 5. Unless otherwise noted, quotations from Ogden's Journal in this chapter are from this source.

earlier. Ogden had made arrangements for a Snake Indian to act as guide for the party, but an entry in his diary for October 7 states that the Indian did not appear. Therefore, it seems without a guide, Ogden traveled slowly along the Malheur River, trapping as he went, and then struck out for the south on October 18. The entries for the succeeding days indicate that the Ogden party was traveling either due south or southeast. On October 23 the party followed Indian tracks for twelve miles, and on the next day received information from a captured Snake Indian that "in 4 days [they] would reach the river with 3 large forks." Undoubtedly, the Indian was referring to the Owyhee River with its tributaries, the Crooked, the Jordan, and the upper Owyhee, the last of which would appear as another fork. The party was probably at least fifty miles to the west of this river system when they received this information.

It seems probable that Ogden and his party traveled southward from the Malheur River to a lake, now known as Alvord Lake, located in the present Harney County of southeastern Oregon. Thus the entry in Ogden's diary for October 26; "Started at day break. Advanced 6 miles and reached a long lake not suspecting the water was salt we advanced . . . when discovering it, we were obliged to retrace our steps to a small brook and camped at 4 P.M. having travelled all day to little purpose. . . . Course S.E." The entry in his diary for the following day, October 27, contains a better description of the lake: "Started at 7 A.M. following the Banks of Salt Lake about 9 miles in length and 4 in breadth as usual without a discharge." Gerald A. Waring, in an article which appeared in 1909 in the *United States Geological Survey Water Supply Paper 231,* described Alvord Lake as being alkaline. Mr. F. W. Libbey, director of the Oregon State Department of Geology and Mineral Industries, states, "We have no analysis of the lake water, but I would assume that during the dry season especially the lake would be classed as saline in character."[58] It must be remembered that the month was October, too late for the spring run-off and a little too early for the winter snows; thus the lake would be considered saline and fit Ogden's description of a long, salty lake.

Another sentence in the entry for October 27 gives almost conclusive evidence that Ogden was in the Alvord Lake region rather than on the Owyhee River: "We passed a hot spring in a boiling state

58 Letter to Gloria Griffen (Cline), April 19, 1952.

strong smell of sulphur, tracks and huts of Indians." Mr. Libbey mentions that "about 2½ miles south of Alvord Lake there are some hot springs, one of which has a rather large flow estimated at about 900 gallons per minute. The temperature is about 97 degrees."[59]

Upon leaving the hot springs, Ogden traveled in a southeasterly direction attempting to find out just where he was. On November 1 he interrogated an Indian but learned little, commenting, "a more ignorant stupid brute I never saw." It seems likely that the Ogden party left what is now southern Oregon and crossed into the present state of Nevada slightly to the east of modern Denio, Nevada. The party encountered a "brook" on October 29, which could be Bilk Creek. Continuing to travel in a southeasterly direction, Ogden and his men camped on "a small stream" on November 2 which was probably Kings River in the vicinity of its junction with the Quinn River, for on November 3, Ogden wrote: "At Day light this Morning I sent off three Men in an Easterly direction and to return this Evening and at 7 A.M. we started I made several attempts to cross but could not the Horses sinking in Mud and Mire, we had not advanced more than three miles when we found three large lakes covered with Wild Fowl." In an entry for the following day, November 4, Ogden mentions that the men whom he had sent out returned with the information that they had followed the river and that it "took a N.E. bend," which is undoubtedly a reference to Quinn River, which follows such a course. Three days later, on November 7, Ogden gives a better description of the Quinn River: "At 7 A.M. we started crossed over the River which from its running through a number of Lakes, I have named River of the Lakes although not a wide Stream is certainly a long one, unfortunately however not a Beaver was in it." The Quinn River passes through a series of shallow lakes and marshes, and thus the name that Ogden applied to it was quite appropriate.

It is very apparent that Ogden and his men had no understanding of the drainage pattern of the region, for an entry in the Ogden Journal for November 5 indicates that Ogden believed himself to be on a tributary of the Snake River. On the following day, November 6, a diary entry shows that Ogden's men supposed themselves to be on a "Branch of Sandwich Island River" rather than in the Great Basin, an area of interior drainage.

[59] *Ibid.*

From the Quinn River, probably in the vicinity of the present Sod House, Ogden and his men crossed to the Little Humboldt River, passing to the south of the Santa Rosa Mountains by a route which is utilized somewhat by the modern State Highway 8A. The Little Humboldt River was reached a short distance above its confluence with the Humboldt in the vicinity of present Winnemucca, Nevada. On November 9, Ogden reached the Humboldt River, one of the most important Great Basin streams, commenting in his diary: "... a fine large Stream apparently well lined with Willows was in Sight. ... I made all speed to reach it and the first thing that presented itself was a Beaver House apparently well stocked a most pleasant sight to me and I hope it will repay us for all the trouble and anxiety it has caused me to reach it."

Ogden gave the name "Unknown" to the river because its source and course were unknown to him. He even speculated that the Humboldt River might be connected with the Owyhee River and thus part of the Snake River drainage system, saying: "Curious as to the course of river—decided to explore a little downstream. Traveled downstream from daylight until 1 P.M. and as far as I could see in advance this River takes a due West Course if it be Sandwich Island River it must almost return from whence it now goes in." The Ogden party's confusion in regard to the drainage pattern of the Humboldt is most clearly shown by a map portraying the Ogden trail of 1829. This map shows the Unknown River as a tributary of the Sandwich Island (Owyhee) River and places both in a most interesting and novel relation to the Great Salt Lake.

The appellation "Unknown" was to last for only a short time until the name Mary, in honor of an Indian wife of one of the trappers, was applied to the stream. Later the name of Paul became associated with it because of the death of Joseph Paul along its banks. When the Walker-Bonneville party of 1833–34 entered what is now the state of Nevada, they struck the Humboldt River, to which Zenas Leonard, a member of the expedition, says "we gave the name of Barren River—a name which we thought would be quite appropriate as the country, natives and everything belonging to it deserve the name."[60] The name that Frémont gave to the river has been the

60 Zenas Leonard, *Narrative of the Adventures of Zenas Leonard*, 111. A recent edition of this 1839 account has been published by the University of Oklahoma Press.

most lasting but probably the most inappropriate; he called it the Humboldt River in honor of the great scholar who never saw the stream that bears his name.

Although Ogden was curious about the course of the Humboldt River, he decided that it was becoming too cold and winter was coming on too rapidly to risk exploring its lower courses. Thus he decided on November 12 to move his men to winter quarters in the buffalo country northeast of the Great Salt Lake. However, Ogden did gain some information regarding the Humboldt River from a group of Indians he encountered along the river somewhere between present Golconda and Valmy, Nevada. These Indians, who spoke the lower Snake language, gave Ogden this information, which he recorded on November 16: ". . . to the sources, not less than ten days march than we shall find five Forks on three of these Beaver, that the river discharges in a large Lake and that Salmon does not ascend this Stream and consequently has no communication with the waters of the ocean, with this I am most pleased as it might interfere with McLeod's Trapping Party." This is the earliest recorded reference to the terminus of the Humboldt River and explains, together with Ogden's visit to the Humboldt Sink in the following year, why the British at such an early date discredited the existence of the San Buenaventura River which supposedly flowed through this very region.

Ogden and his party proceeded up the Humboldt River and on November 16 reached the point where Evans Creek flows into the Humboldt, having traveled about thirty miles east from the point at which they had first struck the river. Nine days later, on November 25, Joseph Paul, a member of the party fell ill in the vicinity of the modern Beowawe, Nevada, and the progress of the party was greatly hampered by this turn of events. For the next few days the Ogden party remained encamped, hoping that the sick man's health would improve. By December 6, Ogden put Paul on horseback and gave orders to move camp. However, progress was painfully slow, and by December 10 it became obvious that Paul could not continue the trip. Therefore, on this day, Ogden, while encamped probably near the site of the present town of Carlin, Nevada, had to make the difficult decision to leave Paul here on the banks of the Humboldt River with two trappers who volunteered to remain with him, while the main party continued eastward in search of game. Although this decision was unpalatable, Ogden related that "there was no alternative. It is impossible for the whole party to remain here and feed on horse flesh for four months."

On December 10, the party procured a guide and continued up the Humboldt River and passed probably Maggie, Susie, and Dixie creeks on this and the following days, for Ogden stated in his journal on December 12: "The River here is nearly as large as when we first discovered it, for we have only as yet seen three small forks which we passed on the 10th & 11th Inst gives me hopes that it is yet far to its sources." Ogden added that the Indian guide wished to leave the Humboldt River at this point. Thus it seems apparent that Ogden and his Snake Country Expedition left the river in the vicinity of the present town of Elko, Nevada, rather than traveling up this stream to its headwaters in the vicinity of the modern site of Wells, Nevada, as has been previously supposed.[61] On December 13, the party crossed the Humboldt River and left this stream as they proceeded into a hilly country south of the river. On the following day, they reached the western face of the Ruby Mountains, for Ogden reports, "We are now near the foot of a Mountain, which appears very high and this we are to cross tomorrow." Undoubtedly Ogden and his men crossed the Ruby Mountains via Secret Pass, which is today utilized by State Highway 11, and then proceeded eastward over a southern spur of the East Humboldt Range. On the sixteenth, they struck a small stream which most probably was what is known today as Franklin River and then passed on to Snow Water Lake.

For the next few days the party traveled in an easterly direction and then on December 19 turned northeasterly, which course was changed to a northern one by December 21. This line of direction undoubtedly took Ogden across Independence Valley, over the Pequop Range via Shafter Pass, and into the Goshute Valley, where they encamped at Johnson Springs. From Johnson Springs the party traveled in a northerly direction by a route which has been followed in more recent years by State Highway 30. The group now passed

[61] David E. Miller, "Peter Skene Ogden's Trek into Utah, 1828–29," *Pacific Northwest Quarterly*, Vol. LI (Jan., 1960), 16–25. Although Professor Miller's information concerning the Ogden route was limited because he used the Laut-Elliott transcriptions of this Snake Country journal, he has done some excellent field work in the eastern Nevada–western Utah region illuminating some of the campsites utilized by Ogden and his party.

near the site of modern Montello, Nevada, and crossed the present political boundary between the states of Nevada and Utah about nine miles northeast of this town. From this point, the party continued eastward, passing around the southern end of the Muddy Mountains before turning almost abruptly northward to reach what has been identified by Professor Miller as Dove Creek Camp on Christmas Eve. On the following day the party traveled in a north-easterly direction and gained the first view of the Great Salt Lake, this being the first time a British brigade had seen this large interior lake.[62] Professor Miller points out that Ogden moved eastward across Park Valley to Ten Mile Spring, which lies on the southeast slope of the Raft River Mountains, a position from which the Ogden party could gain a view of the lake. They now proceeded eastward toward the North Promontory Range and camped on December 28 near the site of present Snowville, Utah, where Ogden recorded in his journal: "Here we now are at the end of Great Salt Lake having this Season explored the half of the North Side of it and can safely assert as the Americans have of the South side that it is truly a barren Country."

The expedition now followed a north-northeasterly course and proceeded across the present boundary line between the states of Utah and Idaho on December 29. The following day they crossed the divide of the Samaria Mountains via Malad Pass and reached the Malad River in the vicinity of modern Malad City, Idaho. On January 1, 1829, while the party was encamped in this region, the two men who had remained with Joseph Paul on the banks of the Humboldt River rode in, reporting that the ill man had died eight days after the main party had departed from the encampment near present Elko, Nevada.

During the course of the next few weeks, the Ogden party explored the region now known as south-central Idaho in an effort to find buffalo. On January 12, Ogden and his men camped on one of the forks of the Portneuf River, thus leaving the Great Basin in favor of the Snake River drainage basin. However, when he learned from Indians that there were no Americans in the Bear River region—"and if there be no Americans in that quarter, as all the Indians agree in saying there are none, I shall certainly be surprised if we do not find Buffalo there"—he decided to steer his course back to the

62 Ogden did not personally see the Great Salt Lake when he visited the Bear-Weber River region on his 1825 expedition to Utah.

Great Basin towards the banks of the Bear. But on the following day, when Ogden noticed that parties of Snake Indians were proceeding toward that Great Basin stream, he decided to remain in the Snake River drainage area and to trap the main branch of the Portneuf River. While encamped on the Portneuf River, Ogden mentioned that the party was now commencing to take its second thousand of beaver and that he expected the group to procure two thousand more before they returned to Fort Nez Percés.

On February 5, 1829, the party broke camp and headed for the Bear River, which was reached on February 7. Thus Ogden and his men left the Snake River drainage system and crossed to the big bend of the Bear River in the vicinity of modern Alexander, Idaho, after having intercepted his 1825 trail into the Great Basin somewhat northwest of that present-day town. The party proceeded down the Bear River for the next several weeks, complaining about the cold weather and the poor condition of their horses. It seems likely that Ogden led his men into Cache Valley, then through Bear River Canyon to the Great Salt Lake Valley, which they reached northwest of the present town of Fielding, Utah. It was probably on March 12 that the group struck the Malad River where it joins the Bear River and recognized it as a stream they had crossed the previous December. It seems that the party now crossed the Malad River, above its confluence with the Bear, and then proceeded in a westerly direction to the north end of the Great Salt Lake, which they reached the latter part of March.

On March 18, when the party was encamped on the lower courses of the Bear River, Ogden speculated in interesting fashion on Bear River and earlier suppositions about the course of this stream, and his speculations are strangely reminiscent of the geographical conceptions of this region laid down by Lewis and Clark. Ogden states that the Bear River makes a

> bend to the Westward and this gave rise to a supposition by the first who descended this River, the late Mr. Bourdon, that it was a fork of the Willamet had he advanced a days' march he would have been undeceived as it discharges in Salt Lake and as that Lake has no discharge there it remained, it is to be regretted that there is no water communication from this Country to the Willamet the South Branch excepted is the only water communication to the Columbia and one fourth of the distance is not navigable for any

kind of Craft and from the winding course it takes it will never be of any advantage for instance from Fort Nez Perces to the discharge of Burnt River in the South Branch the distance can be travelled with loaded Horses in six days and by water with half loaded Craft it will take three weeks.

The Ogden party probably crossed the relatively flat country southwest of the present town of Bear River City, Utah, and then skirted the plain to the north of Bear River Bay, an arm of the Great Salt Lake, utilizing a route which was later employed by the Union Pacific Railroad.[63] Ogden recorded that on March 27 they intercepted their winter trail and thus were able to travel at greater speed; this undoubtedly occurred not far from present Kolmar, Utah. On the following day the Snake River Brigade followed a northwestern course which brought the Great Salt Lake into view, probably in the vicinity of what is now known as Cedar Springs on the western slopes of the Promontory Range. As Ogden proceeded northwestward from the Cedar Springs region, he believed the group to be almost opposite the sources of the Raft River, a correct assumption, and therefore sent a party to this area to trap, stating that he hoped that they would collect four hundred beaver.

On March 31 the Ogden party reached what Professor Miller has identified as Ten Mile Spring, but which was known to Ogden as Foggy Encampment, so named by the latter because of the heavy fogs he had encountered while encamped there the preceding December. Now, from this position, Ogden was able to gain a clear view of the Great Salt Lake and records in his journal that Great Salt Lake "appears surrounded by Mountains, but beyond these Mountains at the West and altho' the Lake has no discharge I am of opinion there must be large Rivers and probably an object worthy of exploring at a future day." Although Ogden makes this positive statement regarding the discharge of the lake and thus refutes the geographical conceptions held by many contemporary geographers, his comment illustrates the fact that he, like others, could not quite believe that a large stream did not exist in the barren country to the west of the Great Salt Lake.

Ogden and his party now continued in a southwestern direction,

[63] This route is probably better known today as that used by the Southern Pacific Railroad.

following their old trail in order to reach the sources of the Humboldt River. Ogden mentioned on April 1 that they were making use of Indian tracks along their route as well in a search for water, a problem which had not caused them much difficulty the preceding December when they were able to melt snow. Nevertheless, the group moved rapidly along their old trail: it is not uncommon to find entries in the Ogden journal for this period indicating that the party was covering twenty-five or thirty miles of country a day, in contrast to the progress of the group between the Humboldt River and the Great Salt Lake four months previously at a rate of less than half this speed.

On April 9, Ogden and a group reached the Humboldt River, probably near present Halleck, Nevada, where they met twelve trappers who had been detached from the main party in the region north of modern Kelton, Utah, on March 31 and ordered to the "Unknown River." On the following day the Snake Country Expedition crossed to the north side of the Humboldt River and also crossed a large fork of this river, undoubtedly the North Fork of the Humboldt. Trapping apparently was not very good in this region, for Ogden wrote, "Beaver are certainly thinly scattered in this River." On April 12, the group must have reached the vicinity of present Elko, Nevada, since Ogden made an entry for this date stating that it was from this area that they left the Humboldt River.

For the next few days the party trapped in the twenty-three-mile area between the modern towns of Elko and Carlin, Nevada, remaining in camp on several occasions because of rainy weather. On the fifteenth, Ogden sent a man to visit Paul's grave in the vicinity of present Carlin, "to ascertain if the Natives had dug up the body, he returned and reported he found all safe." Because of the small catch of beaver, Ogden decided to move his party to the Owyhee River, which the Indians told him lay "four days' travel" to the north. On April 16, the group moved up what is today probably Maggie Creek and pushed northward to reach on the nineteenth the South Fork of the Owyhee River and thus the Snake River drainage south of the present Nevada town of Tuscarora. Apparently trapping did not prove successful in this region either, for on the twenty-first, Ogden mentioned that the trappers came in with thirty-two beaver, "far less than we expected." On the following day, he wrote: "Unfortunately we have sustained the loss of 4 Traps carried off by the

Beaver we are now very low on Traps having sustained a greater loss this year than all former years." The group proceeded up the South Fork of the Owyhee River, but when they found the catch to be small, Ogden, on May 2, decided that the party should retrace its steps to the Humboldt. However, as the group proceeded southward on May 5, they intercepted an Indian trail passing to the west and followed it. This trail took the party to the Little Humboldt River by May 8, and two days later brought them to within three miles of their first encampment on the Humboldt River near present Winnemucca, Nevada.

The party now proceeded down the chief artery of the western Great Basin, this time as far as the Humboldt Sink, south and west of present Lovelock, Nevada. Ogden's diary for May 29 gives the following description of the mouth of the Humboldt River: "Encamped within a mile of a large lake. The river is not half the size it was, no doubt spreading in the swamp we have passed. It is 2½ ft. deep and only 10 yds wide." He mentioned that there was a large swamp about five miles to the east of the Humboldt Sink, and reflected that because of this phenomenon the Humboldt should be known as Swampy River rather than "Unknown," as he called it. This entry in the Ogden diary undoubtedly caught the attention of Aaron Arrowsmith when he was preparing his map of North America in 1834, for he depicts graphically "Swamp Lakes & Is." in the western portion of what became known a decade later as the Great Basin.

On May 30, while the group was encamped near the Humboldt Sink, one of the men who had gone toward the lake returned giving an Indian alarm. He reported that as he proceeded west to the lake, twenty Indians on horseback came after him shouting war cries. As Ogden glanced toward the hills which surround the lower Humboldt, he noticed that these basin ranges were infested with Indians. Shortly the Indians, who were well equipped with arms, came down on the plain and camped about five hundred yards from Ogden's temporary headquarters. Ogden now went out and met the group, giving them a foot of tobacco to appease them. While engaged in conversation with these Indians, Ogden made a most interesting observation, which he included in his journal: "We saw pieces of Rifles, Ammunition Arms and other articles this I am of opinion must be some of the plunder of Smith's Party of ten men who were murdered in the Fall and from Native to Native has reached this. They would not inform me from where they had received these Articles from, this looks suspicious." Of course, Ogden was referring to the Umpqua Massacre, which took place on July 14, 1828, along the banks of the Umpqua River in what is now southern Oregon. Ogden was no doubt familiar with this disaster since Jedediah Smith and the two other survivors took refuge within the walls of the Hudson's Bay Company post of Fort Vancouver and it was Dr. McLoughlin, the Pacific Coast superintendent of the Hudson's Bay Company, who was instrumental in procuring the return of at least a portion of the goods stolen from the Smith party.

The Indians whom Ogden and his party encountered at the Humboldt Sink were quite well informed regarding the geography of the region, and from them Ogden learned of a river which lay about eight days' journey from the Humboldt which had "no Beaver Salmon most abundant." Undoubtedly this was a reference to the Truckee River, which rises on the east slopes of the Sierra Nevada Mountains at Lake Tahoe and flows eastward into the Great Basin lake which was discovered and named Pyramid by John Charles Frémont in 1844. However, Ogden was not able to proceed farther to the west to discover the course of this river because of the lateness of the season and also because he did not wish "to infringe on McLeod's territory . . . . McLeod's territory is the water discharging in the ocean. If McLeod has succeeded in reaching the Bona Ventura he must have crossed the Stream the Indians inform me of."[64]

On June 4, the Snake Country Expedition left on its homeward journey, proceeding up the Humboldt River to the vicinity of present Winnemucca, Nevada, and then turning northward up the Little Humboldt River. By June 11 the group had reached the Quinn River, on which they had encamped the preceding November. From this point the Ogden trail deviated somewhat from the one used in the fall, for the party now went almost due north, passing on the west side of the Santa Rosa Range and near the site of present McDermit, Nevada, following a course which is similarly utilized today by U.S. Highway 95. As the group crossed what is now the political

[64] Entry for May 29. Apparently Ogden had no clear understanding of this western portion of the Great Basin, for this entry indicates that he believed that streams which rose immediately to the west of his position flowed to the Pacific Ocean.

boundary between the states of Nevada and Oregon, they kept somewhat to the west of the route followed by the above-mentioned highway, and finally on June 19 reached the South Fork of the Malheur River and thus the Snake River drainage system to the north of present Follyfarm, Oregon. On July 8, after having traveled along Silvies River and the John Day River and having crossed the Blue Mountains, Ogden wrote in his diary: "As the tracks to Nez Perces is now well known, and no danger is to be apprehended, I shall tomorrow leave with 2 men for the fort. Thus ends my 5th trip to the Snake Country."

Dr. McLoughlin was most pleased with the results of Ogden's fifth Snake Country Expedition, pointing out that Ogden's "returns are better than last year and amount including with what his people trading here and in the Interior to four thousand Beaver, and in my opinion remarkably well dryed and in the highest state of preservation which when it is considered some of these Furs have been carried on Horseback through the Country since last fall, Winter, & Summer certainly does him good credit."[65]

Shortly after his return, Ogden set out on his sixth and last Snake Country Expedition. In many local histories of the West, there is repeated a tradition that Ogden visited the Great Salt Lake region during the course of this expedition, but no information to substantiate the tradition has yet come to light. Unfortunately, the facts concerning this Snake Country Expedition, which is undoubtedly one of Ogden's most interesting from a geographical standpoint, are very meager for the reason that all the maps and journals of the party were lost in the waters of the Columbia River. In a letter written to John McLeod on March 10, 1831, Ogden stated: "I was not successful in my last years Trapping as the year preceding although I extended my trails by far greater distance to the Gulph of California but found beaver very scarce and unfortunately below the main fall of the Col. my own Boat was engulphed in a Whirlpool and 9 men drowned."[66]

By piecing together information contained in letters written after Ogden's return to Fort Vancouver on July 6, 1830, one can define in

[65] Letter, John McLoughlin to the Governor and Committee, Fort Vancouver, August 5, 1829, B. 223/b/5, H.B.C.A.

[66] Alice Bay Maloney, "Peter Skene Ogden's Trapping Expedition to the Gulf of California, 1829–30," *California Historical Quarterly*, Vol. XIX (Dec., 1940), 309.

broad terms the route followed by Ogden on his sixth Snake Country Expedition. It seems quite clear that Ogden, after equipping his party on the Columbia, left this river during the last days of October, 1829, and proceeded southward. In a letter addressed to the governor, chief factors, and chief traders, Ogden said that he "lost no time in making the discharge of Unknown River,"[67] which implies that he followed the track that he had blazed to the Humboldt Sink in the autumn of 1828 and utilized on his return trek in the early summer of 1829. Upon reaching the Humboldt, Ogden found the river covered with ice and snow, which frustrated his plans for a fall hunt; and so he decided to continue southward in hopes of finding better conditions. Two days after reaching the Humboldt Sink a few miles west of the present Lovelock, Nevada, Ogden attempted to procure a guide from the numerous Indians who were encamped there. Although he was unsuccessful in gaining a guide or geographical information concerning the adjacent area, his party now struck south and southwestward into previously unexplored terrain, undoubtedly passing from the Humboldt Sink to the Carson Sink and on to the Walker River, which the group followed down to Walker Lake; thus the comment in Ogden's letter: "six days after discovered a fine large river but destitute of Beaver."[68] Ogden was the first Caucasian to visit this area between the Humboldt and the Walker rivers, Jedediah Smith and his two companions in their return trek to the Great Salt Lake in the spring of 1827 having passed over the rim of the Great Basin just south of Walker Lake, not realizing that excellent river systems lay just a few miles to the north.

From Walker Lake the party continued in a southwestwardly direction, moving out into the barren Great Basin terrain which lies to the south of the present Nevada city of Hawthorne. Ogden said, "I still however persevered in advancing and reached the Great Sandy desert of Great Salt Lake."[69] This statement has caused some confusion in regard to the location of the brigade, and some historians have taken Ogden literally, believing that at this time he was en-

67 Letter, Peter Skene Ogden to the Governor, Chief Factors, and Chief Traders, March 12, 1831, as quoted in "Ogden's Report of His 1829–30 Expedition" (ed. by John Scaglione), *California Historical Quarterly*, Vol. XXVIII (June, 1949), 121–22.
68 *Ibid.*
69 *Ibid.*

camped in what is now central Utah rather than in the western Great Basin close to what was later to become the Nevada-California political boundary.

The party continued southward through this harsh terrain, suffering "severely both from want of food and water." By late January they reached "a range of the rocky Mountains," probably the Inyo Mountains of the region immediately south and east of present Bishop, California. Although it is difficult to determine Ogden's course in this region, it seems quite likely that he struck the Owens River and Lake and then continued southwestward, crossing the Mojave Desert, one of the most barren regions of the Great Basin, before reaching "the South West Branch of the Rio Collarado." He then followed down the Colorado an undetermined distance, perhaps to the mouth of the river where it deposits its waters in the Gulf of California, but, finding beaver very thinly scattered, he decided to return northward.

Remembering the Mountain Green, Utah, incident with Johnson Gardner in 1825 and the subsequent admonition by the governor and committee regarding relations with Americans and Mexicans, Ogden steered his course to the northeast so as to not go "too near the Spanish Settlements." The group probably crossed into the Great Valley of California via Tehachapi Pass before proceeding northward along the eastern foothills of the Sierra Nevada Mountains, where Ogden "could examine the different Streams and at the same time avoid meeting the Spanairds." Ogden now followed up the San Joaquin River to its mouth in San Francisco Bay, then turned back up the estuary to the Sacramento River, thence moved to the Pit River and followed his 1826–27 trail back to Walla Walla through a portion of the Great Basin which he especially disliked.

Upon his return, Ogden found that by orders from Governor Simpson he had been transferred to the trade along the coast in the company of Mr. Finlayson, and thus, in 1830, John Work succeeded him as brigade leader of the Snake Country Expedition. In a letter written from the Columbia River on March 10, 1831, Ogden said: "Our friend Work has succeeded me in the Snake country I accompanied him as far as Nez Perces and gave him a fair starting—surely this man deserves a more substantial reward than he now enjoys it is an unpleasant situation he fills I wish him every success but it is all a Lottery."[70]

It seems apparent that shortly after Work received word that he was to head the Snake Country Expedition, he asked the experienced Peter Skene Ogden for advice, for Ogden wrote to him: "You having requested my opinion relating to the route you should take in quest of Beaver. As I am not authorized to give you instructions I shall merely state the track I intended following had I returned." He mentioned the usual trail to the Snake and the course to the Bear River, where he supposed a few beaver might be found. He then added: "From this you will proceed to unknown River. Indians report another River to the southward of Unknown River, this stream I did not see but am of opinion it can not be very long otherwise in my Journey last year I would have discovered if there be one or not."[71]

The Work Snake Country Expedition which left Fort Nez Percés on August 22, 1830, consisted of thirty-seven men, one slave, two youths, twenty-nine women, and forty-five children, a total of 114 persons; it was a most heterogeneous group, for twenty-six of the party were Canadians, two were Americans, six halfbloods from east of the mountains, two Iroquois, and one Nipissing Indian. The expedition followed the usual route of the Snake River Brigade by going south over the Blue Mountains to the Grande Ronde, Powder, and Burnt rivers and then to the Snake. The party trapped on the Portneuf and Bannock rivers, and when they were encamped on the former, on April 12, 1831, Work "sent two men O'Brien and J. Pickette to visit a little valley, called Mr. Ogden's hole, where formerly a good many beaver were found."[72] From this point the group returned to the Bannock River and then moved to the Raft River on May 4. On May 12 the party separated, Work sending one group to trap the headwaters of the Owyhee River while he and the main party proceeded southward into the Great Basin, which they reached on May 13 north of present Kelton, Utah. As the journal relates, the

[70] Letter, Peter Skene Ogden to John McLeod, March 10, 1831, T. C. Elliott Collection, Oregon Historical Society.

[71] Letter, Peter Skene Ogden to John Work, Fort Nez Perces, August 21, 1830, B. 223/b/6, H.B.C.A.

[72] "John Work's Snake Country Journal, 1830–1831," B.202/a/9 and B.202/a/10. Entry for August 12, B.202/a/10, H.B.C.A.

Work party followed virtually the same route as that taken by Ogden westward from the region of the Great Salt Lake to the Humboldt River in the western Great Basin. However, on May 22 the party deviated from the Ogden trail, for Work states: "This morning we left the usual road to Ogden's river, in hopes to reach the river sooner and fall upon it a few days journey higher up than by the other route."[73] Thus it seems that the Work party followed the Ogden trail to the Snow Water Lake region, but instead of proceeding westward as Ogden had done, Work led his party northwestward and struck the Humboldt River between the sites of modern Wells and Deeth, Nevada. The group then crossed the Humboldt, a few miles to the east of present Deeth, and proceeded up Mary's River. By May 24, Work's Snake Country Expedition was on the North Fork of the Humboldt River, which they trapped for a few days before moving into the Snake River drainage system south and east of present Mountain City, Nevada.

After having trapped for several weeks along the Bruneau and Owyhee rivers, the Work party returned to the Great Basin on June 13 and traveled down to the Humboldt River, which they found to be overflowing and infested with mosquitoes. Work mentions that there were some beaver in the stream, but the water was too high for them to be caught. The party traveled about one hundred miles along the banks of the Humboldt, probably from the region near present Beowawe, Nevada, to modern Winnemucca, for the entries in his diary during this period consistently state that the party was following a northwest course.

Upon nearing the site of present Winnemucca, the party left the Humboldt River, crossed over the mountains, and reached the Little Humboldt River, a route which Work said saved two days' journey from going by way of the confluence of the Little Humboldt and Humboldt rivers. The group now continued northward, finally reaching Silvies Lake on July 2. Following up Silvies River, they crossed to the South Fork of the John Day River on July 10, thus leaving the Great Basin some miles to the south and west of the present town of Silvies, Oregon. The last entry in Work's diary was made on July 20, when he stated that the party had traveled over two thousand miles in the course of this Snake Country Expedition but

---

[73] Entry for May 22, *ibid.*, 15.

had very little to show for their efforts on account of the high water encountered in most of the streams.

Within the next few years, Work again entered the Great Basin, but his movements in this region were not significant since he and his party were traversing an area which had been explored to a great degree. During the course of his second Snake Country Expedition, Work and his party followed much the same route as in the previous year with the exception of a trapping expedition into Montana. Then the group came south to the Payette River and during the latter part of June, 1832, entered the Great Basin and crossed to Silvies River. Only a short time was spent in this region before the party returned to Fort Nez Percés by way of the Burnt and John Day rivers.

On August 17, 1832 John Work set out at the head of another brigade. This expedition, which consisted of one hundred men, women, and children, followed the usual route upon leaving Fort Nez Percés. They crossed the Blue Mountains to John Day River and passed southward to Silvies River, where they again entered the Great Basin. They followed Silvies River down to its mouth in Malheur Lake and then struck out to the west through the sagebrush. Their trail bent to the southwest, and they passed the Great Basin lakes of Alkali and Abert before reaching Goose Lake and thus the Sacramento–San Joaquin drainage system. On October 7, while the party was encamped near Harney Lake, Work mentioned that he had intended to proceed southeastward to the Humboldt River and explore to the southward of this stream, but because of the lateness of the season he felt that he should proceed directly to the "Bonaventura" (Sacramento). Thus again the Great Basin was cheated of further exploration, for the season was late because of the distance involved in reaching the region and because of the harsh physical elements encountered during the winter.

Although little new exploration of the Great Basin by the Hudson's Bay Company took place after 1832, the "Great Company" continued to send individuals as well as parties into this region for the next fourteen years.[74] Therefore, the Hudson's Bay Company and

74 Beginning in 1834, Dr. McLoughlin began sending Hudson's Bay Company employees such as Thomas McKay, Francis Ermatinger, and John McLeod to the American rendezvous; however, their success was limited and therefore of little im-

the Snake Country Expedition deserve an important place in the history of exploration of the Great Basin. From the British point of view, it was an important commercial venture, for the Snake Country Expedition produced steady, if not handsome, profits in the period between 1824 and 1846. As an instrument of empire, it likewise served its purpose, for it converted the Snake country and parts of the Great Basin into a virtual fur desert. Furthermore, the Snake Country Expedition wrote one of the most significant chapters in the history of exploration of the Great Basin. During the first decade and a half after its inception, it made its most important contribution by lifting the shroud of mystery that enveloped parts of the Great Salt Lake region and by adding the Humboldt River and the comparatively barren regions of what is now Nevada to geographical knowledge. Although the expedition continued for better than ten years after the Ogden and Work expeditions, it covered little new territory and its activities are not of great importance. However, no history of exploration of the Great Basin would be complete without the Hudson's Bay Company and its vital organ, the Snake Country Expedition, for from 1818, the date of its inauguration, until 1846, the date of disbandment, this British brigade covered a vast extent of territory and penetrated the Great Basin from the north, south, east, and west in what have become the states of Oregon, Idaho, California, Utah, and Nevada.

portance. (Note that it was Thomas *McKay,* not Thomas McKee, as stated in Phillips, *The Fur Trade,* II, 460–61.) H.B.C.A., B/223/b/11.

7

AMERICAN FUR HUNTERS
BEYOND THE ROCKIES

THE BRITISH ENTERED THE GREAT BASIN as early as 1818, and it was through their efforts that much of the northern part of the Great Basin was explored. Although the British antedated the Americans in the land of interior drainage by six years, the Americans were destined to play a significant role in the discovery of topographical features of the Great Basin. In the few short years between 1824 and 1830, American fur traders roamed over almost every section of the Great Basin and revealed the arid and inhospitable nature of this area.

One of the well-known American fur organizations was the Rocky Mountain Fur Company, founded in 1822 by Major Andrew Henry and General William Ashley. The formation of this enterprise was an important event in Great Basin history, for the roster of this company contained the names of some of the most distinguished men in the history of Basin exploration. It was under the banner of the Rocky Mountain Fur Company that Jedediah Smith entered the Great Salt Lake region in 1824-25 and led the vanguard of the American fur trade into the Great Basin.

Following the organization of the Rocky Mountain Fur Company, an advertisement was placed in the *Missouri Gazette and Public Advertiser* on February 13, 1822, which was to give concrete form to the enterprise:

To Enterprising Young Men

The subscriber wishes to engage ONE HUNDRED MEN, to ascend the river Missouri to its source, there to be employed for one, two or three years. For particulars enquire of Major Andrew Henry, near the Lead Mines, in the county of Washington, who will ascend with, and command the party, or to the subscriber at St. Louis, Wm. H. Ashley.[1]

On April 3, 1822, Henry set out for the mountains with Ashley's advance party. A second boat left St. Louis on May 8, 1822, with Jedediah Strong Smith aboard, who was, without a doubt, the most "enterprising" young man who had answered the advertisement.

Operations on the upper Missouri have been briefly discussed and will not be elaborated upon here since General Ashley and Major Henry's activities in regard to the Great Basin are the chief concern. The important factor is that the Blackfoot hostilities and the Arikara outrage of 1823 caused Ashley and Henry to try to develop operations to the south. The Crows and the Snakes who dwelled along the approaches to South Pass, while occasionally unfriendly, maintained no such policy of uncompromising hostility to the whites as had the Blackfeet ever since the days of Lewis and Clark, and consequently trapping in this area appeared feasible. The Ashley expeditions of 1824–25 mark a new chapter in the history of the western fur trade. Instead of operating in the regions east of the mountains, accessible by the Missouri and Yellowstone rivers, they abandoned that area in the spring of 1824; and by the summer of that year the whole company had been transferred to the waters of the three drainage systems beyond the mountains: the Columbia, the Colorado, and the rivers of interior drainage.

Jedediah Smith led the vanguard of the Rocky Mountain Fur Company into this region shortly after the Arikara campaign. He had been ordered to strike into this heretofore unexplored area, and through the fortunate encountering of the Crow winter camp, he was advised by these Indians to continue across the mountains by way of a route south of Union Pass. Thus, while Major Henry pushed operations into the upper country as quickly as possible and while General Ashley was returning to St. Louis, Smith with a party of eleven men left Fort Kiowa in September and traveled westward across what later was to be known as South Dakota. The party followed the Old Cheyenne Trail northwest to the Powder River; then, continuing south, they crossed the Big Horn Mountains to the Wind River. After wintering at the foot of the Wind River Range, they followed the Indians' advice and crossed the mountains by the later

[1] Morgan, *Jedediah Smith*, 19–20.

famous South Pass. Thus occurred the effective discovery of this superb natural phenomenon which provided a southwestern orientation for the members of the Rocky Mountain Fur Company and led them from the Wind River region into the Great Basin and adjacent areas.

On March 19, 1824, Smith reached the Green River, probably near the mouth of the Big Sandy. Although his party was quite small, he divided the group for the spring hunt. Six of the men he took with him to trap farther to the south, while the other three were left with Thomas Fitzpatrick to trap the headwaters of this river. Unfortunately, we have no firsthand account of Smith's adventures in this region, but he probably followed the Green River as far as Blacks Fork and made his spring hunt on that stream and its tributaries. The name of Blacks Fork perhaps dates from this year. It is also significant that one of the head branches of Blacks Fork has been known for a long time as Smiths Fork. While Smith was trapping in this vicinity, Fitzpatrick's party remained in camp on the Green River until the ice thawed and then left to trap the upstream tributaries.

A small rendezvous was conducted by Smith in the middle of June, 1824, on the Sweetwater River. From this point, Smith sent Fitzpatrick, Stone, and Branch east to take the furs which they had accumulated to General Ashley. The remaining seven men and all of the horses were retained by Smith for a fall hunt that he was planning into an area farther to the west than any one of them had yet gone. To carry out this scheme, he turned back across South Pass early in July, proposing to press his hunt as far as the Columbia. In the Green River Valley he had reached the farthest limits of the British fur frontier, and now he wanted to launch himself into the heart of the British domain.

In the late summer of 1824 in the vicinity of the present town of Blackfoot, Idaho, Smith stumbled upon a party of forlorn Iroquois under the command of Pierre who had been detached on June 12 (not the sixteenth as sometimes stated) from the main Snake Country Expedition of the Hudson's Bay Company, conducted that year by Alexander Ross. The Iroquois had penetrated to the south of the Snake River where they became involved in "a Scrape with the Snakes. In consequence of having a horse Stolen, as the story goes, the prudent Iroquois, Killed a Snake, the natives found it out, &

have gone to revenge it."[2] Smith came upon the Iroquois after the Snakes had dealt with them and so was able to strike a shrewd bargain with them, by which they agreed to turn over their remaining furs to him in return for his conveying them to the vicinity of the Three Tetons (Pierre's Hole), where they would meet Alexander Ross with the main body of the expedition. On their way, they met a search party which had been sent out by Ross to look for the Iroquois. This party now guided the Americans to Ross's headquarters near the confluence of the Salmon and Pahsimai rivers in what is now Custer County, Idaho.[3] Ross records in his diary: "Today Pierre . . . arrived pillaged and destitute. The conduct of this party all along, Since they left us, has been in the highest degree blamable. . . . With these Vagabonds arrived 7 American trappers from the Big Horn River; but whom I rather take Spies than trappers."[4]

It is not known where Smith and his men were during the interval between their parting with Fitzpatrick and their meeting with the Iroquois detachment of the Ross expedition. The only clue to the Smith route was a vague remark made by General Ashley a year and a half later that Smith "stated that he had in the fall of 1824 crossed from the head waters of the Rio Colorado to Lewis' fork of the Columbia and down the same about one hundred miles, thence northwardly to Clarks' fork of the Columbia."[5] This statement has been interpreted to mean that Smith went northwest from the Green River Valley to the Hoback River, down the river to Jackson Hole, across the Tetons by Teton Pass, into Pierre's Hole, across the Snake plain to the Three Buttes, and then on north to the Columbia waters proper. Such a route, however, does not conform in all respects to Ashley's description, and the interpretation rests in part on a confusion of the Three Tetons with the Three Buttes. It is entirely possible that when Smith recrossed South Pass, he headed southwest, returning to the country that he had trapped in the spring.[6] This would have brought him into the eastern portion of

2 Alexander Ross, "Snake Counrty Journals, 1824," H.B.C.A., B. 202/a/1, entry for Sept. 7, p. 48.

3 Harrison Clifford Dale, *The Ashley-Smith Explorations and the Discovery of a Central Route to the Pacific, 1822–1829*, 60–67.

4 Ross, "Snake Country Journal, 1824," H.B.C.A., entry for Oct. 12.

5 Dale, *Ashley-Smith Explorations*, 153.

6 Morgan, *Jedediah Smith*, 128.

the Great Basin, since he would have had to move over the Bear River Divide and follow down the Bear River, one of the principal Great Basin streams, one hundred miles before striking north to the sources of the Blackfoot.

After meeting the Snake Country Expedition in what is now southern Idaho, Smith and his men decided not to turn back to their headquarters, but instead to accompany Ross and his party northward to Flathead House near the site of present Thompson Falls, Montana. This northern excursion would afford Smith an opportunity to examine a region which no Americans since the Astorians had penetrated and also to obtain some information concerning British operations. Smith was successful in learning from Alexander Ross and later from Peter Skene Ogden, whom he met at Flathead Post, that the British had some sixty men trapping the Snake country and in the previous four years had taken out 80,000 beaver weighing about 160,000 pounds.[7]

The return of his Iroquois "trapless and beaverless, naked and destitute of almost everything" was a hard blow for Alexander Ross; he had done well after a poor spring hunt and had counted on the Iroquois for additional hundreds of skins.[8] A heavier blow, however, was the appearance of the Americans and their decision to return to Flathead Post with his party. The Hudson's Bay Company officials had become apprehensive of the expanding American fur trade, and Governor Simpson had reported in a letter to the chief factors of the Columbia River District: "The Columbia District is improving; it may not only defray its expenses, but yield moderate profits if strict economy and exertion are exercised and there is no opposition. The Snake Country Expedition has been fitted out under Mr. Ross, who should be cautioned against opening a road for the Americans."[9] With the appearance of Smith and his men, Ross was unable to comply with the Governor's instructions and of necessity led the Americans into the heart of British territory.

[7] 20 Cong., 2 sess., *Senate Exec. Doc. 67.*

[8] An entry in Ross's journal for September 1, while he was waiting for the return of the Iroquois, illustrates his dependence upon their catch to make a respectable showing: "My hopes therefore of making good returns this year is again blasted, if the Vagabonds do not return." Ross, "Snake Country Journals," H.B.C.A., 47.

[9] *The Journal of Sir George Simpson,* Appendix A, 198.

Upon his return to Flathead Post on November 26,[10] Ross was relieved of his command as leader of the Snake Country Expedition and Peter Skene Ogden was advanced to this position. No doubt the problem of dealing with the Americans was one of the most important considerations in this appointment. Ogden was shrewd and had great ability; and it fell to him to attempt to combat the Americans in the area whence they came, the Green River and Great Basin areas, instead of allowing the competitive battle to take place in the richer areas to the north and in the region of Hudson's Bay Company establishments. Thus the Hudson's Bay Company's Snake Country Expedition took on a new character. Ogden led this spearhead into the Great Basin, discovering and exploring more features in this land of interior drainage than any other explorer save Jedediah Smith.

Ironically, these two explorers of the Great Basin, one British and the other American, proceeded into the Basin virtually together. The Snake Expedition of 1824–25 with Peter Skene Ogden at its head left Flathead Post on December 20, 1824. Since there was no particular danger for the first few days of the journey, Smith and his men did not join the British column until December 29, when they were nearing Hells Gate, near the site of present Missoula, Montana. By January 12 the party had arrived at the foot of Gibbon Pass and spent the next two days crossing over to the Big Hole River. The following month, the combined party negotiated Lemhi Pass and crossed over to the waters of the Salmon River, which was only eight days' march from the Snake, where the spring hunt was scheduled to begin.

On March 19, Smith and his party parted from the British brigade and set out for the Snake. However, the two groups were in sight of each other much of the time as they were both trapping the Snake, being practically bound to that area since the route to the Bear River by way of the sources of the Blackfoot was still snowbound. Even in April when Ogden was trapping on the upper Portneuf, this situation continued.

As Dale Morgan points out, Smith and his party seemed to be familiar with the course to the Blackfoot River, and it was his choice as a route to the Bear River and the Great Basin. The fact that it was

10 Alexander Ross, "Flathead Post Journal," H.B.C.A., B. 69/a/1.

his choice may provide an important clue to how he and his party had reached the Snake River the previous fall. If Smith had known nothing of this region, it seems surprising that he would have chosen this route.[11]

As disclosed in the diaries of Ogden and Kittson, the Ogden party spent about four months in the field before they reached the Great Basin in the vicinity of present Alexander, Idaho. They followed the Bear River in a southern direction and on May 5, 1825, entered the present state of Utah, southwest of modern Franklin. It was formerly believed that the Snake Country Expedition followed Bear River all the way down to its mouth in Great Salt Lake, but in view of the present information, it appears that the party left the main stream to trap Logan River and Blacksmith Fork and then turned south through present Hyrum and entered Ogden Valley by way of Paradise Canyon on May 16.[12]

The Kittson diary throws some light on the activities of the Smith group. Kittson says that the Americans went up the Bear River, while the Ogden party was planning to follow it downstream to ascertain its mouth. Although Smith started up the river, he soon came back down when he learned that some Americans had reached the Bear River the previous fall. They had wintered on the banks of this stream and were at that time engaged in trapping the country below.

The actual identity of the trappers who wintered on the Bear River is one of the obscurities in the history of the fur trade, which abounds in obscurities. To this date no substantial narrative by any member of the party has come to light, and only by piecing bits of information together has any identification been made. William L. Sublette has generally been named as the leader of this group, but it seems more likely that Captain John H. Weber was in command. The party seems to have been part of the spearhead that had started up the Big Horn with Major Henry in the fall of 1823, but which cut loose from its base when Henry abandoned his fort on the Big Horn. Only a few names of the members of the company who camped on the Bear River are known. It seems certain that John Weber, Daniel Potts, and Jim Bridger were among this assemblage, and more or less inde-

11 Morgan, Jedediah Smith, 134–41.
12 Miller, "Ogden's Explorations in the Great Salt Lake Region," *The Western Humanities Review,* Vol. VIII (Spring, 1954), 141.

pendent groups of free trappers attached themselves to them along the way—most notably the one headed by Johnson Gardner. Weber's party, more than likely, crossed over into the valley of the Bear by way of Blacks Fork, as evidenced by Daniel Potts's statement that after they had passed from the Green River Valley, moving in a southwesterly direction, they "had very good travelling over an inconsiderable ridge" and "fell on a considerable river, called the Bear River," on the banks of which stream, its tributaries, and adjacent areas, they took beaver with great success during "the autumn of 1824."[13]

This party has been celebrated chiefly because of two incidents in which it became involved, both of which are of a highly significant character. One, although it has been disputed, was the discovery within the Great Basin of one of the most curious phenomena in the United States, the Great Salt Lake. The other, of great importance in the history of the fur trade and of international relations, was a collision of part of this group with Peter Skene Ogden and his Snake Country Expedition of 1824–25.

It is surprising that the Great Salt Lake should have been unknown for so long. It had appeared on the early maps, and many legends had grown up about it, such as it having been a land of tinkling, golden bells and the home of the Aztecs. The lands adjacent to it had been discovered and explored by Domínguez and Escalante as early as 1776, yet a better understanding of the area had not developed; conversely, Lake Timpanogos with many mystical qualities appeared in its place on contemporary maps.

Credit for the discovery of Great Salt Lake has generally been given to Jim Bridger. He was a member of Ashley's main body of men who were camped in Cache Valley. There was speculation by the group concerning the course and outlet of Bear River, and several bets were made. In order to settle the argument, one man was chosen to follow the course of Bear River to its mouth; this man was Bridger. He descended the stream to the point where it passes through a canyon from Cache Valley into Bear River Valley, near the site of present Cache Junction. Upon emerging from the canyon, he reached the borders of the lake and, after testing its brackish waters, believed that he was on an arm of the sea.

The other contender for the distinction of discoverer of the Great

13 Morgan, *Jedediah Smith,* 142–43.

Salt Lake is Étienne Provost. Provost and his partner, LeClerc, whose first name remains unknown, launched trapping operations northwest from Taos into the Colorado Rockies. It is not known how far north and west the partners penetrated in 1823–24, but we do know that the next year they ranged into the country around the Green River, below the Uinta Mountains. In the fall of 1824, Provost pushed west up Strawberry River and passed into the Great Basin, then continued on until he reached the beautiful river which now bears his name. It seems quite certain that by the late fall he had proceeded as far as the valley of the Great Salt Lake itself. At this point, a band of Snake Indians fell upon his party, but with three or four of his men he managed to extricate himself and fled over the Wasatch Mountains to join LeClerc in the Uinta Basin.[14] The uncertainty regarding the discovery of the lake rests upon whether Provost saw Great Salt Lake during the fall of 1824; if he did, Provost would have to be credited with the discovery, for Bridger did not make his explorations of the Bear River and subsequently the shores of Great Salt Lake until early in 1825.

Even Peter Skene Ogden had some supporters as being the discoverer of Great Salt Lake. The assumption was based primarily on letters written to company officials, which have already been mentioned. Ogden's first reference to a large lake was entered in his diary on May 5, 1825: ". . . our Course this day was west over a fine Plain covered with Buffaloes and thousands of Small Gulls the latter was a Strange Sight to us I presume some large body of Water near at hand at present unknown to us all."[15] It is interesting that the existence of Great Salt Lake was a surprise to them and was still unknown to the party.

The publication by the Hudson's Bay Record Society of the Ogden and Kittson journals of this expedition makes it clear that Ogden did not discover the Great Salt Lake. These journals disclose that although some of Ogden's men saw the lake, he did not see it at this time, and most likely did not see it until December 26, 1828. There

14 *Ibid.*, 147.

15 "Ogden's Journal of His Expedition to Utah, 1825," *Utah Historical Quarterly*, Vol. XX (April, 1952), 171–72. Entry for May 5, 1825, quoted in *Ogden's Snake Country Journals, 1824–25 and 1825–26, Publications* of the Hudson's Bay Record Society, XIII.

is still a question whether Ogden's men visited the shores of the lake, but it seems rather unlikely that they did since neither Ogden nor Kittson makes any reference to the saline qualities of the water.

Ogden was unaware that there were Americans other than the Smith party in this vicinity until May 4, when he met a band of Snake Indians who informed him that a party of Americans had wintered near by and had gone in the direction he was intending to take. Since the Americans had passed down Bear River into the valley of the Great Salt Lake, Ogden and his men continued up the south end of Cache Valley and trapped along several of the small creeks. The group spent several days trapping the upper waters of Ogden River, and camps were established near the present towns of Liberty, Eden, and Huntsville, Utah, in the Ogden Valley. From here, Ogden and his men continued southward, passing over the divide into Weber Valley and striking the Weber River near the modern Utah town of Mountain Green.[16]

On Sunday morning, May 22, when Ogden was breaking camp, one of his trappers rode up with two freemen who had deserted from Flathead Post in 1822. They reported that they belonged to a party of thirty men who had been fitted out by "Spaniards and Traders in the Missouri and St. Louis" and who had wintered in this region. On the following day, May 23, another group visited the Ogden camp. This party of fifteen Canadians and Spaniards headed by Étienne Provost and one François, a Hudson's Bay Company deserter,[17] strained British-American relations somewhat, for the Americans blamed the British for provoking the massacre which had involved Provost and the Snake Indians the preceding fall. The Provost-Ogden meeting, however, is insignificant in comparison with the Johnson Gardner incident that developed that same afternoon.

Here, near present Mountain Green, Utah, the much described meeting and conflict between the British and American trappers took place, at which time twenty-three of Ogden's men deserted to the American camp. Historians have differed regarding the site of

16 This site has been positively identified by Professor David E. Miller of the University of Utah's Department of History.

17 Ogden, "Snake Country Journal of the 1824–25 Expedition," H.B.C.A., B. 202/a/2, 23 and 24. Also quoted in the *Publications* of the Hudson's Bay Record Society, XIII.

this event, but they have usually placed it somewhere in Cache Valley, either in northern Utah or in southern Idaho. With the publication of the Ogden and Kittson journals, it becomes evident that the locale was farther to the south and that the clash took place on the Weber River rather than in Cache Valley.

The journals also shed considerable additional light upon the whole episode. Until recently, there was a question about Jedediah Smith's part in the proceedings, but Dale Morgan's fine researches pertaining to Smith and the publication of the diaries seem to exonerate him. It appears quite possible that members of Smith's party may have been responsible for directing the Rocky Mountain trappers to Ogden's camp, but that Smith himself remained aloof from the whole affair.

On the afternoon of May 23, a party of twenty-five Americans and fourteen Hudson's Bay Company "absent men" led by Johnson Gardner rode into the Ogden Camp and accused Ogden and his men of trespassing, stating that they were on soil of the United States. Gardner announced to the British trappers that regardless of whether they were indebted or engaged, they were now free, and offered to buy their beaver for $3.50 a pound, eight times as much as paid by the Hudson's Bay Company. With such an inducement, some twenty-three of Ogden's men, or half of all the freemen with whom he had started out in December, deserted.

Gardner apparently made grandiose threats against the British also, for Dr. McLoughlin stated in a letter dated August 10 that he had just received word from Mr. Dease of Flathead Post "conveying the Mortifying intelligence of the desertion of our Freemen in the Snakes and of the threats made by Mr. Gardner that the Americans would be at the Flat Heads and Kootonais this fall and would drive us from their Territory."[18] On the same day, Dr. McLoughlin began to make plans to counteract the Americans if they did attempt a drive northward:

"In case the Americans come to the Flat Head Country they must be opposed as much as we can but without if possible wasting property as the right to Remain there will be decided between the

[18] Dr. McLoughlin to Chief Factors and Chief Traders, Fort Vancouver, August 10, 1825, H.B.C.A., B. 223/b/1.

142

Governor Simpson, of the Hudson's
Bay Company, who inaugurated the
company's highly successful "scorched
earth" policy.

Dr. McLoughlin, along with other officials of the Hudson's Bay
Company, accepted many of the fantastic geographical ideas current
at the time.

From Ross's *Fur Hunters* (1855)
Yale University Library

Alexander Ross, whose return to Flathead Post with Jedediah Smith
and his Americans caused Governor Simpson to replace him as
leader of the Snake Country Expedition.

Peter Skene Ogden, the versatile leader of the Snake Country Expedition, 1824–30, who explored vast areas of the Great Basin, from a daguerreotype made in New York about 1852.

Old Fort Walla Walla, commonly called Fort Nez Percés, built in 1818 by Donald Mackenzie, which became a point of rendezvous for the British fur trade of the interior.

Fort Vancouver, to which 30,000 beaver skins and other valuable furs were brought in 1827 by Hudson's Bay Company men.

Captain Bonneville, who was deluded by the idea that he could make a fortune in the fur trade.

Joseph Reddeford Walker, of the Bonneville-Walker party, who explored and established an important segment of the Overland Trail, from a portrait by A. J. Miller.

Pyramid Lake, so called by Frémont because a rock rising out of the lake reminded him of the Pyramid of Cheops in Egypt.

two Governments. I think from Discovery and occupancy we will have that part of the Country, therefore it is not our Interest to spoil the Indians however we must do so if necessary and treat them as liberally as the Americans."[19]

Although Johnson Gardner declared that the Ogden party was on American soil, Ogden believed himself to be in the Oregon country, a region which was open to joint occupation by the British and Americans through the British-American convention of 1818. The boundaries of this area were not clearly defined, but it was generally understood that joint occupation applied to the region lying west of the continental divide, although no southern boundary had been named. Ironically, it seems that the Americans and not the British were the trespassers, for by the terms of the Adams-Onis treaty of 1819 between the United States and Spain, the forty-second parallel was selected as the southern boundary to American claims to the Oregon country. The area in question lay south of this line and therefore in reality was not American territory, but belonged to the recently independent nation of Mexico. England had not been a party to this agreement and so was not bound by it.

That the Mexicans were aware that the British and Americans were in Mexican territory and protested their intrustion is evidenced by a letter written by Dr. McLoughlin to Peter Skene Ogden pointing out that he "should avoid any Collision Either with Americans or Spaniards as much as possible."[20] Correspondence between Governor Pelly of the Hudson's Bay Company and the Honorable George Canning, foreign minister of England, had taken place regarding this Mountain Green, Utah, incident, and the British maintained that according to the convention of October 28, 1790, which settled the Nootka Sound Controversy, Spain had abandoned all claim beyond the region that she held in actual settlement. However, the officials of the Hudson's Bay Company, confused about the exact locale of the incident, developed a conciliatory attitude, as is noted in the following message sent by McLoughlin to Ogden: ". . . in consequence of the Remark the Spaniards made last year that you were on their Territories though we should by no means infringe on the

19 Letter, Dr. McLoughlin to John Work, Fort Vancouver, August 10, 1825, H.B.C.A., B. 223/b/1.
20 Fort Vancouver, November 3, 1826, H.B.C.A., B. 223/b/2.

Rights of others still they must have surer foundation than mere assertion on their part."[21]

The fact that the Hudson's Bay Company did not seek compensation for the Johnson Gardner incident which cost the company approximately £3,000 in loss of furs[22] can best be explained by the fact that the Hudson's Bay Company officials believed that the action had taken place east of the continental divide and thus on American territory. They were laboring under this misapprehension because of Ogden's letter of July 10, 1825, which was written from that side of the mountains and so did not realize that the incident had occurred in the Great Basin on the west side of the divide, south of the forty-second parallel. In a letter written by the governor and committee to Dr. McLoughlin on September 20, 1826, the officials of the company commented about the situation:

> Had the spoilation taken place on the west side of the mountains on the neutral ground [joint-occupation area] which from the statement of Mr. Ogden appears not to have been the fact, we might have submitted such a case to the ministers as might have induced them to seek redress or restitution of the property from the United States Government, but as the transaction took place on United States' territory, we fear we must be compelled to bear the loss unless you are able to prove distinctly that it occurred on the West side of the Rocky Mountains.[23]

The effect of this Mountain Green incident upon Hudson's Bay Company policy can be seen in a letter written by the governor and committee to Governor Simpson in March of 1827:

> We can afford to pay as good a price as the Americans and where there is risk of meeting their parties it is necessary to pay as much or something more to avoid the risk of a result similar to that of Mr Ogden. By attempting to make such expeditions too profitable the whole may be lost and it is extremely desirable to hunt as bare as possible all the Country South of the Columbia and West of the Mountains, but the parties must have positive instructions not to cross to the East of the Mountains South of 49 degrees North lati-

21 *Ibid.*

22 Letter, Dr. McLoughlin to Governor, Chief Factors, and Chief Traders, Fort Vancouver, August 10, 1825, H.B.C.A., B. 223/b/1.

23 Letter, Governor and Committee to John McLoughlin, September 30, 1826, as quoted by Merk in *Oregon Historical Quarterly*, Vol. XXXV (June, 1934), 119.

tude. In the event of our trapping party falling in with any Americans in the Country common to both, the leader ought to have instructions to endeavor to make an amicable arrangement as to the parts of the Country which each will take to avoid giving just cause for accusing our people of any aggression against the Americans or violence except in case of self defense.[24]

From the contents of this letter, it is obvious that the officials of the Hudson's Bay Company were concerned with the broad aspects of their trade in northwestern America and in international developments and consequences; therefore, the effective employment of the "scorched earth" policy was a major concern. The Hudson's Bay Company was interested in amicable relations with the Americans for fear of international repercussions and was accordingly careful to avoid future meetings such as that which took place on the Weber River in the eastern portion of the Great Basin.

Meanwhile, General Ashley of the American Rocky Mountain Fur Company was in St. Louis, preparing to start for the mountains on November 3, 1824, with a party of twenty-five men and fifty pack horses. The group traveled up the Platte and North Platte and crossed the continental divide south of South Pass by utilizing Bridger's Pass. Although the party was small, Ashley divided it into four detachments when they arrived on the banks of the Green River; three were to trap the country and the fourth was to accompany him on a reconnoitering expedition. James Clyman was to return to the tributaries of the Green that he had trapped the previous year, while Zacharias Ham was to go directly west, where no doubt he struck Hams Fork, which still bears his name. Thomas Fitzpatrick was sent south to ascertain whether a stream ran at the base of the Uinta Mountains. The fact that Fitzpatrick knew nothing of the existence of such a stream seems to indicate quite clearly that Smith's spring hunt of 1824 had extended only as far south as Blacks Fork.

Ashley was most anxious to learn whether the Shetskedee[25] (Green River) that he had struck was the Buenaventura or the Colorado of the West, so on April 22, 1825, he began a voyage down this stream. On April 23, the party passed the mouth of the Big Sandy, and by

24 London, March 12, 1827, as quoted in *The Journal of Sir George Simpson*, Appendix A, 286–87.

25 Also known as Seeds-ka-day, Seeds-kee-dee, Seedskeeder, Siskadee, and other similar names.

the third of May had reached Henrys Fork. On June 7, Ashley met Étienne Provost and a party of twelve men, who informed him that Captain Weber had wintered in this region and upon learning of Ashley's arrival had gone in search of him. Provost now guided Ashley and his men to the Weber River by what presumably was the route that he had used when he first entered the Great Basin in the fall of 1824. This trail struck west to the headwaters of Strawberry River and then kept to the northern side of that stream to avoid its tortuous canyons until it reached Strawberry Valley. Provost led the group up to the sources of Strawberry River and here entered the Great Basin.

The party descended Center Creek into the valley where Heber City now stands. They turned north along the foothills and crossed a low divide which brought them to the banks of the Provo River. From this point they crossed Camas Prairie to the Weber River, but descended it only as far as Echo Canyon. There Ashley learned that Johnson Gardner and his party had gone up a small stream which they had just passed. Turning back, Ashley followed Gardner's trail up Chalk Creek Canyon and reached the Bear River a little south of where the Mormon Trail was later to cross it.[26]

General Ashley's preoccupation with the Buenaventura River is interesting. He obviously was well acquainted with contemporary geographical conceptions—those of Lewis and Clark in particular—for he was of the opinion that the Buenaventura was a tributary of the Multnomah and that it subsequently flowed into the Columbia. On Friday, May 8, 1825, he wrote:

> From the head waters of Twinty River [Uinta River], I crossed a range of lofty mountains nearly E. and W., which divide the waters of the Rio Colorado from those which I have represented as the Buenaventura. . . . I proceeded down the waters of the Buenaventura about sixty miles bordered with a growth of willows almost inpenetrable. In that distance I crossed several streams from 20 to 60 yards wide running in various directions. All of them, as I am informed, unite in one in the course of 30 miles, making a river of considerable magnitude, which enters a few miles lower down a large lake, represented on your sketch as Lake Tempagono. This information was communicated to me by our hunters who (as I before told) had crossed to this region in the summer of

26 Morgan, *Jedediah Smith*, 156–70.

1824 and wintered on and near the borders of this lake. They had not explored the lake sufficiently to judge correctly of its extent, but from their own observations and information collected from Indians, they supposed it to be about eighty miles long by fifty broad. They represented it as a beautiful sheet of water, deep, transparent, and a little brackish, though in this latter quality the accounts differ; some insist that it is not brackish.[27] I met several small parties of Eutaw Indians on this side of the last mentioned range of mountains, 100 miles long bearing about W.N.W. and S.S.E. [who said] that a large river flowing out of it on the west side runs in a western direction, but they know nothing of its discharge into the ocean or of the country any considerable distance west of the lake. I also conversed with some very intelligent men who I found with our hunters in the vicinity of this lake and who had been for many years in the service of the Hudson Bay Fur Company.[28] Some of them profess to be well acquainted with all the principal waters of the Columbia, with which they assured me these waters had no connection short of the ocean. It appears from this information that the river is not the Multnomah, a southern branch of the Columbia, which I first supposed it to be. The necessity of my unremitted attention to my business prevented me from gratifying a great desire to descend this river to the ocean, which I ultimately declined with the greatest reluctance.[29]

It is clear from this last statement that Ashley now dissociates the Buenaventura from the Multnomah and Columbia and definitely believes that the stream runs into the ocean after first proceeding through a lake. At the time under discussion, the geographical conceptions of Fathers Domínguez, Escalante, and Garcés had been correlated by cartographers, and the Río de San Buenaventura was pictured by them as a westward-flowing stream proceeding from the Rocky Mountains to the Pacific Ocean.

Ashley had crossed the Uinta Range probably in the vicinity of Bald Peak. The waters that he mentions after crossing the divide and associates with the Buenaventura are probably tributaries of the Weber River. Dale states that not all the streams that he crossed

27 This reference is no doubt to Jim Bridger's descent of Bear River. At the mouth of this stream in Bear River Bay, the salinity of the water varies with the seasons, and thus prompts a discussion regarding the lake's salty quality.
28 No doubt members of Ogden's Snake Country Expedition of 1824–25.
29 Dale, *Ashley-Smith Explorations*, 152–55.

unite to form the Weber River, but instead some of them are branches of the Bear River. Ashley may even have crossed the upper waters of Blacks Fork, which is a tributary of the Green River, a non–Great Basin stream.

General Ashley's confusion about his geographical location was certainly not unwarranted, for within a comparatively small area which is not clearly defined by mountain barriers, streams rise which flow into the Gulf of Mexico by way of the Missouri, into the Pacific by way of the Columbia, into the Gulf of California by way of the Colorado, and into the Great Basin directly by the Weber River or circuitously by the Bear River. Not far to the east of the Green River and south of the Wind River Mountains lies South Pass, which separates the Sweetwater branch of the Platte from the Sandy, a tributary of the Green. It bridges an almost imperceptible watershed which divides the waters of the Missouri-Mississippi system from those of the Gulf of California. To the west of the upper Green River only a low divide separates that stream from Big Gray's River and Salt River, which are tributaries of the Snake and hence part of the Columbia River drainage pattern. Just a little to the south of Big Gray's River, and flowing in almost the same direction, is Bear River; this stream flows into the Great Salt Lake and thus is a Great Basin river. Bear River, like Big Gray's River, is separated from Green River only by an easy, though barren, divide. Indeed, there are few areas in North America more confusing topographically.

By July 1, 1825, all the men who were in Ashley's employ or with whom he had any dealings, "together with twenty-nine who had recently withdrawn from the Hudson Bay Company, making in all 120 men,"[30] were gathered in two camps near each other and only about twenty miles away from the appointed place of rendezvous on Henrys Fork, which Ashley had named in May "Randavouze Creek." Although a small rendezvous had been conducted on the Sweetwater River in 1824, this first general meeting conducted by General Ashley himself during the summer of 1825 is the real prototype of that institution. This rendezvous is probably important for another reason also, for Andrew Henry had dropped out of the Rocky Mountain Fur Company by this time and it seems quite certain that Smith and Ashley made an agreement about partnership at this annual meeting.

After he had collected his furs, General Ashley returned to St.

30 Morgan, *Jedediah Smith*, 170.

Louis by way of South Pass and the Big Horn River. Near the confluence of the Missouri and the Yellowstone rivers, Ashley met Brigadier General Henry Atkinson and Major Benjamin O'Fallon, the leaders of the "Yellowstone Expedition," and returned to St. Louis under their protection, arriving there about October 8. The results of this meeting are expressed in a letter written by Brigadier General Atkinson to Major General Brown. The letter, dated November 23, 1825, states:

> I learn from general Ashley, that there is an easy passage across the Rocky mountains, by approaching them due west, from the head waters of the river Platte; indeed so gentle in ascent, as to admit of wagons being taken over: This point is in about latitude 42, perhaps a little more south.—In going west from this pass, you come to the head waters of a river, which is believed to empty itself into the Pacific, some distance south of the Colmubia River.[31]

On March 8, 1826, Ashley left St. Louis with twenty-five men on another trip to the Great Salt Lake region. The group passed up the valleys of the Platte, North Platte, and Sweetwater rivers and crossed South Pass to the valley of the Green River. An article which appeared in *Niles' Register* concerning the expedition reported:

General Ashley's Expedition. The recent expedition of general Ashley to the country west of the Rocky Mountains has been productive of information on subjects of no small interest to the people of the union. It has proved, that overland expeditions, in large bodies, may be made to that remote region, without the necessity of transporting provisions for man or beast. Gen. Ashley left St. Louis in March last, and returned in September. . . . He went to the station of the party which he had left beyond the mountains, when he came in a year ago, and then descended a river believed to be the Buenaventura, about one hundred and fifty miles to the Great Salt Lake. . . . The whole route lay through a level and open country, better for carriages than any turnpike road in the United States.—Wagons and carriages could go with ease as far as general Ashley went, crossing the Rocky Mountains at the sources of the north fork of the Platte and descending the valley of the Buenaventura towards the Pacific Ocean. The lake which terminated the expedition westward, is a most remarkable body of water, and

31 Quoted in 19 Cong., 1 sess., *House Exec. Doc. 117*, p. 15.

heretofore unknown unless from vague accounts. It is estimated to be one hundred miles long, and sixty or eighty wide. It was coasted last spring by a party of gen. Ashley's men in canoes, who were occupied four and twenty days, in making its circuit. They did not exactly ascertain its outlet but passed a place where they supposed that it must have been.[32]

During General Ashley's absence, his men spent the summer of 1825 trapping the waters of Salt River, Green River, Bear River, and along their tributaries. The parties separated widely in the fall to carry on that season's hunt and then gathered for the winter in Cache Valley. However, in mid-December, supposedly for climatic reasons, William Sublette, who seems to have been in charge of the group, moved them to the shores of the Great Salt Lake.[33] Here, not far from the site of present Ogden, Utah, the group wintered.

In the spring of 1826, upon breaking up winter camp, Jedediah Smith took his party around the head of Bear River Bay and on across the Promontory Mountains. Four men were detached to investigate the lake and to make a close examination of its shores. They were sent to discover any fur-bearing affluents and to locate the river which was supposed to flow from the western side of the lake into the sea. As *Niles' Register* suggested, "They did not exactly ascertain its outlet, but passed a place where they supposed that it must have been."[34] The explorers had evidently observed the opening along the western shores north of Strongs Knob, across which the lake had retreated from the Salt Desert in Pleistocene times. This must have appeared to be a likely outlet, and a closer examination of the area, which undoubtedly would have disclosed the true nature of the opening, was prevented by the shallows in this section of the lake.[35]

Smith's route and explorations northwest of Great Salt Lake are still obscure. The scanty record of the expedition consists of a few notations in Ogden's Journal and an itinerary which was depicted on the Burr map of 1839.[36] From these sources, it seems that Smith

---

32 Issue of December 9, 1826, p. 229.
33 John E. Sunder, *William Sublette*, 61–62.
34 December 9, 1826, p. 229.
35 Dale L. Morgan, *The Great Salt Lake*, 81.
36 *Ogden Snake Country Journals, 1824–26;* David H. Burr, *Map of the United States of North America with parts of the Adjacent Countries* (Washington, D.C., 1839).

and his party penetrated into the arid sections of present eastern Nevada, where he found no beaver and little game or water. He then turned north toward the Snake River, proceeding to Salmon Falls Creek and then following it to the great South Branch. The party trapped north to the Boise and then turned north to the Payette, trapping up it to its source in Payette Lake. Although Smith's course back to Cache Valley in the Great Basin is obscure, from the Burr map it appears that he moved east to Henrys Fork, then around the Tetons to Jackson Hole and down the Snake. From this point he followed either the Salt, Blackfoot, or Portneuf rivers, which brought him back into the Great Basin, to the banks of the Bear River.[37] While Ashley's men were engaged in trapping along Sage Creek, a tributary of Bear River, they learned from Ashley's couriers of his arrival and prepared for the rendezvous.

Although previously published accounts generally give the site for the rendezvous of 1826 as Great Salt Lake, it was held in Cache Valley near the present town of Hyrum, Utah.[38] This rendezvous was to be one of the most important that was ever held in the Great Basin, for it was there that General Ashley sold his business to three of his former associates, Smith, Jackson, and William Sublette, and retired from the trade, retaining only an indirect interest in the fur business. He disposed of the Indian goods that he had on hand at a profit of 150 per cent, the price to be paid within five years in beaver skins at five dollars a pound or in cash. Ashley continued to supply the new firm with goods from the States, and for the next three years sent supply trains to the mountains with these provisions. Even after Smith, Jackson, and William Sublette had sold out to Fitzpatrick, Milton Sublette, and Bridger, Ashley still acted as agent, receiving as much as $3,000 commission in one year.[39]

The three new partners now divided the work and began to prepare for expanding operations. Jackson and Smith remained in the mountains in command of the one hundred or more men who were in their employ. Jackson was named the resident partner, and maintained his headquarters first in the vicinity of the Great Salt Lake and later east of the mountains, near the headwaters of the Sweetwater River. Smith was designated the explorer, and sought out new

[37] Morgan, *Jedediah Smith,* 185–87.
[38] *Ibid.,* 187.
[39] Dale, *Ashley-Smith Explorations,* 168–69.

fields for exploitation; Sublette was appointed to make the trip to St. Louis each year with the year's accumulation of furs and obtain requisite supplies.

Now the three partners undertook to operate in the field which had been opened by Ashley's men two years before. This area was immensely rich in beaver and could support continued trapping for a number of years. It was also a region which had been almost untouched by competition. However, Smith, Jackson and Sublette had visions of pushing their trapping parties even farther west. They were aware that a vast area must lie between the Great Salt Lake and the Pacific Ocean, and they were naturally eager to penetrate this new field. The first step was one of exploration and survey, for it would have been an unsound move to turn a large party of men into an unworked field before its business potentialities had been determined. It was decided, therefore, that Sublette and Jackson should remain in the mountains with the largest part of the company, while Smith with a few men should investigate the new region. It may be possible that Smith had other ideas in addition to his interest in determining the fur-bearing resources of the country to the west; he may have thought of the possibility of shipping furs from one of the ports of California. This was not a novel idea, for John Jacob Astor had inaugurated the practice fifteen years before, and even Ashley himself had had such a project in mind.[40] In a letter which was written about this time, Smith stated that it was "reasonable to suppose the whole of the fur trade west of the mountains will take that direction [to the Pacific] to market as soon as any place on the sea coast may be established to a trade operated about the 43rd degree of latitude."[41]

Smith also stated that he and his party started for the Southwest in the hope of finding beaver, but when they found no streams which provided beaver in sufficient numbers to justify their halting to trap, he was forced to continue on to California since his men had been

[40] The chief fur-trading mart in the world was Canton, China, and thus if furs could be sent directly from the Pacific Coast to the Orient rather than via the circuitous route to St. Louis and around the Horn to Asia, Americans could increase their profits considerably. The Hudson's Bay Company had long shipped furs from its Columbia River posts of Fort George and later Fort Vancouver to London where they were sold at auction. Many of these furs were later consigned to the East India Company for transshipment to China because of the East India Company's monopoly in the Orient.

[41] *American Monthly Magazine*, Vol. XXXIII (Jan., 1906), 329.

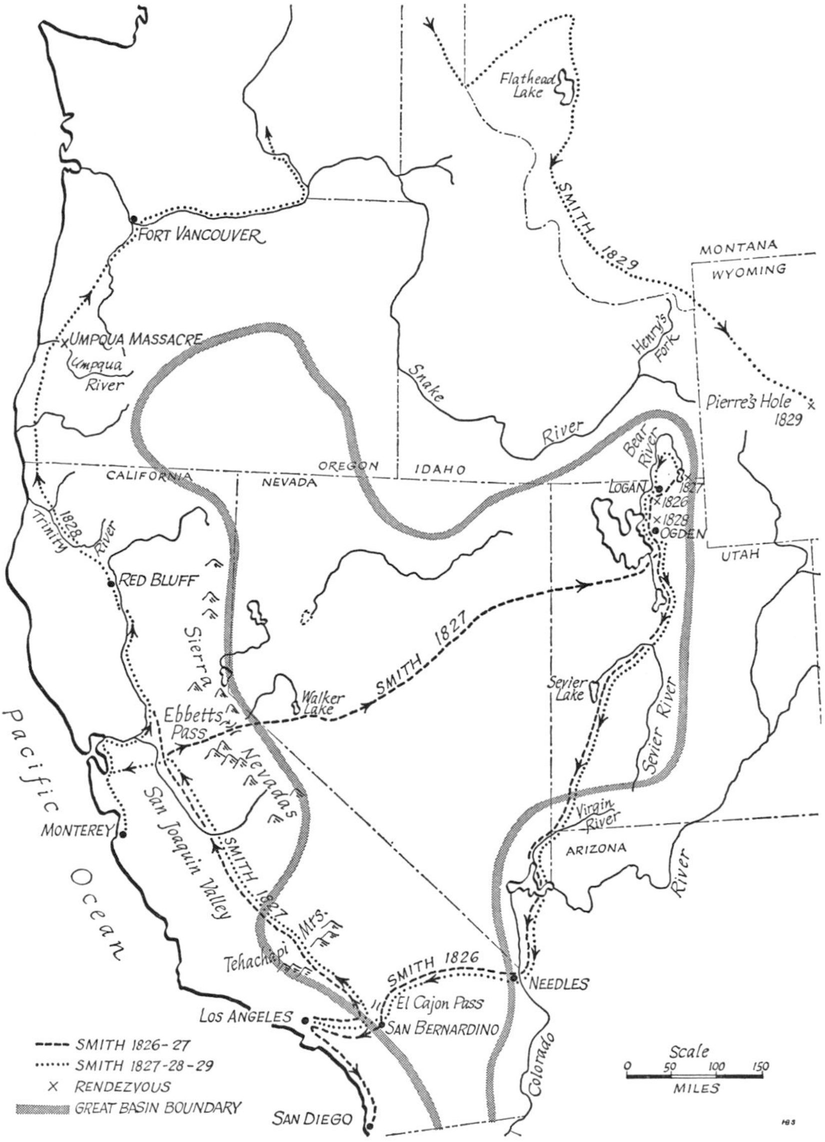
Flathead Lake
SMITH 1829
MONTANA
WYOMING
FORT VANCOUVER
UMPQUA MASSACRE
Umpqua River
Henry's Fork
Snake River
Pierre's Hole 1829
Bear River
OREGON
IDAHO
CALIFORNIA
NEVADA
LOGAN
1827
1826
1828
OGDEN
UTAH
Trinity River 1828
RED BLUFF
SMITH 1827
Sierra Nevadas
Walker Lake
Sevier Lake
Sevier River
Ebbetts Pass
Pacific Ocean
San Joaquin Valley
MONTEREY
Virgin River
ARIZONA
SMITH 1827
River
Tehachapi Mts.
SMITH 1826
NEEDLES
El Cajon Pass
LOS ANGELES
SAN BERNARDINO
Colorado
SMITH 1826-27
SMITH 1827-28-29
RENDEZVOUS
GREAT BASIN BOUNDARY
SAN DIEGO
Scale
0 50 100 150
MILES

Jedediah Smith's Southwestern Expedition, 1826–29

reduced to destitute circumstances. It seems clear, however, that Smith had in mind from the first to push on to the Pacific Coast. Daniel Potts, who was an accurate observer, wrote in a letter to his brother on July 16, 1826 that in a short time he expected "to explore the country lying S.W. of the Great Lake where we shall probably winter. This country has never been visited by any white person— from thence to what place I cannot say, but expect the next letter will be dated mouth of the Columbia River."[42]

The Smith party included Harrison G. Rogers as clerk and the following men: Arthur Black, Robert Evans, Daniel Ferguson, John Gaiter, Silas Gobel, John Hanna, Abraham Laplant, Mauel Lazarus, Martin McCoy, Peter Ranne, James Reed, John Reubascan, and John Wilson. The group left the Cache Valley rendezvous on August 16, 1826. The most direct route down into the valley of the Great Salt Lake is by way of Box Elder Canyon to the site of the present Brigham City, Utah, which is roughly the route followed today by U.S. Highway 91. However, according to the Gibbs and the Burr maps, the party, instead of following the above course, went down the Bear River to the vicinity of Brigham City by a route which is utilized at the present time by U.S. Highway 89.

From this region to the site of present Leven, Smith and his party followed a route that is substantially that which is used today by U.S. Highway 91. He veered slightly northwest in order to reach the Sevier River, meeting it about twenty miles above its great bend. He followed up this river, and then struck Beaver River, which he called "Lost River." He now moved south along what is the present Highway 91 and passed the sites of the modern towns of Paragonah, Parawan, and Cedar City, Utah, before passing over the rim of the Great Basin.[43] At this point he left the Great Basin for a short time when he passed over the divide near Ash Creek, about twenty miles northeast of the present St. George, Utah, and struck the waters of the Colorado drainage system.

There has been some confusion concerning the route followed by Smith in this region. C. Hart Merriam believes that he turned west from Sevier Valley and crossed the range of hills west of Escalante Valley, suggesting that this brought him into the present state of

42 Quoted in Morgan, *Jedediah Smith,* 193.
43 Dale L. Morgan and Carl I. Wheat, *Jedediah Smith and His Maps of the American West,* 161–62.

Nevada near the modern towns of Panaca and Pioche in Lincoln County:

> In conclusion, it may be said with confidence . . . that "Adams River" of Smith is Meadow Valley Wash of eastern Nevada and its continuation the Muddy—not the Virgin, as heretofore misidentified; and that Smith's route after crossing the mountains west of the Sevier lay across the Escalante Desert and thence down Meadow Valley Wash and the Muddy to the lower Virgin, and down it to the Colorado River.[44]

However, other authorities in this field believe that Smith and his men followed down Ash Creek to the Virgin River,[45] and I am inclined to agree with them. In a letter written July 17, 1827 to General William Clark, superintendent of Indian affairs, Smith said:

> My general course on leaving the Salt Lake was S.W. and W. Passing the Little Uta Lake and ascending Ashley's river,[46] which empties into the Little Utah Lake. . . . I passed over a range of mountains running S.E. and N.W. and struck a river running S.W. which I called *Adams River*, in compliment to our President. The water is of a muddy cast, and is a little brackish. The country is mountainous to the East; towards the West there are sandy plains and detached rocky hills. Passing down this river some distance, I fell in with a nation of Indians who call themselves Pa-Ulches. . . . I followed Adams river two days further where it empties in to the Seedekeeden a South East course.[47]

On November 10, 1826, the Smith party, now guided by two runaways from the missions, started westward for the coastal settlements.

[44] C. Hart Merriam, "Earliest Crossing of the Deserts of Utah and Nevada to Southern California: Route of Jedediah S. Smith in 1826," *California Historical Quarterly*, Vol. II (Oct., 1923), 228–36; F. N. Fletcher, *Early Nevada*, 31; Fletcher, in "Eastbound Route of Jedediah S. Smith, 1827," *California Historical Quarterly*, Vol. III (Jan., 1924), 344, also gives his opinion that Smith crossed to Meadow Valley Wash and the Muddy River.

[45] Morgan, *Jedediah Smith*, 197; Chittenden, *The American Fur Trade*, 283; Maurice Sullivan, *Jedediah Smith, Trader and Trail Breaker*, 72; Dale, *The Ashley-Smith Explorations*, 188; Robert Glass Cleland, *This Reckless Breed of Men*, 68.

[46] This is undoubtedly a reference to Sevier River, which, however, does not empty into Utah Lake but into Sevier Lake.

[47] This letter is quoted in full in Dale, *Ashley-Smith Explorations*, 182–90.

They followed a route across the Mojave Desert which was used by the Mojave Indians to bring articles, most specifically, iridescent shells, from the Pacific Slope. This route, through probably the most barren part of the Great Basin, was similar to that used by Father Garcés half a century prior to this crossing. The party struck the Mojave River or the Río de los Martires and called it, quite appropriately, the "Inconstant River." Smith wrote:

> I travelled a west course fifteen days over a country of complete barrens, generally travelling from morning until night without water. I crossed a Salt plain about 20 miles long and 8 wide; on the surface was a crust of beautiful white salt, quite thin. Under the surface there is a layer of salt from a half to one and a half inches in depth; between this and the upper layer there is about four inches of yellowish sand.[48]

After the ordeal of crossing such inhospitable country, Smith and his men reached the San Bernardino Mountains, negotiated them by way of El Cajon Pass, and finally pushed on to Mission San Gabriel, where they arrived on November 26, 1826.

There seems to be no doubt that one of the chief purposes of this southwestern expedition was to determine whether the San Buenaventura River really existed. In the spring, Smith had searched for it in the country west and northwest of the Great Salt Lake to no avail, and consequently believed that if it did exist, it was hidden to the southwest of that body of water. He was determined to travel up the coast in order to ascertain the outlet of this stream on the Pacific Coast. This is evidenced by a letter which he wrote to the United States ambassador plenipotentiary in Mexico on December 16, 1826, in which he states:

> I wrote [undecipherable word], stating to the Gov. Gen. my situation requesting of him some Horses & permission to pass through his coun[try] to the Bay of St. Francisco—I wished to follow up one of the largest Riv[ers] that emptied into the Bay cross the mon [mountains] at its head and from thence to our Deposit on the waters of the Salt Lake.[49]

48 *Ibid.*

49 Letter, Jedediah Smith to the United States Plenipotentiary at Mexico, December 16, 1826, as quoted in Andrew F. Rolle (ed.), "Jedediah Strong Smith: New Documentation," *Mississippi Valley Historical Review,* Vol. XL (Sept., 1953), 308.

Thus when Governor Echeandia ordered Smith to take his expedition out of California by the same route by which he had come, it was a severe blow. Smith decided to circumvent the Governor's orders. He therefore doubled back on his trail as far as the San Bernardino Valley and then turned north along the edge of the Mojave Desert, crossing Antelope Valley and the Tehachapi Mountains; this route led him down into the southern end of the San Joaquin Valley.

The party traveled up the valley and struck a river which they called the Wimmulche after a tribe of Indians who resided on its banks. Authorities have differed in the identification of this stream: Chittenden believes it to be the Merced;[50] Richman refers to it as the Mokelumne;[51] Dale reveals it as the Stanislaus,[52] while Dale Morgan, the erudite Jedediah Smith scholar, is of the opinion that it is the Kings River.[53]

Smith believed that if he followed the western foothills of the Sierra Nevada Mountains, he would come to the Buenaventura River, which he could follow to the Great Salt Lake. He seems to have lost faith in the existence of this river after having traveled three hundred miles to the north of San Gabriel and finding that the Indians were ignorant of such a stream. Since it was time to meet his two partners, Jackson and Sublette, Smith decided to take his expedition over the Sierra Nevada Mountains. In May, 1827, his attempt to take his party over the mountains at the head of the American River failed, and Smith was forced to turn back on his trail seventy-five miles to the Stanislaus. From this point, on May 20, 1827, Smith, together with Silas Gobel and Robert Evans, made a quick dash over the Sierras. The crossing took eight days, and only a mule and two horses were lost. From information ascertained from the Gallatin map of 1836 and the Burr map of 1839, it seems that the Smith party traveled up the north fork of the Stanislaus River and crossed the Sierras by way of Ebbetts Pass. Moving down the eastern slope of the mountains by way of the east fork of the Carson River and the west

50 *The American Fur Trade,* 284.

51 Irving B. Richman, *California under Spain and Mexico, 1535–1847,* map of the Southwest.

52 *Ashley-Smith Explorations,* 189, n. 402.

53 *Jedediah Smith,* 207.

fork of the Walker, the group entered the Great Basin and what is now the present state of Nevada just south of Walker Lake.[54]

In general terms, the route which they followed across Nevada was approximately that which is utilized today by U.S. Highway 6. From Walker Lake, they moved eastward between the Gabbs Valley Range and the Pilot Range and then around the southern end of the Shoshone and Toiyabe mountains and across the Toquima Mountains to the vicinity of the old gold-mining town of Manhattan. Continuing east, they crossed the Monitor Range and struck Hot Creek, and then traveled east along the base of the Pancake Range. Their route was north of Wheeler Peak and led them into the present state of Utah near the modern site of Gandy. They finally reached the Great Salt Lake and skirted its southern shore until they reached the Jordan River. On July 2 they left the lake and turned northeast through the mountains to Cache Valley, where they learned from a group of Snake Indians that the Americans were encamped at Bear Lake.

During Smith's absence, Sublette had initiated the fall hunt to the north in the Snake country, which had a known potential in furs. The party went north to the forks of the Snake, up Henrys Fork, circled the Tetons, and pressed as far as Yellowstone Lake. During this period, Jackson appears to have been trapping the lower reaches of the Snake country.

The rendezvous of 1827 was held at Bear Lake, which lies along the present-day Utah-Idaho boundary line within the great bend of the Bear River. At this rendezvous, Jackson and Sublette delivered to Bruffee, an agent of "W. H. Ashley & Co.," "7,400⅓" pounds of beaver at three dollars a pound. The proceeds of the year's hunt totaled $22,690.[55] This certainly speaks well for Jackson's and Sublette's trapping parties, for the results of Smith's spring hunt were still in California.

The Bear Lake rendezvous broke up on July 13, 1827, ten days after Smith had arrived from California. At this time it was decided that Sublette should take another party north for the fall hunt, this time going all the way to the Blackfoot country. Jackson found it

54 See Francis P. Farquhar, "Jedediah Smith and the First Crossing of the Sierra Nevada," Sierra Club *Bulletin,* Vol. XXVIII (June, 1943), 35–52. Morgan, *Jedediah Smith,* 210.

55 *Ibid.,* 418, n. 41, 211–15.

necessary to make a trip to Missouri, but planned to return and winter in the modern-day Utah region. Smith now outfitted himself with eighteen men and enough supplies to last for two years and left for California to rejoin his men. He planned to trap his way up the Pacific Coast to the Columbia and from that point return to Bear Lake, which was to be the site of the following year's rendezvous.

The eighteen men who accompanied Smith on his second expedition to California were Silas Gobel, Henry Brown, William Campbell, David Cunningham, Thomas Daws, François Deromme, Issac Galbraith, Polette Labross, Joseph Lapoint, Toussaint Marechal, Gregory Ortago, Joseph Palmer, John B. Ratelle, John Relle, Robiseau, Charles Swift, John Turner, and Thomas Virgin. The party headed south from the scene of the rendezvous, going over the ridge which divides Bear Lake from Bear River, and then followed Bear River itself. They veered to the southwest of the Uinta Mountains and reached the Weber River, no doubt by way of Chalk Creek. They took practically the reverse of Ashley's route of 1825 as far as the Provo River, and then followed the banks of this stream down into Utah Valley.

Smith dismisses his route to the Colorado River in a few words, but it seems that he laid the way for the future U.S. Highway 91 west of present St. George, Utah: ". . . and then turning S.W. I crossed the Mountain without any difficulty and crossing the low Ridges struck a Ravine which I followed down to the bed of the dry River [Beaverdam Wash] which I call Pautch Creek which I followed down to Adam's River about 10 miles below the Mou^tn."[56]

Upon arriving at the banks of the Colorado River, Smith found the Mojaves, with whom he had spent fifteen days the previous year, most unfriendly. While the Indians were employed in the task of transporting Smith and his party to the western banks of the river on rafts made of bundles of reeds, they treacherously fell upon the white men and only nine of the eighteen escaped. Smith with the survivors struck westward for the desert and shortly came to the Mojave or Inconstant River, as Smith called it. In continuing his journey, he states, ". . . instead of traveling East around the bend of the stream I struck directly across the Plain Nearly S.S.W. to the Gape of the Mountain."[57] Thus Smith crossed the mountains by way

56 *Ibid.*, 238.
57 *Ibid.*, 243.

of El Cajon Pass and reached the San Bernardino Valley on August 28, 1827. He now traveled to the north by the route he had taken in the previous year and rejoined his men encamped on the Stanislaus.

Traveling up the Great Valley, Smith lost faith in the existence of the Buenaventura River which was supposed to have its headwaters in the Great Salt Lake region. It is believed that when Smith struck the waters of the Sacramento River, he felt that he was on the banks of a large stream, but after his expedition of the preceding year across the Great Basin, he seems to have been skeptical of the fact that this river had its source in the Rocky Mountains. Nevertheless, he named this river the Buenaventura, although he seems to have had in mind a combination of the Domínguez-Escalante and Lewis and Clark geographical conceptions, for he apparently thought that this river (the Sacramento) was a tributary of a northern river, probably the Columbia. Dale states that when Smith was in this area, he sought information concerning the upper courses of the Sacramento River, for knowledge of this region was meager. Smith may have obtained information from Don Luis Arguello's men, who claimed that they were acquainted with the Columbia River; they further declared that in 1821 they went almost to that river and were convinced that the Sacramento River must be a branch of the Columbia. This bit of information when correlated with the Lewis and Clark geography would indicate that this river was the unnamed tributary of the Multnomah which Ashley believed was the Buenaventura; consequently Smith applied this name to the river.

There seems to have been confusion in regard to the Buenaventura even in the mind of Smith, for after he left San Jose he went northeast and east and records on January 1, 1828, that he was "encamped on the Buenaventura River which sometimes is called by the Spaniards the Piscadore."[58] Dale says that this is not the Sacramento River but the Old River Branch of the San Joaquin River. Also on the Wilkes map of 1841 the concept of the Buenaventura as a stream running parallel to the Pacific Coast is adopted, but Wilkes shows the Buenaventura both as the Sacramento and as the Salinas River.

Mr. Smith's party was then 21 strong (though soon after two men deserted) with sufficient supplies to have lasted him back to the Little Lake. He moved on slowly up the Bonadventure, which was generally N.N.W. . . . We then struck off N.W., leaving the

[58] *Ibid.*, 257–58.

Bonadventure running N.E. and coming out of a large range of mountains impassable, until we came to the sea-coast.[59]

By July 13 the party had reached the Umpqua River, and the worst part of the journey to the north appeared to be over. However, on the following morning one of the worst massacres in the history of the fur trade took place, and only Smith, John Turner, and Arthur Black survived. Making their way to Fort Vancouver, the three men were received hospitably by Dr. McLoughlin and other Hudson's Bay Company men, who were instrumental in the return of some of the goods and furs lost by Smith and his party on the banks of the Umpqua.[60] At this post the three Rocky Mountain Fur Company men remained until March, when they left to rejoin Jackson and Sublette at the summer rendezvous.

Disaster followed disaster for the firm of Smith, Jackson and Sublette. During Smith's absence, the partners had maintained about one hundred men in the field, who had been divided into groups and who had trapped the usual streams of the Great Basin and adjacent territory. However, the Hudson's Bay Company's Snake Country Expedition had been doing its work most effectively, and the catches of the Rocky Mountain Fur Company brigades became smaller and smaller as the British trapped out these streams.

One detachment under Samuel Tullock fell in with Ogden's men and was detained four months because the men could not buy the snowshoes needed to push through to their headquarters; because of this delay a part of a season's hunt was lost. Besides the loss of Tullock's men and the massacre on the Umpqua, misfortune befell another group who were crossing from the Columbia to Great Salt Lake. Four of the men had left the main detachment to explore several small streams along the way and were never heard from again.

None of the rendezvous are so little known as that of 1828. It has never been accurately located, but it appears to have taken place somewhere in the valley of the Great Salt Lake. There was no supply

[59] "Brief sketch of accidents, misfortunes, and depredations committed by Indians on the firm of Smith, Jackson, and Sublette, since July 1, 1826 to the present, 1829," as reprinted in *ibid.*, 237.

[60] Only a portion of Smith's goods were recovered. Letter, Dr. McLoughlin to J. S. Smith, Sept. 17, 1828, in which McLoughlin states: "I am extremely sorry to hear from Michel [LaFramboise] that your property is so scattered that there is little probability of recovering it." H.B.C.A., B. 223/6/4.

caravan from St. Louis this year since the company's goods had arrived the previous fall. The year's accumulation of furs was not sent East at this time either, William Sublette setting out with these in the fall of 1828. This seems to have been the last rendezvous which was conducted by the firm of Smith, Jackson and Sublette in the Great Basin, for they held their 1829 meeting on the Popo Agie and the 1830 rendezvous on the Wind River.

The reason for abandoning Bear Lake or Great Salt Lake as the place of rendezvous is not apparent, but it seems that it was a matter of expediency. The firm of Smith, Jackson and Sublette was now operating more and more to the north, in the vicinity of their old fields around the upper Missouri and its tributaries. These areas were much more accessible from the States by way of the Big Horn Basin than by way of Great Salt Lake. The shift to the north seems to have been a direct outgrowth of geographical factors. By this time, 1828, the greater part to the south and west of the Great Salt Lake had been explored and it had been learned that its fur-bearing resources were meager. The streams north and west of Great Salt Lake had been and were being effectively and efficiently trapped out by the men of the Snake Country Expedition. Thus only the area to the north and east of Great Salt Lake remained a land of profitable hunting, and therefore the shrewd partners changed their location to take advantage of the altering conditions.

The firm of Smith, Jackson and Sublette had begun competing in the fur trade in the Great Basin itself. Ashley's successors, however, could not expect to continue to reap large sums of money from this enterprise. The first year alone they cleared $20,000; by 1828 the total value of all the furs brought out to that date either by Ashley himself or by his successors amounted to approximately $220,000, according to Ashley's estimates.[61] There had been no American competition in the Great Basin until 1827, when Joshua Pilcher, representing the interest of the old Missouri Fur Company, entered the field. Soon the American Fur Company began to undermine the monopoly that Smith, Jackson and Sublette was enjoying; it even owned a half-interest in the supply train which Ashley had dispatched to the mountains in the spring of 1827. This caravan, which left St. Louis in March, 1827, is notable because it included, besides the regular goods, a piece of artillery, a four-pounder, mounted on a

[61] Dale, *Jedediah Smith*, 170–71.

primitive carriage. This was drawn over the now familiar route to the Great Salt Lake by way of the North Platte, South Pass, and Green River and was the first wheeled vehicle to be brought into the Great Basin.

By 1830, the Santa Fe trade offered much greater opportunity for wealth than the fur trade. In the latter, competition was constantly increasing, furs were becoming scarcer and more difficult to procure, and, most important, the market price was declining. Therefore, in that year, at the Wind River rendezvous, Smith, Jackson and Sublette sold their business to Thomas Fitzpatrick, Milton Sublette— the brother of William Sublette—James Bridger, Henry Fraeb, and Baptiste Gervais. These men continued operations as the Rocky Mountain Fur Company until 1834, when they were forced to dissolve their partnership, their business being no longer profitable.

After almost six years in the Great Basin, Jedediah Smith left the Great Salt Lake region for the East, and, shortly thereafter, the Southwest. During this comparatively short period, he had explored almost every important geographical feature within the Great Basin and had achieved for himself a niche in history as the greatest pathfinder in the exploration of the land of interior drainage. In 1824 he had led the way through South Pass, and shortly after, with General Ashley, set the trail to the Great Salt Lake. Although the Great Salt Lake was to terminate the expedition for Ashley, it marked only a halfway station for Smith; from this point he marked out a trail the remaining distance to the coast, first by a southern and then by a central route. This was, indeed, a great feat, for, although Lewis and Clark had established a northern crossing of the continent twenty years before, they had the advantage of being able to follow the courses of large rivers for almost the entire distance from St. Louis to the mouth of the Columbia; on the other hand, Ashley and Smith had to cross from one complicated drainage area to another and traverse mountain barriers as well as some of the most barren stretches of desert country that exist in the United States to establish a route to the Pacific Coast.

8

THE GREAT BASIN,
THE CORRIDOR TO CALIFORNIA

IN THE DECADE 1820–30 almost all the streams of any size and importance as well as the other physical features of the Great Basin had been explored by the mountain men. American fur trade activity was centered in the Great Salt Lake area, and through the efforts of these trapping brigades most of the present state of Utah was explored. The Snake Country Expedition of the Hudson's Bay Company was especially vigorous under the firm hand of Peter Skene Ogden, who, between 1825 and 1830, led his men into the northern sections of the Great Basin and discovered many of its topographical features, particularly those in what is now the present state of Nevada. Therefore, by 1830 the British and American fur brigades had explored much of the Great Basin and had found it to be an inhospitable region, especially the western portion, where trappers had difficulty subsisting.

The harsh physical characteristics of the Great Basin, together with the "scorched earth" policy of the Hudson's Bay Company—the systematic trapping out of streams—made the land of interior drainage less inviting to the trapper. In addition to these conditions, more trappers were entering the field, making competition for the gradually diminishing beaver colonies greater and the catches smaller. Trappers were forced to roam over larger areas in search of furs. The Great Basin after 1830 was no longer one of the principal trapping grounds in itself, but merely part of an area which was combed in the quest for pelts. For this reason many trappers left the mountains and entered other fields of endeavor.

The mountain men were especially attracted by events in the Southwest. A new era had opened when Mexico achieved her independence from Spain in 1821 and friendly trade with Americans was invited. Development of the Santa Fe Trail from Missouri with its prairie commerce and further extension of trade into the mountains and even to California became possible.[1] The course of the trail between Santa Fe and Los Angeles became known as the Old Spanish Trail and is of interest since it passed through the southern portion of the Great Basin.

This trail, which had been envisaged in the late eighteenth century to serve as a link to connect Spain's peninsulas of settlement during the Colonial period, reached its height during the 1830's and 1840's. At this time annual caravans brought woolen blankets from New Mexico to be traded in California for horses and mules. Although the Old Spanish Trail was never more than a trail for pack animals, it was entirely practical as a route for such commerce during the spring and fall seasons.

The general course of the Old Spanish Trail on its eastern side was pioneered by Fathers Domínguez and Escalante in 1776. The section between the Green River of the Colorado drainage system and the Sevier River in the Great Basin was established by the Arze-García party in 1813. Exploration along the trail site was extended to the west when Jedediah Smith left the Great Salt Lake region in 1826 and passed southward to the Sevier and Beaver rivers. He then proceeded to the Virgin River and continued down it to the Colorado. Here, near present Needles, California, Smith intersected the trail used by the Mojave Indians on their bartering expeditions to the Pacific Coast; this was also the trail followed in 1776. Thus it was that three of the most important expeditions in the history of Great Basin exploration traced the general course of the Old Spanish Trail and prepared a lane for barter and commerce through the barren stretches of the land of interior drainage.

Travel began over the general course of the Old Spanish Trail in August, 1829, when a trapping party under Ewing Young set out from Taos to the head of the Salt River and then trapped down it to its junction with the Río Verde. Upon reaching the Colorado, the

[1] The great story of the Santa Fe trade is Josiah Gregg's *Commerce of the Prairies: The Journal of a Santa Fe Trader, during Eight Expeditions across the Great Western Prairies, and a Residence of Nearly Nine Years in Northern Mexico* . . . .

group continued to California over the Garcés trail.[2] Transportation and exchange of goods between New Mexico and California were begun by Antonio Armijo in 1829–30.[3] The route which Armijo followed on his journey to California varied slightly from the Old Spanish Trail, for he struck the Amargosa River of the Great Basin as well as the Mojave when crossing the desert stretches between the Colorado River and the Sierra Nevada Mountains.

However, the first party to journey the entire distance over substantially the route of the Old Spanish Trail was led by William Wolfskill[4] and George C. Yount[5] in the winter of 1830–31. Although there was no diarist for the expedition, it is possible to piece together a satisfactory narrative from accounts of members of the party and from Wolfskill's overland ledger.[6] This party, consisting of twenty men, went from Abiquiu to the San Juan and Dolores rivers along the Escalante route. They then crossed the Green River and the Wasatch Mountains to reach the Sevier River and the Great Basin near Salina Canyon. In ascending the Sevier, they appear to have gone up Clear Creek Fork, a variation of the Smith route. It is probable that they came out of the mountains by the canyon that debouches near Little Salt Lake.

The Old Spanish Trail was the first charted track across the Great Basin. Although fur trappers had followed Indian trails along the streams of this region and had browsed through the country in their

[2] J. J. Hill, "Ewing Young in the Fur Trade of the Far Southwest, 1822–1834," *Oregon Historical Quarterly*, Vol. XXIV (Jan., 1923); J. J. Hill, *The History of Warner's Ranch and Its Environs*.

[3] The Armijo diary of the outbound trip was published in the *Registro Oficial del Gobierno* of June 19, 1830. This diary has been reproduced in LeRoy R. Hafen and Ann W. Hafen, *The Old Spanish Trail*, 158–65. For an annotated account, see LeRoy R. Hafen, "Armijo's Journal," *Huntington Library Quarterly*, Vol. XI (Jan., 1947), 87–101, and *The Colorado Magazine*, Vol. XXVII (April, 1950).

[4] See Henry Dwight Barrows, "William Wolfskill, the Pioneer," *Southern California Historical Quarterly*, Vol. V (Dec., 1903), 287–94.

[5] See "The Chronicles of George C. Yount" (ed. by Charles Camp), *California Historical Quarterly*, Vol. II (April, 1923), 3–68. Also see a typescript of the Yount narrative written by Rev. Orange Clark which is now in the Bancroft Library. It has some missing pages, but contains material not seen by Charles Camp when he edited the above.

[6] Wolfskill's ledger, a photostat of which is now in the Huntington Library, was brought to public attention by Frederick Webb Hodge in "Pioneers and Prices," *Southern California Historical Quarterly*, Vol. XXVIII (Sept., 1946). For accounts of the journey, see Bancroft, *History of California*, III, 388.

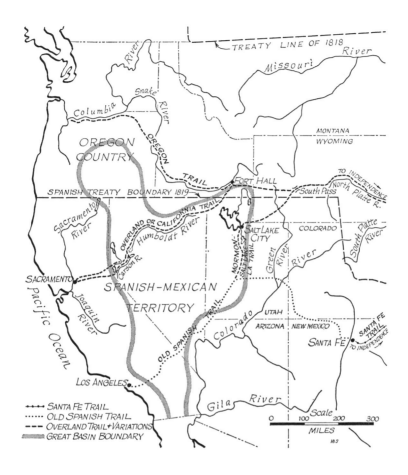

The Great Basin, Corridor to California

search for beaver, their routes had been circuitous. Jedediah Smith had crossed from California to the Great Salt Lake area in 1827 in a direct course, but the region which he traversed was too arid to provide water and forage for any number of men and animals. Therefore, the journeys of Ewing Young, Armijo, and, more important, the Wolfskill-Yount party, mark the beginning of travel along an established trail from New Mexico to California. Because the Pacific Slope was acquiring greater economic significance, travel westward was given impetus. As a result, the Great Basin, embracing the arid stretches between the Wasatch and the Sierra Nevada Mountains, became a corridor to California.

But the southern section of the Great Basin, through which the Old Spanish Trail passed, was not the only corridor to California; within the next two decades, 1830–50, thousands of emigrants were to pass through the northern part of the Basin on their way to California. Here the famous Overland Trail was established. It was marked by the graves of the Great Basin's first permanent settlers, those who perished on their journey to the Pacific.

An important section of the Overland Trail was explored and later established by Joseph R. Walker of the Walker-Bonneville party.[7] The expedition was of a curious nature since it was led by a Frenchman, Captain Bonneville, who was an officer in the United States Army. Benjamin Louis Eulalie de Bonneville was graduated from West Point in 1819 and was assigned to duty on the western frontier. There he became deluded with the idea that he could make a fortune in the fur trade, and accordingly began to look for an opportunity to gratify this ambition. The result was his famous expedition of 1832–35.

Bonneville secured a leave of absence from the army from August, 1831, to October, 1833, with permission to spend it in the unexplored regions of the Far West. The letter from the War Department which granted Bonneville his leave stated that it was

> . . . for the purpose of carrying into execution your design of exploring the country to the Rocky Mountains and beyond, with a view of ascertaining the nature and character of the several tribes inhabiting those regions; the trade which might be profitably car-

7 See Douglas Sloane Watson, *West Wind: The Life Story of Joseph Reddeford Walker, Knight of the Golden Horsehoe.*

ried on with them; the quality of the soil, the productions, the minerals, the natural history, the climate, the geography and topography, as well as the geology of the various parts of the country.[8]

It was understood that Captain Bonneville's expedition was to be of no expense to the United States government.

This leave provided the opportunity for which Bonneville had been waiting, and his romantic Gallic mind immediately developed bold schemes:

> One of these was to carry his expeditions into some of the unknown tracts of the Far West, beyond what is generally termed the buffalo range. . . . Another favorite project was to establish a trading post on the lower part of the Columbia River, near the Multnomah Valley, and to endeavor to retrieve for his country some of the lost trade of Astoria. The first of the above mentioned views was, at present, uppermost in his mind—the exploring of unknown regions. Among the grand features of the wilderness about which he was roaming, one had made a vivid impression on his mind, and been clothed by his imagination with vague and ideal charms. This is a great lake of salt water, laving the feet of the mountains, but extending far to the west-southwest, into one of those vast and elevated plateaus of land, which range high above the level of the Pacific.[9]

Bonneville made arrangements with Alfred Seton of New York, one of the old Astorians, and some of his associates to provide the funds for a mountain expedition, whose operations in the field Bonneville was to conduct. In order to carry out this program, the Captain organized a party of 110 men with two principal assistants, Mr. J. R. Walker and Mr. M. S. Cerré. Wagons were to be used on this expedition, contrary to the usual practice of the mountain traders. There were to be twenty of these vehicles drawn by oxen and mules. The whole expedition was to be conducted on a strictly military basis, and from all outward appearances the enterprise would make a great showing in the mountain trade.

The final organization of the expedition took place ten miles from Independence, Missouri, at Fort Osage. The group finally set out

[8] Chittenden, *The American Fur Trade*, I, 397.
[9] Washington Irving, *The Adventures of Captain Bonneville*, 220–21.

from this point on May 1, 1832. The route was the usual one up the valleys of the Platte and Sweetwater rivers and then on to Pierre's Hole rendezvous. From this point the party went south to the Green River, where Captain Bonneville decided to erect a trading post with the evident purpose of making a permanent settlement. The site Bonneville selected was on the west bank of the river, four miles above the mouth of Horse Creek. This fort became known in western history as Fort Bonneville or Bonneville's Old Fort, but the trappers called it "Fort Nonsense" or "Bonneville's Folly." This was a poor place for a permanent post because the altitude was high and the winters severe. Finally Bonneville was convinced that he had erred in selecting this location, and the group moved to the Salmon River area to establish new winter quarters.

In making arrangements for the next year, Bonneville's principal move was to be, according to his own representation as recorded by Irving, a thorough exploration of the Great Salt Lake and the country around it:

> As you ascend the mountains about its shores, you behold this immense body of water spreading itself before you, and stretching further and further, in one wide and far-reaching expanse, until the eye, wearied with continued and strained attention, rests in the blue dimness of distance, upon lofty ranges of mountains, confidently asserted to rise from the bosom of the waters. . . . To have this lake properly explored, and all its secrets revealed, was the grand scheme of the Captain for the present year; and while it was one in which his imagination evidently took a leading part, he believed it would be attended with great profit, from numerous beaver streams with which the lake must be fringed.[10]

Little did Bonneville realize that this had been one of the favorite trapping grounds for the mountain men for almost a decade and consequently had been pretty well trapped out.

George Nidever, who accompanied the expedition and who was fully aware of Bonneville's purpose to a great extent, says nothing of an intended survey of the lake. This idea probably arose in Bonneville's mind when reciting his adventures to Irving. The only comment that Nidever makes is: "Upon breaking up of the rendezvous

10 *Ibid.*, 221–23.

we started southward, intending to trap a short time on the Marys River."[11]

Nevertheless, as Bonneville related his adventures, he proposed exploration of the Great Salt Lake: "This momentous undertaking he confided to his lieutenant, Mr. Walker, in whose experience and ability he had great confidence."[12] Walker was the proper man to select for that sort of work for he had had a long and varied experience in the Santa Fe and Missouri trade. Also, he was well acquainted with the Indians and was particularly fond of new adventures. In later years, Walker became a conspicuous character in California history.

The Bonneville party reached the Great Salt Lake by way of the Bear River. In the first part of November, it is said that when

> . . . crossing an elevated ridge, Captain Bonneville now came upon Bear River, which, from its source to its entrance into Great Salt Lake, describes the figure of a horseshoe. Proceeding down this river, the party encamped, on the 6th of November, at the outlet of a lake about thirty miles long, and from two to three miles in width, completely imbedded in low ranges of mountains, and connected with Bear River by an impassable swamp. It is called the Little Lake, to distinguish it from the great one of salt water.[13]

Bonneville now decided to go to the Snake River in order to meet a band of free trappers that he had detached in this region the previous July. He then proceeded northward to the Hudson's Bay Company post of Fort Nez Percés, following the usual route of the Snake Country Expedition along the Powder and Grande Ronde rivers and over the Blue Mountains.

While Bonneville was going north, Joseph Walker and his men were on the trail westward. Reports vary concerning the number of men engaged in the expedition. Irving states that "the brigade of forty men set out from the Green River Valley, to explore the Great Salt Lake,"[14] while George Nidever places the number at thirty-six:

11 George Nidever, *The Life and Adventures of George Nidever* (ed. by William Henry Ellison), 32.
12 Irving, *Captain Bonneville*, 224.
13 *Ibid.*, 284.
14 *Ibid.*, 385.

"In the spring, there were a large number of trappers gathered at the rendezvous in Green River valley and among them Capt. Walker and Company, bound for California. We joined him, making a party in all of 36."[15] Zenas Leonard, however, who was the clerk for the expedition and thus should have been in a position to know the actual number of men in the party, places the number at nearly sixty.[16] Perhaps Walker's men numbered between thirty-six and forty and a few others joined the group en route.

The party went directly to the valley of the Great Salt Lake, where they stopped to lay in their final supply of buffalo meat. They killed their last buffalo on August 4, and three days later proceeded to leave that area. They left the western extremity of the lake and took a westerly course into the barren plains. After crossing the Salt Lake Desert, they finally reached the East Humboldt Range in what is now eastern Nevada. The route that they followed west from Great Salt Lake no doubt closely paralleled that used by Peter Skene Ogden in 1828 and 1829 and by John Work in 1831 and is roughly the course utilized today by the Southern Pacific Railroad.

Irving relates that "After a time they came upon a small stream leading directly towards these mountains. Having quenched their burning thirst, and refreshed themselves and their weary horses for a time, they kept along this stream, which gradually increased in size, being fed by numerous brooks. . . . The stream on which they had thus fallen is called by some, Mary River, but is more generally known as Ogden's River."[17] This passage, of course, records the striking of the Humboldt River, which they called the "Barren River" because of the comparatively barren country through which it flows.

The party traveled down the Humboldt until they reached the Humboldt Sink on October 4. Here an event occurred which cast a lasting odium upon the expedition. Zenas Leonard tells about it:

. . . we continued traveling down the river, now and then catching a few beaver. But as we continued extending our acquaintance with the natives, they began to practice their national failing of

15 Nidever, *Life and Adventures,* 32.
16 Leonard, *Narrative,* 102.
17 Irving, *Captain Bonneville,* 387.

stealing. So eager were they to possess themselves of our traps that we were forced to quit trapping in this vicinity and make for some other quarter. The great annoyance we sustained in this greatly displeased some of our men, and they were for taking vengeance before we left the county—but this was not the disposition of Captain Walker. These discontents being out hunting one day, fell in with a few Indians, two or three whom they killed and then returned to camp, not daring to let the captain know it. The next day while out hunting they repeated the same violation, but this time were not so successful, for the Captain found it out, and immediately took measures for its effectual suppression.[18]

When the party arrived at the Humboldt Sink, they noticed a great number of Paiute Indians and feared trouble. Leonard estimated that there were eight or nine hundred Indians in all, although Nidever gave a somewhat more conservative figure.[19] After the whites gave a demonstration of their guns, the Indians disappeared and the Walker party had a peaceful night's sleep.

Early the next morning Walker and his men resumed their journey along the banks of the Humboldt Sink without seeing any Indians. About sunrise, however, large parties of Indians began appearing and asking the Caucasians to smoke with them. Walker believed that the Indians were attempting to delay his party so that their whole force would have time to reach the place. Finally he gave the order to his men to fight. Thirty-two members of his party dismounted and closed in on the Indians. The result of the battle was the death of a number of red men and the overwhelming of the remainder of the group. Although Leonard placed the losses of the Indians at thirty-nine killed,[20] the number varies according to the account; Nidever put it at thirty-three,[21] whereas Irving said twenty-five.[22] The number was probably somewhere between Irving's and Nidever's estimates. Leonard's figures, whether they refer to the number composing the expedition, the number of Indians involved in battle, or the number of casualties, seem a little extravagant.

In justification of the action taken, Leonard said:

[18] Leonard, *Narrative*, 110–11.
[19] Nidever, *Life and Adventures*, 32.
[20] Leonard, *Narrative*, 116.
[21] Nidever, *Life and Adventures*, 34.
[22] Irving, *Captain Bonneville*, 388–89.

The severity with which we dealt with these Indians may be revolting to the heart of the philanthropist; but the circumstances of the case altogether atone for the cruelty. It must be borne in mind that we were far removed from any succor in case we were surrounded, and that the country we were in was swarming with hostile savages, sufficiently numerous to devour us. Our object was to strike a decisive blow. This we did, even to a greater extent than we had intended.[23]

Whether the Walker incident could have been avoided or not is a matter of speculation. The important factor is that it did occur, and therefore makes the Walker-Bonneville party significant in the history of the Great Basin. This was the first time that a battle between two such large groups, Indian and white, had taken place in the area of interior drainage, and not until Nevada territorial days would there be a similar occurrence. To commemorate this so-called fight in self-defense, the name "Battle Lakes" was applied to the shallow ponds or sink near which Walker and his men fought the Indians.

The party now crossed to the Carson Sink. It is believed that they followed a small flow of water that proceeds from the Humboldt Sink to the Carson Sink. This diminutive stream bed may still be seen and contains water in the early spring. However, it is likely there may have been water in this wash when the Walker party passed along its banks since the years 1833–34 are reputed to have been wetter than the preceding or succeeding ones.

Walker and his men followed this stream bed to the Carson Sink and then struck westward over the Sierras in order to reach the San Joaquin Valley. In the fall of 1833 the party ascended the eastern flank of the Sierra, probably by one of the southern tributaries of the East Walker River. According to Leonard, on the second day after leaving their encampment in the valley, they reached a small lake or pond and on the following day passed a number of small lakes. The former has been identified by some historians as Grass Lake beyond Luther's Pass and the small lakes as Twin Lakes near Carson Pass; but it seems more likely that the Walker party crossed the Sierra a number of miles to the south of this area.

The party endured great suffering because provisions became almost exhausted and the terrain was exceedingly difficult. One ac-

[23] Leonard, *Narrative,* 117.

count mentions that the party had to let their horses down by ropes over a long slope of loose rocks. Their experience after crossing the summit of the Sierras indicates that they were lost for several days in a maze of mountains and lakes. This description fits the character of the region near what has become known as Virginia Canyon. From here the party no doubt crossed the Tuolumne River, perhaps near Conness Creek. They passed Lake Tenaya and probably followed a course similar to that utilized today by the Tioga road. The party now found its way down from the mountains into the lower canyon of the Tuolumne River and thence passed into the San Joaquin Valley.[24]

By October 30 the party had reached the foot of the main range. In the course of the next few days, they passed certain natural features which aid in an identification of their route when one is familiar with the region. Shortly after leaving the base of the mountains, they passed "some trees of the Redwood species, incredibly large—some of which would measure from 16 to 18 fathom round the trunk at the height of a man's head from the ground."[25] Francis P. Farquhar states, "To my mind, there is not the slightest doubt that the reference is to the Tuolumne or Merced Grove and that this is the first published mention of the Big Trees of California."[26]

It seems most likely that the Walker party reached the rim of what is now known as Yosemite Valley in Yosemite National Park, but did not penetrate to the valley floor. Dr. L. H. Bunnell, in his book *Discovery of Yosemite*, reported that on one occasion he told Captain Walker that the Indian Ten-ie-yea had said that "a small party of white men once crossed the mountains on the north side [who] were so guided as to not to see the valley proper." According to Bunnell, the Captain smiled and replied, "That was my party, but I was not deceived, for the lay of the land showed there was a valley below, but we had become nearly barefoot, our animals poor and ourselves on the verge of starvation, so we followed down the ridge to Ball Creek where, killing a deer, we went into camp."[27]

The group arrived in California in November and spent the winter there. The returning party consisted of 52 men, 365 horses,

24 Fletcher, *Early Nevada*.
25 Leonard, *Narrative*, 136.
26 *Exploration of the Sierra Nevada*, 6–7.
27 Page 39.

47 beef cattle, and 30 dogs, together with an outfit of provisions. Preparations for the return trip were finally made, and the group set out on February 14, 1834. The Walker party traveled through the San Joaquin Valley at a leisurely pace to a point where they hired two guides. They then followed up the Kern River and negotiated the mountain chain by what thereafter became known as Walker's Pass and entered the Great Basin for a second time, south of Owens Lake. They proceeded up Owens Valley and arrived at some hot springs which are easily identified as the present Benton Hot Springs. The course which they followed is approximately the course that was later taken by the now extinct railroad that connected Benton, California, and Sodaville, Nevada.

After journeying to a point somewhere in the vicinity of present Sodaville, Captain Walker thought he recognized a landmark. He decided to take the group across the barren stretches to the north and east of his present location in order to reach the Humboldt River by the shortest possible route. This decision almost brought ruin to the expedition, since once away from the mountains there was no water, wood, or grass, and the members of the group were about to perish when their horses led them to a stream. This stream can be no other than the Walker River. Evidently the party had left the mountains not far north of Sodaville and had traveled into the desert east of Walker Lake. In their search for water, the group had turned back and reached the river north of the lake. According to Leonard, it required several days of constant traveling to reach their old trail. This seems to indicate that they had gone up the river almost as far as Antelope Valley before turning north and intersecting their outgoing trace near Carson Sink.

When the group reached the Humboldt Sink (their "Battle Lakes"), they apparently met the same band of Indians with whom they had dealt so severely. Leonard wrote:

> All along our route from the mountains we had seen a great number of Indians, but now when we reached the vicinity of the place where we had had the skirmish with the savages when going to the coast, they appeared to rise in double the numbers that they did at that time, and as we were then compelled to fight them, we saw by their movements now that this would be the only course to pursue. We had used every endeavor that we could think of to

reconcile and make them friendly but all to no purpose. We had given them one present after another, made them all the strongest manifestations of a desire for peace on our part, by promising to do battle against their enemies, if required, and we found that our own safety and comfort demanded that they should be severely chastised for provoking us to such a measure. Now that we were a good deal aggravated some of our men said hard things about what they would do if we should again come in contact with these provoking Indians; and our captain was afraid that, if once engaged, the passions of his men would become so wild that he could not call them off while there was an Indian left to be slaughtered. Being thus compelled to fight, as we thought, in a good cause and in self-defense, we drew up in battle array and fell on the Indians in the wildest and most ferocious manner as we could, which struck dismay throughout the whole crowd, killing fourteen besides wounding a great many more as we rode right over them. Our men were soon called off, only three of whom were slightly wounded. This decisive stroke appeared to give the Indians every satisfaction they desired, as we were afterwards permitted to pass through their country wihtout molestation.[28]

Thus again the Indians met the wrath of the Caucasians, and the Humboldt Sink earned its name of Battle Lakes for the second time.

The party retraced their route until they reached a point at the north end of the Ruby Mountains. They now turned north, going up Bishop Creek to Thousand Springs Valley and thence to Raft River, part of the Snake River drainage system. The supposition regarding this course of the Walker-Bonneville party is strengthened by the fact that ten years later Walker guided the Chiles party from Fort Hall down this route, retracing his present east-bound course and establishing a route from the Snake River to the Humboldt which was later extensively followed by emigrants making their way to the Pacific Coast. From the Snake River, Walker and his party made their way to the appointed rendezvous on the Bear River, where they arrived about the first of June.

The Walker expedition was a great disappointment to Bonneville, who attributed its failure to disobedience of orders. In this he not only was unjust, but also misrepresented the whole affair. The evidence is overwhelming that the expedition left the Green River

28 Leonard, *Narrative*, 214–15.

rendezvous with the full and primary expectation of going to the Pacific Coast, as is clearly shown by Mr. Leonard's statement: "I was anxious to go to the Pacific and for that purpose hired with Mr. Walker as clerk, for a certain sum per year."[29] Bonneville's one-sided report did not give Walker the credit that was due him for a really remarkable achievement in exploration.

As far as commercial results were concerned, the enterprise was a complete failure. Bonneville was not trained in business, particularly the kind of business which was transacted in the mountains. He was unduly afraid of Indians, was unwilling to take risks, and held himself above using some of the methods of those he considered irresponsible traders. The final outcome was a loss to his backers of many thousands of dollars. This is not surprising in the light of what was happening in the fur trade in general.

With competition becoming greater and greater and the beaver colonies diminishing, even those who had been engaged in trapping for many years felt that this business was becoming unprofitable. By 1834 the owners of the Rocky Mountain Fur Company felt the lines of competition tightening about them and could see the American Fur Company gaining ground. In this year, Fraeb and Gervais retired. With the departure of these two, a new partnership was formed under Fitzpatrick, Sublette, and Bridger, but the new company, resigned to the inevitable, signed away their independence from the start. An agreement was made with Lucien Fontenelle, who was in charge of the American Fur Company's forces in the field, for the disposition of the furs of the three partners, and they were thus reduced to the status of agents. Late in that year or early in the spring of the following year, the partners bought Fort William from Sublette and Campbell, and here Fitzpatrick seems to have stationed himself while Bridger ranged the mountains with a group of trappers in the search for beaver.[30]

The scientific aspects of Captain Bonneville's expedition were even more of a failure than the commercial aspects. Chittenden states that the Captain never reported to the War Department as he had promised, probably because he had nothing of value to report, but a letter from Captain Bonneville to Lewis Cass, secretary of war, is

29 *Ibid.,* 105.
30 LeRoy R. Hafen and W. J. Ghent, *Broken Hand: The Life Story of Thomas Fitzpatrick,* 109–14.

proof to the contrary. In this letter Bonneville apologizes for his long absence and gives a good description of the western areas.[31] The Captain's notes upon the nature of the country are limited, however, and of no great value. His astronomical observations for latitude and longitude were little better than wild guesses.

However, Bonneville must be credited with two maps of the western country. One of these is of the region about the sources of the Missouri, Yellowstone, Snake, Green, Wind, and Sweetwater rivers, including the region of the Great Salt Lake. The other, on half the scale, included the country westward from the region embraced in the first map to the Pacific Ocean. These maps have won for Captain Bonneville a degree of credit for promoting discovery to which he is in no sense entitled, for nearly all of the valuable features appeared on Gallatin's map and were further brought to public notice by Gallatin's memoir which accompanied the map. Although this is true, there are three important additions to geographical knowledge which must be credited to the Bonneville maps: the location of the Humboldt River and the Humboldt Lake or Sink, the location of the San Joaquin River, and the approximately correct topography of the country around the sources of the Big Horn and Green rivers. Even though the Bonneville maps are not of great importance from a general geographical standpoint, they are significant in the history of the Great Basin, for they showed that the Humboldt River was the best course to follow in a journey across the Basin.

More important to the history of the Great Basin, Captain Bonneville was responsible for the Walker expedition, which deserves great prominence in this connection. Captain Walker and his men crossed the Great Basin in its exact center twice and established, in part, the Overland Trail which within a decade was to be used by many parties of homeseekers. Although Jedediah Smith had crossed the Great Basin previously and Peter Skene Ogden and John Work had explored the Humboldt River quite thoroughly, no white man up to that time had recorded movement southward to the Carson Sink and Walker River or, of even greater significance, had discovered a mountain pass over the Sierra Nevada which is used even today. In later years Captain Walker's chief concern was to be known as the

---

[31] Captain Bonneville to Lewis Cass, secretary of war, September 30, 1835, as quoted in the *Washington Historical Quarterly*, Vol. XVIII (July, 1927), 221–25.

discoverer of Yosemite Valley, but his greatest honor lies in the fact that he was one of the important pathfinders of the West.

The feats of the Walker-Bonneville party, so ably presented by Washington Irving, as well as the fame of the fur trade of the Northwest and the romance of the explorations of the Astorians and the members of the Hudson's Bay company, attracted the attention of many people living east of the Rocky Mountains. Tales of these adventures suggested possibilities of developing this virgin country. One person who was particularly fascinated by these thrilling stories was a youth named John Bidwell. Because of his interest in and enthusiasm for what lay beyond the Rockies, he was to lead the first emigrant train through the Great Basin over a large section of the trail that Joseph Walker had established.

Bidwell loved the West to such a degree that he accepted a teaching post close to the frontier in what was then Kansas Territory. While he was teaching there, five miles from the little town of Weston, he met the old frontiersman, Antoine Robidoux,[32] who regaled the young man with tales of the Pacific Coast which greatly stimulated Bidwell's already growing enthusiasm. He described the meeting in the following manner:

> In November or December of 1840, while still teaching school in Platte County, I came across a Frenchman named Roubideaux who said he had been to California. He had been a trader in New Mexico, and had followed the road traveled by traders from the frontier of Missouri to Santa Fe. . . . His description of California was in the superlative degree favorable, so much that I resolved if possible to see that wonderful land, and with others helped to get up a meeting at Weston and invited him to make a statement before it in regard to this wonderful country. Roubideaux described it as one of perennial spring and boundless fertility, and laid stress on the countless thousands of wild horses and cattle. . . . He said that the Spanish authorities were most friendly, and that the people were the most hospitable on the globe; that you could travel all over California and it would cost nothing for horses or food. Even the Indians were friendly. His description of the country made it seem like a Paradise.[33]

[32] Robidoux or, sometimes, Roubideaux. See William Swilling Wallace, *Antoine Robidoux, 1794–1860; A Biography of a Western Venturer.*
[33] Rockwell Hunt, *John Bidwell,* 22–23.

The group that met in Weston was almost overwhelmed by Robidoux's glowing account and began to formulate plans to travel to the Pacific Coast. They created an organization called the Western Emigration Society to carry out their plans. It was the purpose of this organization to invite people to go overland to California and to collect data relating to the routes and methods of travel. However, it seems obvious that the society failed miserably in gaining geographical information concerning the western region, for Bidwell later stated, "Our ignorance of the route was complete. We knew that California lay west, and that was the extent of our knowledge."[34]

The movement that started with so much vigor and warmth in the autumn was brought to a sudden collapse with the winter winds. By spring, of the five hundred persons who had originally signed the pledge to make the journey, only sixty-nine remained, and these met at the appointed place of rendezvous, Sapling Grove. Here is a list of those who made the trip to the West:

John B. Bartleson	W. P. Overton
Talbot H. Green	George Simpson
John Bidwell	V. W. Dawson
George Hinshaw	Andrew Kelsey
Charles Hopper	Benjamin Kelsey and family
James P. Springer	Edward Rogers
A. G. Patton	D. F. Hill
Nicholas Dawson	A. Cook
Josiah Belden	N. Dawson
J. M. Jones	Jones
J. W. Chandler	Carroll
John DeSwart	James Ross
Henry S. Brolaske	Henry Huber
Michael C. Nye	John Roland
Elias Barnet	William Belty
Major Walton	Thomas Jones
A. Walton	Augustus Fifer
Green McMahon	James John
John McDowel	Robert Richman
Robert H. Thomas	H. Peyton
Elisha Stone	Joseph B. Chiles

[34] John Bidwell, "The First Emigrant Train to California," *Century Magazine*, Vol. XLI (Nov., 1890), 3.

Isaiah Kelsey and family	Charles Weaver
William Towler	James Shotwell
Richard Williams and family	Samuel Kelsey and family[35]
E. W. Flugge	

The group chose Bartleson as captain of the company, not because he was the best man for the position, but because he would not go if he were not put in charge of the expedition. They felt obliged to select him because he had seven or eight men with him, and they did not want their party to be diminished any further. John Bidwell was chosen secretary and historian for the journey.

Probably no group ever started out so ill-informed as this Bidwell-Bartleson party; however, they were most fortunate in that they met another group shortly after the beginning of the trip. This second group was led by the able Thomas Fitzpatrick, who was in this case acting as guide to Father De Smet, who was returning to the Northwest to establish a permanent mission. From Sapling Grove to the Bear River in the Great Basin the two parties kept together, but when they arrived at Soda Springs on the northernmost bend of the Bear River, the groups separated. Bidwell reported:

> Thirty-two of our party, becoming discouraged, now decided not to venture without path or guide into unknown and trackless regions toward California, but concluded to go with the missionary party to Fort Hall and thence find their way down the Snake and Columbia Rivers into Oregon. The rest of us—also thirty-two in number, including Benjamin Kelsey, his wife, and little daughter —remained firm, refusing to be diverted from our original purpose of going direct to California.[36]

On Wednesday, August 11, 1841, this entry is found in Bidwell's diary: "The two companies, after bidding each other a parting fare-well, started and were soon out of sight, several of our company however went to Fort Hall to procure provision and to hire if possible, a pilot to conduct us to the Gap in the California Mountains, or at least, to the head of Mary's river,[37] we were therefore to move on slowly 'till their return."[38]

[35] John Bidwell, *A Journey to California*, 1.
[36] H. H. Bancroft, *History of Utah*, 97–98.
[37] Humboldt River.
[38] Bidwell, *Journey to California*, 14.

Meanwhile, the group turned south at what is now Alexander, Idaho, and followed the Bear River for several days to a point near the site of present Corinne, Utah. From this point their course was northwest until they turned west around the north end of the Great Salt Lake.[39]

Bidwell related:

In about ten days our four men returned from Fort Hall, during which time we had advanced something over one hundred miles toward Salt Lake. They brought the information that we must strike out west of Salt Lake—as it was even then called by the trappers—being careful not to go too far south, lest we should get into a wasteless country without grass. They also said we must be careful not to go too far north, lest we should get into a broken country and steep canyons, and wander about, as trapping parties have been known to do, and become bewildered and perish.[40]

On Monday, August 23, Bidwell made an entry in his diary which seems to indicate that the group must have been at the summit of the pass through the Promontory Range near the modern site of Promontory, Utah, for Bidwell says: "At evening we arrived in full view of Salt Lake."[41]

Slowly the group moved on. On August 27, Bidwell reported:

Daylight discovered us a spot of green grass on the declivity of the mountain toward which we were advancing. Five miles took us to this place, where we found, to our great joy, an excellent spring of water and an abundance of grass. Here we determined to continue, 'til the route was explored to the head of Mary's river, and run no more risks of perishing for want of water in this desolate region.[42]

The location described by John Bidwell was undoubtedly Pilot Spring, south of the present site of Snowville, and about thirty miles to the north of what is known as Salt Wells.

On August 29, Captain Bartleson and C. Hopper started out to explore the route to the head of the Humboldt River. On September

39 Charles Kelley, *Salt Desert Trails*, 30.
40 Fletcher, *Early Nevada*, 98.
41 *Journey to California*, 17.
42 *Ibid.*, 18.

9, the two men returned bringing news that they had found the river, which was distant about five days' travel. This information had a rejuvenating effect upon the tired, foot-sore group, who immediately resumed their journey. At this point many of the members of the party were forced to abandon their wagons because the animals could no longer pull them. Therefore, they now made pack saddles and placed all their possessions on their horses.

After leaving Pilot Peak, the party turned to the southwest and followed roughly the route which has since been utilized by the Southern Pacific Railroad through Silver Zone Pass and into Steptoe Valley. In this valley, they found water on what was later known as the Johnson Ranch. After traveling west through this valley, they crossed the Pequop Range and soon came to the South Fork of the Humboldt River. They followed this tributary down to the point where it enters the main stream, a short distance to the west of present Elko, Nevada.

On October 7, while the group was encamped on the banks of the Humboldt River, probably some miles to the west of present Winnemucca, Nevada, Captain Bartleson decided that if the party was to cross the mountains before winter set in, they must hurry. He was determined to cross the Sierras soon, and, therefore, with eight of the company, he left the main party to depend upon their own resources and to follow as best they could. Bartleson's men killed an ox, and taking double their share of the meat, started off. Those in Bidwell's party who were in charge of the cattle were unable to follow rapidly, and much bad feeling ensued. Benjamin Kelsey now came to the front to lead the emigrants to California.

Kelsey's group followed the Bartleson trail for two or three days, but after they had crossed over to the south side of the Humboldt River, the tracks were obliterated. The group proceeded down the Humboldt and crossed from the western reaches of the stream to the drainage system of the Carson River, for Bidwell stated in his journal:

> As soon as we reached what we supposed to be the furthest sink of the Humboldt but which I am now inclined to think must have been what Fremont afterwards called Carson Lake, we endeavored to make our course more westerly; for we knew that the Pacific Ocean lay to the west. . . . The first stream crossed was that now known as Walker's River, so-called by Fremont in 1844, I think.

This river we ascended to the foot of the high mountains whence it came. Here we deemed it best to give our animals a rest, for men and animals were much in need of it. In the meantime men were sent to scale the mountains to the west, to discover if possible a pass. They were gone a day and a night, and reported that the mountains were barely passable. While thus engaged, the party who had deserted nine days before, came up, weary and halting, from the east. They had gone south too far, probably as far as Walker Lake, and now returned crest-fallen and weak with dysentery brought on by pine nuts and fresh fish given them by the natives.[43]

The Bidwell camp on the Walker River where the Bartleson party rejoined them was probably near present Coleville, California, which is located on the modern highway, U.S. 395. The Indians pointed out the place to Frémont in January of 1845, telling him that a party had passed that way a few years previously, utilizing a pass that was open only in the summer. Undoubtedly the pass to which the Indians referred is that which is now known as Sonora Pass.

On October 17 the Bidwell group set out from their camp on the Walker River. After several days of struggle, they finally passed over the divide and down to the tributaries of the Stanislaus River. They proceeded down the Stanislaus until they reached the valley near present Sonora, California, the county seat of Tuolumne County. From this point the party traveled northwestward before reaching, several days later, the ranch of Dr. John Marsh at the foot of Mount Diablo.

The Bidwell-Bartleson party is of significance to the history of the Great Basin because it was the first group of emigrants who saw the Great Salt Lake and the Humboldt River as well as other prominent physiographic feature of the land of interior drainage. It is also important because the members of this party were the first to bring covered wagons into the present states of Utah and Nevada, and thus traversed a large part of the Great Basin by means of this wheeled vehicle. Benjamin Kelsey's wife and daughter accompanied the group and so were the first white women to enter the Great Basin. Of even greater import is the fact that the journey of this party revealed that the crossing of western America, even of some of the

43 "Bidwell's California, 1841–8," MS, Bancroft Library, 32–33.

desolate stretches of the Great Basin, could be accomplished by emigrants. Thus they set the stage for the great westward movement which was soon to follow.

While the Bidwell-Bartleson party was making its trek to the Pacific Coast through the northern part of the Great Basin, another group was proceeding through the southern portion of this region with virtually the same destination, California. This was the Workman-Rowland party, which had set out from Santa Fe in early September; however, their motive for making the journey was entirely different from that of the Bidwell-Bartleson party.

Both William Workman and John Rowland, the leaders of this 1841 emigrant party, were well-established men in Santa Fe, but the times in that city were unstable. Rumors had reached New Mexico that Texas planned to make her claim to the Río Grande as a boundary and thus intended to extend her authority over Santa Fe and the rest of New Mexico which lay east of the river. During the summer and fall of 1841, reports were numerous regarding the Texas invaders, and many persons were suspected of being in sympathy or in league with them.

It has never been established to what extent, if any, William Workman and John Rowland were sympathetic towards Texas or involved in revolutionary schemes, but they were under suspicion. They therefore deemed it necessary to leave New Mexico. These two men, who were both acquainted with California through the reports of traders, formed an emigrant party which was composed of twenty-five men. Most were Americans who had resided in New Mexico for some years, a few were new arrivals over the Santa Fe Trail, and several were natives of New Mexico of Spanish or Indian blood.

Although the Workman-Rowland party is worthy of mention since it was the first emigrant party to reach California by way of the Old Spanish Trail, it does not compare in significance with the Bidwell-Bartleson party. The latter charted its own trail through wide stretches of the Great Basin, while the former crossed only a small section of the land of interior drainage and followed, as Bancroft put it, "the same route taken by Wolfskill in 1831."[44] However, the emigrant parties, which began with Bidwell and Bartleson and Workman and Rowland, played an important role in the history of the Great Basin, for it was they who linked together the explora-

[44] *History of California,* IV, 276–78.

tions of the mountain men and who made a trail through this area of confusing topography.

The stream of emigration which began with the Bidwell-Bartleson party did not reach considerable proportions until 1849; but a number of notable parties crossed the Basin, the corridor to California, prior to this date.[45] The second emigrant party to enter the land of interior drainage over what was substantially the Overland Trail was known as the Walker-Chiles group and traveled to California in 1843. One of its leaders was Joseph Walker, the mountain man who had achieved fame with the Walker-Bonneville party; another was Joseph B. Chiles, who had been a member of the Bidwell-Bartleson party of 1841.[46] This group followed the usual route to Fort Hall, and there separated. Some of the men with Chiles followed a new route by way of Fort Boise and the Malheur and Pit rivers to the Sacramento Valley.[47] Joseph Walker was left in charge of the families and the wagons and was told to lead them to California through what was later to become known as the Great Basin. Thus Walker with the majority of the group traveled to the Snake River, thence to the Raft River and down Thousand Springs Valley to the Humboldt River, following the route that he had established in 1834 on his return from the Pacific Coast. The party continued down the Humboldt River to its sink and then turned southward to Walker Lake. They traveled southward, negotiating the Sierra Nevada Mountains by Walker's Pass, discovered by Walker in 1834. This party was the first to bring wagons overland to California through the Great Basin, proving that the land of interior drainage was an adequate corridor to California, one in which wheeled vehicles could be used.

Many of the emigrants who were on their way to Oregon were met at Fort Hall and encouraged to go to California by way of the Great Basin. In 1844, Caleb Greenwood encountered many of these travelers at Fort Hall and produced a letter from Captain Sutter telling of the

45 Two hundred and fifty persons in five distinct companies traveled across the Great Basin in 1845. It has been estimated that the number of homeseekers crossing the Great Basin in 1846 equalled that of the five preceding years. Hafen and Rister, *Western America*, 322.

46 Joseph B. Chiles, "Visit to California," MS, in Bancroft Library. Louisa Thompson, "The Days of 1846: Recollections . . . ." This was written by Miss Thompson from the dictation of Joseph B. Chiles in 1877 and includes a brief mention of his journey to California in 1843. MS, Bancroft Library.

47 H. H. Bancroft, *History of Nevada, Wyoming, and Colorado*, 55.

advantages of California.[48] The most important group that took Sutter's advice was led by Elisha Stevens, but was better known as the Murphy company. This company, composed of fifty emigrants, traveled south from Fort Hall, following substantially the trail used by the Walker-Chiles party in the preceding year. They passed down Thousand Springs Valley and reached the Humboldt River near the present Wells, Nevada, and then proceeded down the banks of this stream to the Humboldt Sink, west of present Lovelock, Nevada. At this point, the Stevens-Murphy group deviated from the trail established by Joseph Walker. Here they struck out directly to the west, crossing the barren stretches of the Forty Mile Desert before reaching the Truckee River near present Wadsworth. The group had difficulty following up this stream since the walls of its canyons are so narrow that they were forced to drive their wagons in the bed of the stream in many places. Although their route from the Humboldt River to the Truckee River and up the latter to Donner Pass had many obstacles, it became an important variation to the famous Overland Trail and was used by thousands in their journey across the Great Basin to California. Today this route is utilized by the Southern Pacific Railroad and one of the best-known transcontinental highways, U.S. Highway 40.

Even though the Great Basin became a corridor to California during the 1830's and 1840's, the travelers passing over the Old Spanish Trail and the Overland Trail did not achieve any true understanding of the geographical nature of the land of interior drainage. Most of the members of emigrant parties held erroneous geographical conceptions, for in general they followed maps portraying the mythical rivers. Therefore, although many parties of homeseekers crossed the barren stretches of the Great Basin during this period, it was not until 1844, the same year in which the Stevens-Murphy party crossed the present states of Utah and Nevada, that John Charles Frémont, while traversing much of the same region, made his important pronouncement—the area lying between the Wasatch and the Sierra Nevada Mountains is an interior-drainage basin.

[48] Charles Kelley, *Old Greenwood: The Story of Caleb Greenwood, Trapper, Pathfinder, and Early Pioneer of the West.* Also interview with Carroll D. Hall, curator of Sutter's Fort Historical Museum, Sacramento, California.

9

MYTH CONQUERS REALITY

DURING THE 1840's the Great Basin became a corridor to California through which a great number of emigrants passed. It was pointed out in the previous chapter that many of these people who traversed the barren stretches of the land of interior drainage had little understanding of the geographical nature of the area. Most of the emigrant groups were given a false impression of the Great Basin since they were in possession of maps that showed apochryphal rivers and other mythical topographical features.

Perhaps the best example of the prevailing ignorance of the emigrants in this respect is John Bidwell's statement about the Bidwell-Bartleson party of 1841:

> Our ignorance of the route was complete. We knew that California lay west, and that was the extent of our knowledge. Some of the maps consulted, supposed of course to be correct, showed a lake in the vicinity of where Salt Lake now is; it was represented as a long lake, three or four hundred miles in extent, narrow and with two outlets, both running into the Pacific Ocean, either apparently larger than the Mississippi River. An intelligent man with whom I boarded—Elam Brown, who till recently lived in California, dying when over ninety years of age—possessed a map that showed these rivers to be large, and he advised me to take tools along to make canoes, so that if we found the country so rough that we could decend one of those rivers to the Pacific.[1]

It seems almost incredible that, after more than three decades of exploration which penetrated into the heart of the Great Basin, such ignorance could exist. This situation can be attributed to the

[1] "The First Emigrant Train to California," *Century Magazine,* Vol. XLI (Nov., 1890), 3.

cartographic extravaganza which dominated geographical circles during the first half of the nineteenth century. Governor Simpson of the Hudson's Bay Company described the geographical state of affairs plainly and accurately in these words:

> I have examined with much attention the different charts and maps that have appeared of this Country but none of them give anything like a correct idea there of Rivers Lakes Mountains Plains and Forests being introduced and disposed as suited the fancy and taste of the Draftsmen and some of the writers have had the effrontery to Gull the public with the produce of their own fertile imaginations differing widely from the truth and with descriptions of Countries they have never seen and which had not been explored when their works came from the Press.[2]

Although there were no penetrations of a scientific nature into the Great Basin during the first decades of the nineteenth century, there were two—one on the north and the other on the south and east of this area—which were of primary importance in the cartographic extravaganza which was centered in the latitudes of the Great Basin. These were, of course, the remarkable expeditions of Lewis and Clark and Zebulon Pike, described earlier. Shortly before and while these men were in the field, another scientist, Alexander von Humboldt, was working in the archives of Mexico, and his findings had a pronounced influence upon the cartographic reports of the two previously mentioned expeditions. The triumvirate of Lewis and Clark, Pike, and Humboldt,[3] each of whom produced maps which were important in cartographic history, not only wrought changes in the works of one another but also set the course for future cartographers portraying western North America.

It is not surprising that the works of Pike, Humboldt, and Lewis and Clark, all of which were published in the few short years between 1810 and 1814, should be of such great import. Prior to this time there had been only two well-documented expeditions into the Great Basin, both of them Spanish; and these had remained unknown

2 *The Journal of Sir George Simpson,* 112.

3 William Clark, "Map of Lewis and Clark's Track . . . ." Zebulon Pike, "A Map of the Internal Provinces of New Spain," in *Account of an Expedition to the Sources of the Mississippi and through the Western Parts of Louisiana . . . and a Trip through the Interior Parts of New Spain,* ed. by Elliott Coues. Alexander von Humboldt, *"Carte du Mexique et Pays Limitrophes . . . ."*

to the contemporary world until through the efforts of Baron von Humboldt the findings of these Spanish expeditions were reported graphically, and the errors of Bernardo Miera y Pacheco, the cartographer of the Domínguez-Escalante expedition, were brought to public attention and were perpetuated.

Although no important expeditions had entered the Great Basin between 1776 and the third decade of the nineteenth century, interest developed in this area because of the work of Humboldt, Pike, and Lewis and Clark. The cartographic mistakes which were made by Miera and copied by Humboldt were also copied by Pike and Lewis and Clark and, in this way, disseminated. Their maps were published almost simultaneously and became the model for European cartography dealing with this area, exerting great influence upon the cartographers of the world.

As a result of the work of these four men, the Great Basin was not a blank spot on a piece of paper as Aaron Arrowsmith portrayed it in 1795 on the first of many editions of his notable map of North America, nor was it a space which bore an inscription stating that the area was unknown. It was now the land of Lake Timpanogos and the locale of the remarkable San Buenaventura River. With these models in front of them—two by the leaders of expeditions that had made great entries into the Trans-Mississippi West and the third by one of the greatest scholars of that day—cartographers were quick to grasp at the new materials which were available.

Aaron Arrowsmith, the head of the well-known English family of cartographers, was one of the first to take immediate advantage of the achievements of Baron von Humboldt. He was a well-trained cartographer rather than a scientific geographer, but he understood map projection in all its branches. His training enabled him to utilize, in a way peculiarly his own, the store of information and material that was placed at his disposal. He was a close friend of Dalrymple and Rennell and was well acquainted with the directors of the Hudson's Bay and East India companies, both of which proved to be wonderful sources of information of a geographical nature.

In 1810, Arrowsmith produced a map which showed the Garcés and Domínguez-Escalante findings as perpetuated by Font and Miera through the works of Mascaro and Costanso and, more important, those of Humboldt. Although Humboldt's published work was dated 1811, it is apparent that Arrowsmith had access to his findings, for Humboldt's influence is clearly shown on the Arrowsmith map which was published on October 5, 1810. Here for the first time is drawn a dotted line from the Great Salt Lake region through the central and western Great Basin to the Pacific Ocean to denote an extension of Domínguez and Escalante's San Buenaventura River. Thus, in the unexplored regions of the Great Basin, Arrowsmith hesitantly tied together the geographical conceptions of Garcés, Domínguez and Escalante, and Humboldt, and produced one of the last vestiges of the mythical water passage through the North American continent.

Arrowsmith took immediate advantage of the publication of the Lewis and Clark map of 1814, and on his edition of his map of North America for that year he carefully portrayed the discoveries of the two captains. Brué, in Paris, also did likewise in the same year, and in this way these two European maps brought the Lewis and Clark findings to wide public attention. Both cartographers used materials which they obtained from Northwest Company explorers also, and therefore their maps represented an important step in the general understanding of the nature of western America.

Other cartographers were quick to follow suit, among them John Melish, who emigrated from Scotland and settled in Philadelphia. He was the author of a two-volume work, *Travels in the United States of America, in the years 1806 & 1807, and 1809, 1810 & 1811*. He published the first edition of his well-known map of the United States in 1816.[4] This map followed closely the Lewis and Clark map for the Northwest; however, farther south Melish followed Pike. There is an interesting similarity between his map of 1816 and Aaron Arrowsmith's map of 1810, for both depict the San Buenaventura River as a dotted line. Melish shows the Buenaventura flowing into a large unnamed lake with a dotted line extending westwardly to San Francisco Bay. On the map he wrote the legend, "Supposed course of a river between the Buenaventura and the Bay of San Francisco which will probably be the communication from the Arkansas to the Pacific Ocean."[5]

In 1819 there appeared a map drawn by Dr. John Hamilton Rob-

4 *Map of the United States with Contiguous British and Spanish Possessions* (Philadelphia, 1816). Lawrence Martin, formerly director of the Map Division of the Library of Congress, reported twenty-two issues of this map between 1816 and 1823. Carl I. Wheat, *Mapping the American West, 1540–1857,"* 70, n. 6.

5 *Ibid.,* 70.

inson which is the antithesis of the Cook-Vancouver geography, for it brings the conceptions of Arrowsmith and Melish to their predictable conclusion. Robinson had been with Pike; later he became a brigadier general in the Mexican revolutionary army. On his map, which was entitled *Mexico, Louisiana and the Missouri Territory*, he states that he had used several manuscript maps which he had obtained in Mexico as references. His map seems to have been derived in part from that of Lewis and Clark and in part from Pike's map; it also shows the influence of Font and Miera. Escalante's and Garcés' journeys are shown in detail through the Great Basin, as well as the trail of Font. The most interesting feature of the Robinson map, however, is that it does not show the mythical rivers as dotted lines, but depicts them as streams of great magnitude flowing across the desert stretches of the Great Basin and over what is now known to be the highest portion of the Sierra Nevada Mountain chain.

The year 1822 is interesting and important in the history of cartography of the Great Basin because it witnessed the publication of Henry Schenck Tanner's monumental map of North America. Tanner, who was trained as an engraver, was endowed with the combination of scientific and artistic sense that identifies the true cartographer, and this in turn led him ultimately to produce what for his time were the outstanding maps of the territory of the United States based upon a critical study of the sources. In spite of his skill, Tanner was imbued with the idea which was prevalent at that time that there were several large rivers flowing to the west from the Rocky Mountains, and these he reproduced on his map of 1822. In an accompanying memoir, Tanner stated that he had used the maps of Humboldt, Pike, and Long,[6] as well as Don Juan Pedro Walker's "map of New California"[7] in the preparation of his work. On this

[6] Stephen H. Long had been an officer of the United States Topographical Engineers and had made a celebrated expedition in 1820 to the Rocky Mountains and the sources of the Platte and Arkansas rivers. Pike, it will be recalled, saw a distant stream and identified it with the Yellowstone, but Long identified it with the headwaters of Lewis Fork of the Columbia. Long's map is considered an excellent depiction of the areas that he had visited; thus, together with the map of Lewis and Clark and to lesser degree that of Pike, it became one of the progenitors of an entire class of maps of the American West.

[7] Don Juan Pedro Walker was a most interesting person. He was born in Louisiana when it was under Spanish rule, and in manhood became an officer in the Mexican Army. He was one of the two Spanish officers who signed the receipt

map, in the North and Northwest, one finds Lewis and Clark geography, with Long's Lewis River heading near the sources of the Platte, Río Grande, and Colorado. The Multnomah, which Lewis and Clark had pictured as a river of great magnitude flowing from the interior of the continent, is reduced to reasonable size, but, conversely, Lake Timpanogos is shown with two rivers, the Los Mongos and the Timpanogos, flowing from it to the Pacific Ocean. South of Lake Timpanogos a "Salt Lake" is depicted, from which the Buenaventura flows to the ocean; still farther south, Garcés' "R. St. Felipe" flows from the same lake. Even the exotic Mojave River is given grandeur under the name of "R. de los Martires" which Garcés had applied to it. It is shown flowing to the coast not far north of the site of San Diego. However, after investing the Great Basin with streams of such magnitude, Tanner does qualify them by a legend which he placed in the Pacific Ocean. It states that the materials Tanner used for the rivers "was not of that authentic character which distinguished nearly all the other materials" used in constructing the map. "It is therefore very doubtful," he adds, "whether the representation afforded by it, of the courses and magnitude of those streams, should be relied on as correct."[8]

Although the maps of Arrowsmith, Melish, Robinson, and Tanner, as well as many others, may appear strange today, they should not be too harshly criticized for their portrayal of the far western regions. It is evident that the cartographers attempted to use the available source material with care and intelligence. It must be remembered that almost another third of a century was to elapse before a cartographer would be able to develop an understanding of the intermontane region and adjacent areas and present a reasonably accurate picture of the entire western region. Indeed, these works seem even

for Pike's papers when the latter was interned in Chihuahua, and from this source and from the sketch that Pike made for General Salcedo, it seems that Walker became acquainted with Pike's geographical conceptions, for his maps resemble those of Pike. On his map of 1805, Walker follows the theory so dear to Pike's heart that several continental rivers have their sources in a common area, and so portrayed the Columbia, Missouri, Arkansas, and Río Grande as rising within common ground. Father Garces' unknown river is shown off to the west and southwest of Escalante's Lake Timpanogos, but little other Escalante material seems to have been used.

8 Wheat, *Mapping the American West*, 75, n. 15.

more remarkable when one realizes that their land of apocryphal streams had not yet been discovered!

Of course, it is impossible to estimate the full effect that these maps had upon the actual course of exploration of the Great Basin, but it seems safe to assume that they had some influence, probably more than is realized at first glance. It must be remembered that the explorers of the 1820's of this basin of interior drainage were members of the fur trade, and had two selfish reasons for wanting to discover the mythical rivers which were purported to flow from and through the Great Basin. They thought that if they found one of these rivers, it would be rich in fur-bearing animals and its waters could be used to float the beaver pelts to the Pacific Coast, where they could be sent directly to the fur mart in Canton, China, instead of being shipped by the circuitous route via St. Louis.

The vanguard of the Rocky Mountain Fur Company entered the Great Basin in 1824, and its leader, General Ashley, made his entrance in the following year. The influence of the various contemporary cartographic productions upon Ashley's thinking is shown by the fact that when he arrived on the banks of the Green River on April 19, 1825, he believed it to be the Buenaventura, making the same mistake that Escalante had made fifty years before. Ashley, however, believed this stream to be a tributary of the Multnomah, which he supposed flowed into the Columbia. This belief clearly illustrates a composite of the Lewis and Clark conclusions and those of the Domínguez-Escalante expedition, no doubt as disseminated by Humboldt. Ashley stated:

> I proceeded down the waters of the Buenaventura about sixty miles bordered with a growth of willow almost impenetrable. In that distance I crossed several streams from 20 to 60 yards wide running in various directions. All of them, as I am informed, unite in one course of 30 miles, making a river of considerable magnitude, which enters a few miles lower down a large lake, represented as Lake Tempagono.[9]

That his idea that the Buenaventura was connected with the Multnomah underwent a metamorphosis after he conversed with several members of the Ogden Snake Country Expedition of 1824–25 is shown in the statement below:

[9] Dale, *Ashley-Smith Explorations*, 147–48.

195

Some of them profess to be well acquainted with all the principal waters of the Columbia, with which they assured me these waters had no connection short of the ocean. It appears from this information that the river is not the Multnomah, a southern branch of the Columbia, which I first supposed it to . . . . The necessity of my unremitted attention to my business prevented me from gratifying a great desire to descend this river to the ocean, which I ultimately declined with the greatest reluctance.[10]

However, to ascertain whether the Buenaventura had an outlet after flowing into "Lake Tempagono," as he called it, Ashley sent a group of men to make a circuit of the Great Salt Lake, and in this case the creations of the cartographers gave impetus for the first circumnavigation of this body of water.

On July 18, 1826, General Ashley retired from an active part in the fur trade and relinquished his interest in the Rocky Mountain Fur Company to Jedediah Smith, David Jackson, and William Sublette. The new firm was made up of young and energetic men who were anxious to make a success of their undertaking. It seems apparent that the three were interested in extending their operations into new fur-bearing regions, and shortly after the business deal was consummated, Jedediah Smith was sent out into the country south and west of Great Salt Lake, perhaps to search for the San Buenaventura River. This expedition was to lead Smith southward into the Colorado drainage system and ultimately to Mission San Gabriel before he traveled up the Great Valley of California and crossed the Sierra Nevadas to rejoin his partners at Bear Lake, the place chosen by the three partners as the site for the summer rendezvous of 1827.

Smith's belief in the existence of the San Buenaventura was strong at this time, as is shown in a letter which he wrote in 1826 while in California: "I wrote [undecipherable word], stating to the Gov. Gen. my situation and requesting of him some Horses & permission to pass through his coun[try] to the Bay of St. Francisco—I wished to follow up one of the largest Riv[ers] that emptied into the Bay cross the mon [mountains] at its head and from thence to our Deposit on the waters of the Salt Lake."[11] Smith's confidence in the existence of

10 *Ibid.*, 150–51.

11 Letter, Jedediah Smith to the United States Plenipotentiary at Mexico, Port of Landing, Province of New California, December 16, 1826, quoted in Rolle (ed.),

this river began to wane as he traveled northward. He had felt that if he followed the western foothills of the Sierra Nevada Mountains, he would come to the San Buenaventura River, which he could follow up to the Great Salt Lake; but after he had journeyed three hundred miles to the north of Mission San Gabriel and found that the Indians were ignorant of such a stream, he seems to have lost faith in it entirely.

Again in 1827, Smith made a trek to California by almost the same route that he had used the preceding year. It is believed that when he struck the waters of the Sacramento River, he felt that he was on the banks of a large stream, but after the expedition of the year before, he seems to have been skeptical of this river's having its source in the Rocky Mountains. Nevertheless, he named this river the Buenaventura. He probably, however, had in mind a combination of the Domínguez-Escalante geographical conceptions, for he seemed to imagine a connection of this river (the Sacramento) with a northern river, probably the Columbia. Dale relates that when Smith was in this area, he sought information concerning the upper courses of the Sacramento River, which at this time were vaguely known. Smith may have obtained information from one of Don Luis Arguello's men who claimed that they were acquainted with the Columbia River; they further declared that in 1821 they went almost to that river and that they were convinced that the Sacramento River must be a branch of it. This bit of information when correlated with the Lewis and Clark geography would give one the impression that this river would be the unnamed tributary of the Multnomah, which Ashley believed was the Buenaventura, and therefore Smith applied this name.

While the Rocky Mountain Fur Company trappers were exploring the Great Basin and adjacent areas, the Hudson's Bay Company was sending brigades southward. Thus within a period of five years all of the most prominent physiographical features of the Great Basin were revealed by the Americans and the British. The Great Salt Lake or "Lake Timpanogos" was discovered by Jim Bridger in 1825, and almost simultaneously Jedediah Smith and his band of trappers made known most of what is now the present state of Utah and parts of the modern state of Nevada through which their path led in the

"Jedediah Strong Smith: New Documentation," *Mississippi Valley Historical Review*, Vol. XL (Sept., 1953).

spring of 1827. With the advent of the Snake Country Expedition, parts of Utah, such as the site of the present city of Ogden and the Ogden River Valley, were explored, as well as the important Humboldt River which lies within the political boundaries of the state of Nevada. Shortly after the expiration of this first five-year period of primary exploration, the Walker-Bonneville party plotted a trail across the Great Basin, using the Humboldt River as a guide, as did Ogden, but extending this track to the Carson Sink and over the Sierra Nevada Mountains. The return of Walker and his men by way of what is now known as Walker's Pass and the Walker River added to the knowledge of the western portions of the Great Basin.

Thus one would conclude that, with the exploration of this basin of interior drainage, the cartographic extravaganza which had centered in these latitudes would terminate. Such was not the case. Unfortunately, most of the information that was acquired by the mountain men filtered out from the West piece by piece, and little of the fund of knowledge which they had acquired in their wanderings was brought to public attention.

William Kittson, who was the clerk on Ogden's 1824–25 Snake Country Expedition, did draw a map showing the area through which the party traveled, which, of course, included much of what is now known as the Utah region of the Great Basin; but his sketch map was to lie in the Hudson's Bay Company's archives for over a century and a quarter, until it was reproduced recently by the Hudson's Bay Company's Record Society in *Ogden's Snake Country Journals, 1824–25 & 1825–26*. The pencil sketch map by Peter Skene Ogden on his historic 1828–29 Snake Country Expedition met a similar fate and is still in the repository of the Hudson's Bay Company, being reproduced for the first time in this book.

Jedediah Smith drew at least two maps during the course of his western travels; one was a sketch of his 1826 route to California, which he made for Father Sánchez at Mission San Gabriel, and the other was a sketch drawn for Dr. McLoughlin at Fort Vancouver in August of 1828. It also appears that Smith sent to General Ashley, at some time between 1829 and 1831, a more general representation of his explorations, a map which was no doubt drawn upon, directly or indirectly, by both Albert Gallatin and David H. Burr in constructing their maps of the West. It is also believed that Smith was preparing an elaborate map when he was in St. Louis in 1830–31 for the purpose of illustrating his journals, which he intended to publish. However, to date no original Jedediah Smith map has been discovered.[12]

Notwithstanding the fact that no original map drawn by Jedediah Smith has come to light, it is apparent that certain contemporary maps were influenced by him. The earliest map which has so far been uncovered that reveals Smith's influence is one that was produced in Paris in 1833 by the cartographic firm of A. H. Brué. Brué was an erudite cartographer who gathered material from many sources, one of which was Alexander von Humboldt, as Brué stated in his great atlas of 1830. Unfortunately, Brué was stricken with cholera and died of this illnes on July 16, 1832.[13] His widow published posthumously the maps that appeared with his name after this date. The Brué map of 1833 was a monumental reproduction of North America, largely of the traditional type like those of his predecessors, Robinson and Tanner. It shows Lewis and Clark's apocryphal Multnomah as a stream of great magnitude which is at one point labeled "R. Mackay" in honor of Thomas Mackay, one of Peter Skene Ogden's associates in the Hudson's Bay Company. Brué makes this stream the outlet of Lake Timpanogos. The Sacramento River is also shown and is declared to be navigable by large vessels for fifty leagues. The Spanish lakes of Timpanogos and Teguayo are clearly depicted with two rivers, Ashley and Adams, off to the southwest of them. Ashley and Adams, of course, were the names which Jedediah Smith had applied to the Sevier and Virgin rivers on his trek to the Pacific Coast in 1826. The name which Smith had given to the Green-Colorado drainage system was "Seeds Keeder," and this appellation appears no less than three times on the Brué map. Even the rock-salt cave that Smith had briefly mentioned is depicted. It seems apparent, therefore, that Brué was acquainted with the explorations of Jedediah Smith.

Brué must have acquired this information in quite a round about fashion. It will be recalled that on July 12, 1827, when Smith was encamped at Bear Lake in the Great Basin, he wrote a letter to General William Clark, superintendent of Indian affairs, narrating his first journey to California. A condensed version of this letter was, in turn, published in the St. Louis *Missouri Republican* on October

12 Morgan and Wheat, *Jedediah Smith and His Maps*, 15.
13 Mm. Michaud (ed.), *Biographia Universelle, Ancienne et Moderne,* 671.

11, 1827, and was ultimately widely reprinted. In 1828 a French version of the letter was printed in *Nouvelles Annales des Voyages* under the title of *"Excursion a l'ouest des Monts Rocky, extrait d'une lettre de M. Jedediah Smith ...."*[14]

In the following year, 1834, another map was published by the firm of A. H. Brué.[15] This one is particularly noteworthy, for it appears to be the earliest attempt by a cartographer to display Smith's actual route on a map. This large map of Mexico is similar to the Brué map of North America of 1833, as it includes virtually the same legends. However, the 1834 map varies from its predecessor in one important aspect: it includes several dotted lines which are significant because they denote the Smith trail. One, which leads southwestward from Adams River, has the title *"Route de Smith en 1826"* while another, which bears slightly northeast of King's River (here given Smith's appellation of "Wimmelche") is labeled *"8 Journées"* and crosses "Mt. St. Joseph." East of "Mt. St. Joseph" or the Sierra Nevada Mountain Range is a legend which gives a more accurate description of the Great Basin: *"Pays desert, aride et sablonneux sans Gibier et habité par quelques bandes d'Indiene. 20 jours. Route de Smith en 1826."*[16] Of course, this mention of the year 1826 is an error, for Smith made his trek across the center of the Great Basin in the spring of 1827.

In the same year that the Brué map was published, Aaron Arrowsmith, across the Channel, produced an important atlas which contained a map of North America which is of particular interest. This map shows "Swamp Lakes & Is." in the Great Basin area into which flows a Buenaventura River, and from this point a dotted line proceeds westward to an unnamed Sacramento River which is labeled higher on its course "R Buenaventura N[orthern] Bra[nch]." Ashley River is shown as well as "Unknown R." This map is of interest because it suggests that some information derived from the Hudson's Bay Company explorers was used in its preparation. It appears to contain the first large-scale cartographic mention of "Swamp Lakes & Is." and could very easily have originated with the Ogden Snake

14 Morgan and Wheat, *Jedediah Smith and His Maps*, 16.

15 A. H. Brué, *Nouvelle Carte du Mexique et d'une partie des provinces unies de l'Amérique Centrale* (Paris, 1834). A large reproduction is in Morgan and Wheat, *Jedediah Smith and His Maps*, 18.

16 *Ibid.*, 18.

Country Expedition of 1828–29. The Ogden map of 1829, which is a sketch of the Snake River, Great Salt Lake, and Humboldt River drainage area, denotes a "Swamp" lake on the lower course of "Unknown River" or the Humboldt. In addition, Ogden made several notes in his diary indicating the swampy characteristics of the lower courses of the Humboldt, such as the entry for May 27, 1829 when the party was encamped near Humboldt Sink: "Encamped within a mile of a large lake. The river is not half the size it was, no doubt spreading in the swamp we have passed. It is 2½ ft. deep and only 10 yds. wide."[17] At this point Ogden and his men learned from the Indians about a river which lay about eight days' march from the Humboldt River, which may account, in part, for Arrowsmith's dotted line between these lakes and the unnamed Sacramento. Unfortunately, because of the lateness of the season, Ogden was not able to proceed farther to the west to discover the course of this river; also he did not wish "to infringe on McLeod's territory . . . . McLeod's territory is the water discharging in the ocean. If Mr. McLeod has succeeded in reaching Bona Ventura[18] he must have crossed this stream."[19] It must be remembered that Aaron Arrowsmith was hydrographer to the king as well as a close friend of the directors of the Hudson's Bay Company, and it would seem quite likely, therefore, that he had access to this very journal, which is still in the Hudson's Bay Company Archives and has remained unpublished with the exception of the passages which have been quoted in this volume.

This Arrowsmith map is of importance, for it apparently formed the basis for a number of future outstanding American maps. The first map to reproduce some of Arrowsmith features was prepared in 1838 by Captain Washington Hood of the Corps of Topographical Engineers and was to accompany Senator Linn's report on a bill to "Authorize the President to occupy the Oregon Territory."[20] Hood made a few additions and emendations of no great moment, but he retained almost all the Arrowsmith details in the Oregon country. "Swamp Lakes and Islands" are included; however, Ogden's name has been added to the Unknown River, while the appellation "Lake

17 Entry in Ogden's diary for May 27, 1829, "Peter Skene Ogden's Snake Country Journal, 1828–1829," B. 202/a/8, H.B.C.A., 47.

18 Ogden here is referring to the Sacramento River.

19 "Ogden's Snake Country Journal, 1828–29," entry for May 29, 1829, B. 202/a/8, H.B.C.A.

20 25 Cong., 2 sess., *Senate Bill 206.*

Bonneville" is used in addition to Arrowsmith's name for the Great Salt Lake.[21]

In 1836, Albert Gallatin published an important map to illustrate an article which he had written, entitled, "A Synopsis of the Indian Tribes within the United States East of the Rocky Mountains, and in the British and Russians possessions in North America."[22] In this article Gallatin stated that "several geographical innovations have been introduced in the small map annexed to this Essay." A study of the various features of this map indicates that Gallatin had one of the lost Smith sketches before him as he prepared his map for publication. He depicts "Ashley L.," "Lost R.," and "Adams R." quite accurately and shows the Mojave River as a short river west of the Colorado bearing the name that Smith applied to it, "Inconstant R." He also shows two dotted lines joining east of the Great Salt Lake or "Timpanogo" and continuing down the east side of the Colorado before crossing to the vicinity of Mission San Gabriel. This, of course, is to denote Smith's trail of 1826. Gallatin's map is important because it is the earliest published attempt in the United States to represent Smith's explorations. It is also the earliest map from which an inference can be made that an actual Smith map was used as a basis. Although this map is crude, it is superior to Brué's map of 1834, and discloses that more than a published letter was used in its preparation.[23]

There are other aspects of the Gallatin map which are of interest in a study of the Great Basin. On this reproduction of North America, Gallatin decreased the Multnomah greatly in size and stated in his accompanying essay, "It will be seen by this, that the sources of the Multnomah do not reach farther south than the forty-third degree of latitude."[24] This statement completely outdates the Lewis and Clark conception of a large river which they believed had its sources in the interior of the continent, in the area that was to become known as the Great Basin.

Gallatin had more to add concerning the Great Basin, for he con-

21 Wheat, *Mapping the American West*, 86–87.

22 Published in *Transactions and Collections* of the American Antiquarian Society, II, 529–30.

23 Morgan and Wheat, *Jedediah Smith and His Maps*, 19.

24 Gallatin, "Synopsis of the Indian Tribes," *Transactions and Collections* of the American Antiquarian Society, II.

tinued: "The Lake Timpanogo has been found, and is laid down, in the same latitude and longitude nearly, as had been assigned to it by Baron Humboldt. It received two rivers from the east, which issue from the mountains west of the Colorado, is known to the Americans by the name of Great Salt Lake, and has no outlet whatever towards the sea."[25] In this statement Gallatin more or less set forth the principle of an interior drainage basin, but even though he introduced the principle, it was many years before the idea of such a phenomenon was universally accepted.

Another aspect of the Gallatin map is of special interest, though it seems to have gone completely unnoticed. This feature is Gallatin's depiction of the Owyhee River, which he shows connected to the Humboldt River. Of course, this makes it plain that there was no clear understanding of the internal-drainage qualities of the Great Basin; even Gallatin, who did so well with the Great Salt Lake region, shows the Humboldt River, one of the most important Great Basin streams, as part of the Snake River drainage system. Gallatin's arrangement of these two streams indicates that he was also supplied with information from a British source, since Peter Skene Ogden and John Work had visited this region on many occasions prior to 1836. However, it was Ogden, when he discovered the Humboldt River on November 4, 1828, who hinted at a connection with the Owyhee when he said: "Should this river flow to Sandwich Island River I trust we shall have full time to trap it."[26] In the following year, 1829, the Ogden map graphically illustrates a definite connection between the "Sandwich Island River" (Owyhee) and the Humboldt, which Ogden knew as "Unknown River."

In the year following the publication of the Gallatin essay and map, Washington Irving published his *Bonneville,* which included two important maps. The first of these dealt with the sources of the great rivers and the Great Salt Lake region, which was here termed "Lake Bonneville." This was considered to be by far the best map of the fur trade country to date. The second map was an excellent reproduction of the country to the west of the Rocky Mountains. Bonneville later wrote to Lieutenant Warren indicating that he was the person who had prepared these maps, to which Warren replied

25 *Ibid.*
26 "Ogden Snake Country Journals, 1828–1829," H.B.C.A., 7.

that they were "the first to correctly represent the hydrography of this region west of the Rocky Mountains."[27]

In the northern part of the Great Basin, Bonneville improved upon the Gallatin map of the previous year, for he dissociated the Owyhee and Humboldt rivers and gave a fairly good representation of the course of the latter. Warren continues to discuss these maps as follows:

> Although the geographical positions are not accurate, yet the exist-ence of the great interior basins, of Mary's or Ogden's river [named afterwards Humboldt by Captain Frémont], of the Mud Lakes, and of Sevier river and lake was determined by Captain Bonne-ville's maps, and they proved the non-existence of the Rio Buena-ventura and of other hypothetical rivers. They reduced the Willa-muth or Multnomah [Willamette] river to its proper length, and fixed approximately its source, and determined the general extent and direction of the Sacramento and San Joaquin rivers.[28]

Although Lieutenant Warren was rich in praise of Bonneville's maps and there is merit in what he said, it was to be almost another decade before many of these facts would be considered and accepted.

Smith's influence is also shown on the map of 1839 prepared by David H. Burr, who was geographer to the House of Representatives. This monumental work, entitled *Map of the United States*,[29] sets forth in considerable detail Smith's travels, together with Smith's own legends and place names. Therefore, it seems that there can be no doubt that Burr had before him an original Smith map while he worked on his portrayal of the West. Since General Ashley was a member of the House of Representatives from 1831 to 1837 and Burr was geographer to that body, it seems reasonable to assume that Ashley offered him an opportunity to examine a Smith manuscript

27 Wheat, *Mapping the American West,* 85; also G. K. Warren, "Memoir to Ac-company the Map of the Territory of the United States from the Mississippi River to the Pacific Ocean . . . ," which appeared in *Reports of Exploration and Surveys to Ascertain the Most Practicable and Economical Route for a Railroad from the Mississippi River to the Pacific Ocean,* XI.

28 *Ibid.,* 33.

29 David H. Burr, *Map of the United States of North America with Parts of the Adjacent Countries.* For a large reproduction, see Morgan and Wheat, *Jedediah Smith and His Maps,* back pocket.

map. Regardless of where Burr obtained his information, he seems to have used it intelligently and effectively.

Another feature of the Burr map is that it depicts General Ashley's travels in the West. With the loss of Ashley's own maps, this Burr map is the only firsthand cartographic representation of Ashley's whereabouts in the mountains during the winter of 1824–25. Along the Owyhee River appears the inscription "Route of Ogden & McKay of the Hudson Bay Co. 1826," which is apparently the first cartographic mention of this important expedition.[30] Thus Burr's map was in every way a cartographic milestone.

It is most surprising, in view of these facts, that in the year following the publication of his splendid *Map of the United States,* Burr produced a work which was a complete throwback. This map, which was drawn to illustrate Robert Greenhow's *Memoir on the North West Coast,* depicts Arrowsmith's "Swamp Lakes and Islands" and even goes so far as to show the Sacramento River flowing from them. It also shows a great east-west range of mountains called the "Snowy Mountains" which extend from the Pacific Coast to the Great Salt Lake. The production of this map in 1840 seems almost unexplainable, and the only solution seems that it was prepared before the Burr map of 1839.

In 1841 the celebrated Wilkes expedition to the Pacific Ocean visited the Oregon country, and several parties were sent out to explore the Cascades; one group was even dispatched overland to California. The results of this expedition were two maps which display a composite of the geographical conceptions that were then current, and, in this way, they exhibit the general cartographic resources which existed at the time the maps were drafted. In depicting the northern portions of the Great Basin and the Snake country, Wilkes was obviously influenced by Arrowsmith, but certain other features seem to indicate the use of a Smith map. Wilkes uses the term "Great Sandy Desert" in the Great Basin and also the legend, "The Country is extremely Rocky and rough, the Rivers running through Clift Rocks," which is obviously Smith language.

We know that it is Smith language because of a map that was recently discovered by Carl Wheat which bears notations from a map that Smith must have drawn not long before he departed for Santa Fe

[30] Morgan and Wheat, *Jedediah Smith and His Maps,* 21, 37–38.

in 1831. This map, which is in reality the Frémont map of 1845, is the basis for the important Smith notations which George Gibbs, the well-known writer and cartographer, placed upon it, and for that reason it is referred to as the "Frémont-Gibbs-Smith" map. This map has great historical significance, for on it appears far more Smith information than is to be found on any other map which Smith influenced.

In examining the "Frémont-Gibbs-Smith" map, one is able to ascertain what this great explorer had actually learned about the immense area through which he wandered. It seems that Smith was fully aware of the character of the Great Salt Lake region and depicts it as a self-contained basin with such features as Bear River, Bear Lake, the Weber River, and the dependent relationship of Utah Lake. He also shows, to the south, Sevier River and Sevier Lake; and the Beaver River and the Virgin River are correctly shown in relation to each other and to the general character of their drainage. This is important, for these streams lie in the region of the southern border of the Great Basin, and so it is essential to differentiate between the Sevier and Beaver rivers, which are streams of the interior basin, and the Virgin River, which is part of the Colorado drainage system. As Morgan and Wheat eloquently put it, "Escalante in 1776 had seen most of these physiographic features, but had possessed insufficient background and information to interpret them as a whole, and time and fantasy had wrought wonders with the facts he brought back from his entrada into the Great Basin."[31]

However, one of the most important understandings that Smith had acquired was that of the relationship of the Great Basin to the Central Valley of California, and therefore he depicted the Sierra Nevada Range as a wall separating the two. With these Smith representations we now have a distinct drainage pattern of the Great Basin with the exception of the Humboldt, Truckee, and Carson systems. In this manner Smith clarified the problem of the Great Basin.

It is most unfortunate that Smith's findings did not manage to reach the light of day, for, as Dale Morgan says:

Overall this Smith map constitutes a remakable geographic advance. Had Smith lived to publish it, say in 1832, backed by a book

[31] *Ibid.*, 40.

describing his travels, it would probably stand today as a landmark in American cartography. For the first time someone had come to grips with the most complicated drainage area of this nation, the entwined watersheds of the Platte, Yellowstone, Missouri, Green, Colorado, Snake and Great Basin, had disentangled them, and had set forth their major features as they exist in fact. Smith dealt with the central area, the point of merger for the Lewis and Clark, Long, Pike, de Miera, and Garces maps where error had been most prevalent, and he straightened them all out.[32]

With Smith's death on the Santa Fe Trail in late May of 1831, the development of western cartographical knowledge was retarded by half a generation. It seems strange that none of the contemporary cartographers grasped the significance of his tremendous exploratory achievements. They were apparently ignorant of, or resisted the importance of, the work of Brué and Gallatin, and they were not as fortunate as Burr and Wilkes in having a Smith map to guide them. Thus by far the majority of the commercial maps of the West during the early 1840's were of dubious geographical merit and still followed the patterns set by Lewis and Clark, Pike, Long, and Humboldt at the beginning of the century.

[32] *Ibid.*, 96–97.

10

THE REVELATION OF THE GREAT BASIN

THE MAPS OF NORTH AMERICA made by the cartographers of the world not only attracted the attention of future emigrants but also were of great interest in political circles. The mythical rivers as portrayed by Robinson, Arrowsmith, and Brué, to mention only a few, showed the Great Basin latitudes as a more attractive route through western North America than the northern one followed by Lewis and Clark. There is strong indication that these fictitious rivers helped to kindle interest in the western area, especially in the harbor of San Francisco.

While the Bidwell-Bartleson party was still on the trail, an expedition under Commander Wilkes of the United States Navy entered San Francisco Bay. This celebrated expedition visited the Oregon country and California, surveying these parts of the Pacific Coast of North America in an attempt to discover if a river of sizable magnitude entered the Pacific Ocean south of the Columbia. Two maps resulted from this expedition, and on them Wilkes displayed his skepticism about the existence of a river which had its source in the Great Salt Lake region.

Not satisfied with the findings of the Wilkes expedition with relation to the apocryphal streams, in the next year another scientific expedition took to the field. This was the first expedition led by John Charles Frémont, who was destined to become one of the most controversial figures in western American history. The expedition materialized through the efforts of Thomas Hart Benton, father-in-law of Frémont, when he brought the matter of western territories before Congress in 1842. This expedition, which included Charles Preuss as topographer and Kit Carson as guide, proceeded up the Platte to the Sweetwater and reached South Pass on August 8, 1842, before exploring the Green River region and the Wind River mountain chain.

Of far greater importance to the history of the Great Basin was Frémont's Second Expedition, which had the ostensible object of connecting his explorations of the previous year with the surveys of Commander Wilkes along the Pacific Coast. The party left Kaw Landing (Kansas City) on May 29, 1843, and followed up the northernmost fork of the Kansas River before reaching the Oregon Trail on the banks of the Sweetwater. Frémont states that "By making this deviation from the former route, the problem of a new road to Oregon and California, in a climate more genial, might be solved."[1]

Upon reaching South Pass, Frémont and his men journeyed to the Green River, thence to the Bear River of the Great Basin, and then proceeded down to Great Salt Lake. That Frémont believed in the existence of a river flowing from this region to the Pacific Ocean is indicated in a statement he made concerning a certain "important river":

The great object of the expedition would find its point of commencement in the termination of the former, which was at the great gate in the ridge of the Rocky mountains called the South Pass, and on the lofty peak of the mountain which overlooks it, deemed the highest peak in the ridge and from the opposite side of which four great rivers take their rise, and flow to the Pacific or Mississippi.[2]

From an entry in his *Report,* it appears that Frémont was conversant with the maps and reports of Gallatin and Bonneville, but these seem to have left him undaunted, as he makes the following statement in regard to the Great Salt Lake: "It was generally supposed that it has no visible outlet; but among the trappers, including those in my own camp, were many who believed that somewhere on its surface was a terrible whirlpool, through which its waters found their way to the ocean by some subterranean communication."[3] This entry illustrates the strength and power of these apocryphal rivers. Although exploration was increasing the doubt as to their reality and even proving that their existence was impossible,

[1] Fremont's *Report,* 106.
[2] *Ibid.*
[3] *Ibid.,* 132.

some people—including even those familiar with the local topography—continued to believe in them and, moreover, contributed further to the illusive qualities of these streams.

The Frémont party left the Great Salt Lake and went north to Fort Hall on the Snake River. They proceeded to The Dalles and then turned south from the Columbia River and struck Klamath Lake. As he passed south from this area, Frémont said:

> In our journey across the desert, Mary's lake, and the famous Buenaventura river, were two points on which I relied to recruit the animals, and repose the party. Forming, agreeably to the best maps in my possession, a connected water line from the Rocky mountains to the Pacific Ocean, I felt no other anxiety than to pass safely across the intervening desert to the banks of the Buenaventura.[4]

Frémont seems to have firmly believed in the existence of the Buenaventura River, and while traveling through this area, momentarily expected to discover it. On January 3, almost four weeks after the preceding entry, he wrote:

> We had reached and run over the position where, according to the best map in my possession, we should have found Mary's lake or river. We were evidently on the verge of the desert[5] which had been reported to us; and the appearance of the country was so forbidding, that I was afraid to enter it, and determined to bear away to the southward, keeping close along the mountains, in the full expectation of reaching the Buenaventura river.[6]

Frémont's continual reference to "Mary's lake or river" seems curious, for there were only a few streams in the Great Basin which bore this name, and none of them had any physical qualities which would be worthy of this degree of attention. When Ashley first saw the Yampa River, which lies in the modern state of Utah, he applied the name "Mary," and this same thing was done when Ogden discovered the Humboldt River. It seems, however, that Frémont had in

[4] *Ibid.*, 205.

[5] The party was in the northwestern corner of what is now the state of Nevada and was, no doubt, warned about the Black Rock Desert and its extension, Smoke Creek Desert, in the vicinity of the modern Gerlach, Nevada.

[6] *Report*, 214.

mind a stream of considerable size when referring to Mary's River, and this river seems to have been located, according to his calculations, in the vicinity of the Humboldt River. Another fact can be put forth for the case of Mary's River being an enlarged version of the Humboldt, for Frémont refers also to "Mary's lake." The lake perhaps originated with the Humboldt Sink, which no doubt would have been referred to as "Mary's" since that was the name of the river that deposited its waters in the Humboldt Basin. There is one last vestige of the name "Mary" in this region, and that is preserved by a tributary of the Humboldt River in the vicinity of the site of present Deeth, Nevada.

In his search for the apocryphal streams, Frémont had discovered some areas of the Great Basin which had been previously unknown. After he had completed the first part of his journey, that of making an accurate survey of the emigrant trail to Oregon, he turned to the south and re-entered the Great Basin, this time in south-central Oregon. It will be remembered that Peter Skene Ogden and his Snake Country Expedition had explored this area in 1826 and 1827, but they had not proceeded southward into what is now the south-eastern section of Oregon and the northwestern portion of Nevada. This Frémont did, and on December 25, 1843, he encamped on a body of water which he chose to call "Christmas Lake" in honor of the day of discovery. There is no longer a lake by this name because this body of water coalesced with Lake Anderson to form what is now called Warner Lake. On December 26, the Frémont party pitched their camp on about the forty-second parallel, which now forms the boundary between the states of Oregon and Nevada.

On January 10, Frémont and Carson pushed on in advance of the main party, which was then encamped at Mud Lake. This was the lower eastern lobe of a valley which had for its western lobe Smoke Creek Desert, with Granite Creek Desert as a neck between it and Black Rock Desert at the north. At the lower end of Mud Lake Valley, Frémont and Carson found a grassy hollow in the Lake Range, and after leaving a message or signal here for the following party to pitch camp at this location, they continued up the hollow to see where it led and what lay beyond. When they arrived at a point where they could look into the country ahead, they suddenly found themselves looking down about two thousand feet upon a vast sheet of greenish water. They made their camp opposite an odd-shaped rock rising out of the waters on the eastern side of the lake. This strangely shaped formation which Frémont had been observing with much curiosity for miles reminded him so much of the Pyramid of Cheops that he named this body of water "Pyramid Lake," by which name it is known today.

The group traveled to the southeast end of Pyramid Lake to a site which is now occupied by the Nixon Indian School and near by found the waters of the Truckee River discharging into the lake. They followed up this stream to about the site of present Wadsworth, Nevada, where they made camp. At this point the Truckee River, which had previously followed a course almost due south, makes a decided turn to the west, for its waters flow from Lake Tahoe, which lies in the Sierra Nevada Mountains on the western fringe of the Great Basin. From this area, Frémont and his party left the Truckee River and marched southward about twenty miles until they came to what is known as the Carson River.

On January 18, since the horses were in serious condition and it seemed to be impossible to find the Buenaventura River, Frémont decided to cross the Sierra Nevada Mountains in order to reach the Sacramento Valley by the most practical pass that could be discovered. From their camp on the Carson River, Frémont and his men struck out to find a way through the labyrinth of peaks and valleys. On the following day, January 19, Frémont and his men went up the Carson River, made a circuit around a small mountain, and camped that night on the same river near the site of present Fort Churchill. Continuing the next day up the same stream, they again camped close to the Pine Nut Range near modern Markleeville, California, in Antelope Valley. They proceeded through this valley and finally made camp on the East Walker River, just below the forks in Bridgeport Valley, which is approximately three or four miles below the present-day town of Bridgeport, California.

After wandering around in the Devils Gate area and making little or no progress, they secured a capable Indian guide. He led them north through Diamond Valley to the East Carson River and then on to Markleeville Creek. The group struggled up the mountains, trudging through heavy snow, and camped near Carson Pass. With Preuss, Frémont climbed the highest mountain and from its summit viewed for the first time Lake Tahoe.

On February 21, the group started down the mountains, following in a direction north-northwest along a ridge between the Silver Fork of the American River and Strawberry Creek, a tributary of the same river.[7] Frémont still believed in the existence of the Buenaventura River even though he had not found it, for he states:

We saw a shining line of water directing its course towards another, a broader and longer sheet. We knew that these could be no other than the Sacramento and the bay of San Francisco . . . . On the southern shore of what appeared to be the bay could be traced the gleaming line where entered another large stream; and again the Buenaventura rose up in our minds.[8]

After spending a number of days at Sutter's Fort recuperating, the little group resumed their journey. They left the fort on March 22 and headed for Walker's Pass in the southern portion of the Sierras. Going southward, they soon struck the Tuolumne River, and then on April 7 reached Kings River, the principal tributary of Tulare Lake. After crossing the Kern River, the expedition held a southeasterly course approximately on the line of the present Southern Pacific Railroad. While the party was encamped on Cottonwood Creek, an Indian rode into their camp and offered to guide them. He led them into the mountains and over a pass which is now known as Tehachapi Pass and is today utilized by the rails of the Atchison, Topeka and Santa Fe as well as the Southern Pacific Railroad. After leaving the mountains, they skirted the desert to the south, and on the afternoon of April 20 struck the Old Spanish Trail a few miles north of El Cajon Pass, through which it came from Los Angeles. They followed this trail, and on April 28 reached a large creek of salty and brackish water which probably was the Amargosa River of the Great Basin.

After spending the night of the thirtieth at a place now called Resting Springs, they pushed on until they reached water at the springs at Las Vegas. When several days had passed and the group had recovered sufficiently, they started on a sixteen-hour uninterrupted march to the Muddy River. On May 6, they crossed to the Virgin River and worked their way up this stream until two days

[7] Frederick S. Dellenbaugh, *Frémont and '49,* 192–99; 204–29.
[8] Frémont, *Report,* 236.

later they camped on Beaverdam Creek at the point where it enters the Virgin River. From this position, they struck northeast into the Beaverdam Mountains and camped for the night on the Santa Clara Branch of the Virgin River in what is now the very southwestern corner of the state of Utah. On May 16, the group left the Old Spanish Trail and moved north to reach the Sevier River on May 23 and Utah Lake on May 24.[9]

Frémont's encampment at Utah Lake is one of great significance in the history of the Great Basin as well as in the history of the entire West. It was here that Frémont made his pronouncement in regard to the Buenaventura River and the other apocryphal streams and thus struck a death blow to one of the most durable and provocative myths of western American history. Frémont said:

> In arriving at the Utah Lake, we had completed an immense circuit of twelve degrees diameter north and south and ten degrees east and west . . . . The rivers of the San Francisco bay, which are the largest after the Columbia, are local to the bay, and lateral to the coast, having their source about on a line with the Dalles of the Columbia, and running each in a valley of its own, between Coast range and the Cascade and Sierra Nevada range. The Columbia is the only river which traverses the whole breadth of the country, breaking through all the ranges, and entering the sea.[10]

He continued this discourse by stating:

> This fact in relation to the rivers of this region gives an immense value to the Columbia. Its mouth is the only inlet and outlet to and from the sea; its three forks lead to the passes in the mountains; it is therefore the only line of communication between the Pacific and the interior of North America.[11]

One of the most important maps in the history of western American cartography was the product of Frémont's Second Expedition. On this map Frémont included a significant legend concerning the Great Basin: "Diameter 11° of latitude, 10° of longitude: elevation above the sea between 4 and 5,000 feet: surrounded by lofty mountains:

[9] Dellenbaugh, *Frémont and '49*, 230–63. Hafen, *Old Spanish Trail*, 285–300.
[10] Frémont, *Report*, 274.
[11] *Ibid.*, 275.

contents almost unknown, but believed to be filled with rivers and lakes which have no connection with the sea."[12] Thus, while Frémont was encamped at Utah Lake on May 23, 1844, near the place where the Domínguez-Escalante party had stayed sixty-eight years before, he came to the conclusion that the vast interior between the Wasatch and the Sierra Nevada Mountains was a land of interior drainage, truly a "great basin," and he so named it.

This must have been a reluctant conclusion for Frémont to reach, since it demolished one of the most influential myths in American exploration. Frémont had believed in the San Buenaventura, so his father-in-law said; and, of course, Thomas Hart Benton believed in it, too. There was no stronger advocate of the water route to the Orient than Benton, and although his orientation followed Jefferson's up the Missouri, it did not rule out the possibility of another water passage, which Frémont had been commissioned to explore. However, both Benton and Frémont were quick to "embrace the new faith" and endeavored to help Americans appreciate the changes in climate and topography beyond the one hundredth meridian. Although the maps of Gallatin, Bonneville, and Burr, all published prior to 1840, reflected the discoveries of the fur trappers which hinted at an interior drainage basin, it was not until the Frémont Expedition, with its scientific basis and the support of the national government, that the people of the United States received their first comprehensive idea of the true nature of the area lying inland from the Pacific Coast; more specifically, the region lying between the great mountain barriers of the Wasatch and the Sierra Nevada chains.

Frémont's contributions to geographical knowledge cannot be measured by a mere recital of his discoveries, for it must be remembered that very little of his exploratory work was accomplished in regions not previously visited by civilized men; however, he will always be celebrated in the history of exploration as the first person to write an adequate and accurate account of the general physical features of the region between South Pass and the Pacific Ocean. As Allan Nevins aptly puts it, "He was not a 'Pathfinder'; he was a Pathmarker."[13]

[12] *Map of an Exploring Expedition to the Rocky Mountains in the Year 1842 and to Oregon and North California in the Years 1843–44,* Bancroft Library.
[13] *Frémont, the West's Greatest Adventurer,* II, 703.

Frémont's descriptions of the routes across the continent are comparable with Lewis and Clark's accounts of their northern trek to the Pacific Coast. His descriptive narrative of the best routes across the Great Basin and of the passes over the Sierra Nevada Mountains, combined with his glowing accounts of California, did much to stimulate emigration into that area. The descriptions show that Frémont was not only a great explorer; he was also a geographer with a real understanding of the concept of a region as a natural unit. Frémont's surveys of South Pass, the Great Salt Lake, the Humboldt River, and Donner Pass were all valuable additions to geographical knowledge. But his greatest scientific achievement was the discovery of the true nature of the Great Interior Basin of North America.

BIBLIOGRAPHY

MANUSCRIPTS

Applegate, Jessie. "Views of Oregon History." MS, Bancroft Library.

Barrett, I. M. "McKenzie, McDonald and Ross in the Snake River Country," unpublished M.A. thesis, Department of History, University of California, 1924.

Bates, Lana Louise. "Historical Geography of California, 1542–1835," unpublished M.A. thesis, Department of History, University of California, 1928.

Bidwell, John. "A Journey to California," MS, Bancroft Library.

———. "California, 1841–1848: An Immigrant's Recollections of a Trip across the Plains and of Men and Events in Early Days including the Bear Flag Revolution," MS, Bancroft Library.

Brereton, George. "Overland to California in 1841," unpublished M.A. thesis, Department of History, University of California, 1926.

Chiles, Joseph B. "Visit to California," MS, Bancroft Library.

Cutter, Donald C. "Moraga of the Military: His California Service, 1784–1810," unpublished M.A. thesis, Department of History, University of California, 1947.

Dalrymple, Alexander. "Plan for promoting the fur trade and securing it to this country by uniting the operations of the East India and Hudson's Bay companies," MS, Bancroft Library, 1789.

Davies, Jessie Hughes. "The Expedition of Peter Skene Ogden in the Snake River Region," unpublished M.A. thesis, Department of History, University of California, 1926.

Douglas, Sir James. "Journal of Sir James Douglas, 1840–41, Fort Vancouver and the Northwest Coast," MS, Archives of British Columbia.

Durán, Narciso. "Diario de la expedición de reconocimiento hecha en el mes de Mayo de 1817 por el Señor Comandante del real presidio de Nuestra Padre San Francisco, Teniente Don Luis Arguello, 1817," MS, Bancroft Library.

Edwards, Lyman Elmer. "Trail Making in the Great Basin since 1840," Berkeley, 1916, MS, Bancroft Library.

Elliott, T. C. "Folio of Letters," Oregon Historical Society, Portland, Oregon.

———. "Peter Skene Ogden," MS, Oregon Historical Society Collection.

Hudson's Bay Company Archives.
>   Of central importance were the following collections of documents:
>   B.223/b—Fort Vancouver Correspondence Books.
>   B.202/a—Snake Country Journals, of which B.202/a/8, Ogden's Snake Country Journal of 1828–29 was of chief significance.
>   B.202/a/1—Alexander Ross's Snake Country Journal of 1824.
>   B.202/a/9 and B.202/a/10—John Work's Snake Country Journals of 1830–31.
>   B.69/a—Flathead Post Journal.

Leader, Herman Alexander. "The Hudson's Bay Company in California," unpublished Ph.D. dissertation, Department of History, University of California, 1927.

Moraga, Gabriel. "Diario de la tercera expedición . . . a los rios del Norte . . . ," Sept. 25–Oct. 23, 1808, MS, Bancroft Library.

Morgan, Dale. Documents relating to the Missouri River . . . fur trade, 1818–32, selected by Dale Morgan from the Adjutant General's Office and Office of the Secretary of War in the National Archives, Microfilm, Bancroft Library.

New Mexico Archives Documents, 155 vols., Bancroft Library.

O'Neil, Marion. "The North West Company on the Pacific Slope," unpublished Ph.D. dissertation, Department of History, University of California, 1940.

Payeras, Mariano. "Noticia de las Misiones que ocupan los Religiosas de N.P.S. Francisco Misioneros Apost (olic)os del Colegio . . . de San Fernando de Mexico . . . 1815 y 1816 . . . ," MS, Bancroft Library.

Smith, Jedediah Strong. "Journal," Bancroft Library.

Snow, William James. "The Great Basin before the coming of the Mormons," unpublished Ph.D. dissertation, University of California, 1923.

Thompson, John Henry. "The Truckee and Carson Drainage Region," unpublished Ph.D. dissertation, Department of Geography, University of Washington, 1949.

Thompson, Louisa. "The Days of 1846: Recollections . . . ," MS, Bancroft Library.

U.S. Congress. 25 Cong., 2 sess., *Senate Bill 206.*

U.S. House of Representatives. 19 Cong., 1 sess., *Executive Document 117.*

U.S. Senate. 20 Cong., 2 sess., *Executive Document 67;* 33 Cong., 2 sess., *Executive Document 78.*

Wiley, Francis A. "Jedediah Smith in the West," unpublished Ph.D. dissertation, Department of History, University of California, 1941.

BOOKS

Alaskan Boundary Tribunal Atlas Accompanying the Case of the United States before the Tribunal convened at London. Washington, D.C., Gov't. Printing Office, 1903.

Alter, J. Cecil. *James Bridger, Trapper, Frontiersman, Scout, and Guide: A Historical Narrative.* Salt Lake City, Shepard Book Co., 1925.

Armand, Louis, Baron de Lahontan. *Memoirs of North America.* Vol. I in John A. Pinkerton (ed.), *A General Collection of . . . Voyages and Travels, q.v.*

Atwood, Wallace W. *The Physiographic Provinces of North America.* Boston, Ginn & Co., 1940.

Bancroft, Hubert Howe. *History of California, 1825–1840.* San Francisco, The History Co., 1886.

———. *History of California, 1840–1845.* San Francisco, The History Co., 1886.

———. *History of Nevada, Colorado, and Wyoming.* San Francisco, The History Co., 1890.

———. *History of the Northwest Coast.* 2 vols. San Francisco, The History Co., 1886.

———. *History of Oregon.* San Francisco, The History Co., 1886.

———. *History of Utah, 1540–1886.* San Francisco, The History Co., 1889.

———. *History of Washington, Idaho, and Montana.* San Francisco, The History Co., 1890.

Bandelier, Fanny, and Adolph Bandelier (eds.). *Journey of Alvar Núñez Cabeza de Vaca and His Companions from Florida to the Pacific, 1528–1536.* New York, A. S. Barnes & Co., 1905.

Barrow, John. *A Chronological History of Voyages into the Arctic Regions; undertaken chiefly for the purpose of discovering a Northeast, Northwest, or Polar Passage between the Atlantic and the Pacific . . . .* 3 vols. London, J. Knox, 1765.

——— (ed.). *The Life, Voyages, and Exploits of Sir Francis Drake.* London, J. Murray, 1843.

Bartlett, Richard A. *Great Surveys of the American West.* Norman, University of Oklahoma Press, 1962.

Beazley, Sir Charles Raymond. *The Dawn of Modern Geography.* 3 vols. London, H. Froude, 1905–1906.

Beckwith, Edward Griffin. *Report of Exploration of a Route for the Pacific Railroad, near the 38th and 39th parallel of latitude from the mouth of the Kansas to Sevier River in the Great Basin.* Washington, D.C., Gov't. Printing Office, 1855.

Beckwourth, James P. *The Life and Adventures of James P. Beckwourth.* New York, Harper & Bros., 1856; ed. by T. D. Bonner, Los Angeles, U. S. Library Association, 1932.

Benton, Thomas Hart. *Thirty Years' View.* 2 vols. New York, D. Appleton & Co.; Boston, F. Parker, 1854–56.

Biggar, Henry Percival (ed.). *A Collection of Documents relating to Jacques Cartier and Sieur de Roberval.* Ottawa, Public Archives of Canada, 1930.

———— (ed.). *The Precursors of Jacques Cartier, 1497–1534: A Collection of Documents Relating to the Early History of the Dominion of Canada.* Ottawa, Gov't. Printing Bureau, 1911.

———— (ed.). *The Voyages of the Cabots and of the Corte-Reals to North America and Greenland, 1497–1503.* Paris, Macon, Protat frères, 1903.

Blackwelder, Eliot.*The Great Basin, with Emphasis on Glacial and Postglacial Times.* Salt Lake City, University of Utah Press, 1948.

Bolton, Herbert Eugene. *Anza's California Expeditions.* 5 vols. Berkeley, University of California Press, 1930. Vol. I was published separately as *Outpost of Empire.* New York, Alfred A. Knopf, 1939.

————. *Coronado on the Turquoise Trail: Knight of Pueblos and Plains.* Albuquerque, University of New Mexico Press, 1949.

————. *The Early Explorations of Father Garcés on the Pacific Slope.* New York, Macmillan, 1917.

————. *Spanish Borderlands.* New Haven, Yale University Press, 1921.

————. *Spanish Exploration in the Southwest, 1542–1706.* New York, Scribner's, 1925.

———— (trans. and ed.). *Pageant in the Wilderness: The Story of the Escalante Expedition to the Interior Basin, 1776.* Salt Lake City: Utah Historical Society, 1950.

Bourne, Edward Gaylord. *Spain in America, 1450–1580.* New York, Harper & Bros., 1904.

Brimlow, George F. *Harney County, Oregon, and Its Range Land.* Portland, Oregon, Binfords & Mort, 1951.

Bryce, George. *Remarkable History of the Hudson's Bay Company,*

Including That of the French Traders of N. W. Canada and of the N. W., X. Y., and Astor Fur Companies. London, S. Low, Marston & Co., Ltd., 1910.

Bunnell, L. H. *The Discovery of Yosemite.* Chicago, F. H. Revell, 1880.

Burpee, Lawrence J. *An Historical Atlas of Canada.* Toronto & New York, Thomas Nelson & Sons, Ltd., 1927.

———. *The Search for the Western Sea.* London, Alston Rivers, Ltd., 1908.

Cartografía del Ultramar. 2 vols. Seville, Spain, Servicious Geográfico e Histórico del ejército, 1957.

Carvalho, S. N. *Incidents of Travel and Adventure in the Far West with Colonel Frémont's Last Expedition.* New York, Derby & Jackson, 1857.

Carver, Jonathan. *Travels through the Interior Parts of North America in the Years 1766, 1767, and 1768.* London, printed for the author and sold by J. Walter, 1778.

Chapman, Charles Edward. *The Founding of Spanish California.* New York, Macmillan, 1916.

———. *History of California: The Spanish Period.* New York, Macmillan, 1921.

Chittenden, Hiram Martin. *The American Fur Trade of the Far West.* 3 vols. New York, F. P. Harper, 1902.

Clark, Dan Elbert. *The West in American History.* New York, Thos. Y. Crowell Co., 1937.

Cleland, Robert Glass. *From Wilderness to Empire: A History of California, 1542–1900.* New York, Alfred A. Knopf, 1947.

———. *Pathfinders.* Los Angeles & San Francisco, Powell Pub. Co., 1929.

———. *This Reckless Breed of Men.* New York, Alfred A. Knopf, 1950.

Clyman, James. *James Clyman, American Frontiersman, 1792–1881.* Ed. by Charles L. Camp. San Francisco, California Historical Society, 1928.

Cook, Captain James. *A Voyage to the Pacific Ocean. Undertaken by the Command of His Majesty, for Making Discoveries in the Northern Hemisphere . . . in the Years 1776, 1777, 1778, 1779, and 1780.* 3 vols., London, W. & A. Strahan for G. Nicol & T. Cadell, 1784.

Costanso, Miguel. *The Narrative of the Portolà Expedition of 1769–1770.* Ed. by Frederick J. Teggart and Adolph van Hemert-Engert. Berkeley, University of California Press, 1910.

Coues, Elliott (ed.). *Forty Years a Fur Trapper on the Upper Missouri.* 2 vols. New York, F. P. Harper, 1898.

——, and H. C. Yarrow. *Report upon the Collections of Mammals made in portions of Nevada, Utah, California, Colorado, New Mexico, and Arizona* . . . . In Vol. V of *U.S. Geological Surveys West of the 100th Meridian.* Washington, D.C., Gov't. Printing Office, 1875.

Cox, Ross. *Adventures on the Columbia River.* London, H. Colburn & R. Bentley, 1831. A more recent edition, ed. by Edgar I. and Jane R. Stewart, Norman, University of Oklahoma Press, 1957.

Crespi, Fray Juan. *Fray Juan Crespi, Missionary-Explorer on the Pacific Coast, 1769–1774.* Trans. and ed. by Herbert Eugene Bolton. Berkeley, University of California Press, 1927.

Crouse, Nellis M. *In Quest of the Western Ocean.* New York, W. Morrow & Co., 1928.

——. *La Vérendrye, Fur Trader and Explorer.* Ithaca, Cornell University Press, 1956.

——. *The Search for the Northwest Passage.* New York, Columbia University Press, 1934.

Dale, Harrison Clifford. *The Ashley-Smith Explorations and the Discovery of a Central Route to the Pacific, 1822–1829.* Cleveland, Arthur H. Clark, 1918.

Davidson, Gordon Charles. *The North West Company.* Berkeley, University of California Press, 1918.

Dellenbaugh, Frederick S. *Frémont and '49.* New York, G. P. Putnam & Sons, 1914.

De Smet, Pierre Jean. *Letters and Sketches, with a Narrative of a Year's Residence among the Indian Tribes of the Rocky Mountains.* Philadelphia, M. Fithian, 1843.

De Voto, Bernard. *The Course of Empire.* Boston, Houghton Mifflin, 1952.

Dobbs, Arthur. *An Account of the Countries adjoining Hudson's Bay* . . . . London, printed for J. Robinson, 1744.

Espejo, Antonio de. *Expedition into New Mexico Made by Antonio de Espejo, 1582–1583.* Trans. and ed. by George P. Hammond, Agapito Rey, and Diego Pérez de Luxán. Los Angeles, Quivira Society, 1929.

Fages, Pedro. *Expedition to San Francisco Bay in 1770: Diary of Pedro Fages.* Ed. by Herbert Eugene Bolton. *Publications* of the Academy of Pacific Coast History. Berkeley, University of California Press, 1911.

——. *A Historical, Political, and Natural Description of Cali-*

fornia. Trans. and ed. by Herbert I. Priestley. Berkeley, University of California Press, 1937.

Farquhar, Francis P. *Exploration of the Sierra Nevada.* San Francisco, California Historical Society, 1925.

Favour, Alpheus H. *Old Bill Williams, Mountain Man.* Chapel Hill, University of North Carolina Press, 1936.

Fernández Dura, Cesareo. *Don Diego de Peñalosa y su descubrimiento del reino de Quivira.* Madrid, Manuel Tello, 1882.

Ferris, Warren Angus. *Life in the Rocky Mountains, 1830–1835.* Ed. by Herbert S. Auerbach. Salt Lake City, Rocky Mountain Book Shop, 1940.

Fischer, Jos., and Wieser, R. V. (eds.). *Die Alteste Karte mit dem Namen Amerika aus dem Jahre 1507 und die Carta Marina aus dem Jahre 1516 des M. Waldseemüller.* Innsbruck, Wagner'sche Universitats-Buchhandlung, 1903.

Fleming, R. Harvey (ed.). *Minutes of Council, Northern Department of Rupert Land, 1821–31.* Toronto, Champlain Society, 1940.

Fletcher, F. N. *Early Nevada: The Period of Exploration, 1776–1848.* Reno, A. Carlisle & Co., 1929.

Flint, Richard Foster. *Glacial Geology and the Pleistocene Epoch.* New York, John Wiley & Sons, Inc., 1947.

Font, Pedro. *The Anza Expedition of 1775–1776: The Diary of Pedro Font.* Ed. by Frederick Teggart. *Publications* of the Academy of Pacific Coast History. Berkeley, University of California Press, 1913.

———. *Font's Complete Diary: A Chronicle of the Founding of San Francisco.* Trans. and ed. by Herbert Eugene Bolton. Vol. III of *Anza's California Expeditions.* Berkeley, University of California Press, 1931.

Franchère, Gabriel. *Narrative of a Voyage to the Northwest Coast of America in the Years 1811, 1812, 1813, and 1814 . . . .* Trans. and ed. by J. V. Huntington. New York, Redfield, 1854. Also volume VI in Thwaites' *Early Western Travels, q.v.*

Forbes, Jack D. *Apache, Navaho, and Spaniard.* Norman, University of Oklahoma Press, 1960.

Frémont, John Charles. *Geographical Memoir upon Upper California in Illustration of His Map of Oregon and Caifornia.* 30 Cong., 1 sess., *Senate Misc. Doc. 148,* (1848).

———. *Memoirs of My Life.* New York, Belford, Clarke & Co., 1887.

———. *Report of the Exploring Expedition to the Rocky Mountains in the Year 1842, and to Oregon and North California in the Years 1843–44.* 28 Cong., 2 sess., *House Exec. Doc. 166* (1845).

223

Freytas, Nicholas de. *Expedition of Don Diego Dionisio de Peñalosa.* New York, J. G. Shea, 1882.

Galbraith, John S. *The Hudson's Bay Company as an Imperial Factor, 1821–1869.* Berkeley and Los Angeles, University of California Press, 1957.

Garcés, Francisco. *On the Trail of a Spanish Pioneer: The Diary and Itinerary of Francisco Garcés.* Ed. by Elliott Coues. 2 vols. New York, F. P. Harper, 1900.

Gates, Charles M. (ed.). *Five Fur Traders of the Northwest.* Minneapolis, University of Minnesota Press, 1933. Pub. for the Minn. Society of the Colonial Dames of America.

Ghent, W. J. *The Road to Oregon.* London and New York, Longmans, Green & Co., 1929.

Gilbert, Edmund William. *The Exploration of Western America, 1800–1850.* Cambridge, Eng., Cambridge University Press. 1933.

Gilbert, Grove Karl. *Lake Bonneville.* Washington, D.C., Gov't. Printing Office, 1890.

Greenhow, Robert. *Geography of Oregon and California and the Other Territories on the North-West Coast of North America.* New York, M. H. Newman, 1845.

———. *History of Oregon and California.* London, John Murray, 1844.

———. *Memoir, Historical and Political, on the Northwest Coast of North America and the Adjacent Territories.* New York and London, Wiley & Putnam, 1840.

Gregg, Josiah. *Commerce of the Prairies: The Journal of a Santa Fe Trader during Eight Expeditions across the Great Western Prairies and a Residence of Nearly Nine Years in Northern Mexico . . . .* 2 vols. New York, H. G. Langley, 1844. A recent one-volume edition has been edited by Max L. Moorhead, University of Oklahoma Press, 1954.

Hackett, Charles Wilson (ed.). *Historical Documents Relating to New Mexico, Nueva Vizcaya, and Approaches Thereto to 1773, Collected by Adolph F. A. Bandelier and Fanny A. Bandelier.* 3 vols. Washington, Carnegie Institution, 1923–37.

Hafen, LeRoy, and W. J. Ghent. *Broken Hand: The Life Story of Thomas Fitzpatrick.* Denver, Old West Publishing Co., 1931.

Hafen, LeRoy R., and Ann W. Hafen. *The Old Spanish Trail.* Glendale, Arthur H. Clark, 1954.

——— (eds.). *To the Rockies and Oregon, 1839–1842.* Glendale, Arthur H. Clark, 1955.

Hafen, LeRoy, and Carl Coke Rister. *Western America.* New York, Prentice-Hall, 1941.

Hakluyt, Richard. *Divers Voyages Touching the Discovery of America and the Islands Adjacent.* London, Hakluyt Society, 1850.

———. *The Original Writings and Correspondence of the Two Richard Hakluyts.* Ed. by E. G. R. Taylor. London, Hakluyt Society, 1935.

———. *The Principal Navigations, Voiages, Traffiques, and Discoveries of the English Nation.* 8 vols. New York, E. P. Dutton & Co., 1907.

Hammond, George P., and Agapito Rey (eds.). *Don Juan de Oñate, Colonizer of New Mexico.* 2 vols. Albuquerque, University of New Mexico Press, 1953.

Hastings, Lansford. *Emigrants' Guide to Oregon and California.* Cincinnati, G. Conclin, 1845.

Heawood, Edward. *A History of Geographical Discovery in the Seventeenth and Eighteenth Centuries.* Cambridge, Cambridge University Press, 1912.

Henry, Alexander. *New Light on the Early History of the Greater Northwest.* Ed. by Elliott Coues. 3 vols. New York, F. P. Harper, 1897.

Heylyn, Peter. *Cosmography in 4 books containing the chorography and history of the whole world . . . improved with an historical continuation to the present times . . . .* London, printed for E. Brewster, R. Chiswell, B. Tooke, T. Hodgkin, & T. Bennet, 1703.

Hill, Joseph J. *Ewing Young in the Fur Trade of the Far Southwest, 1822–1834.* Eugene, Oregon, Koke-Tiffany Co., 1923.

———. *The History of Warner's Ranch and Its Environs.* Los Angeles, Young & McCallister, 1927.

Hines, Rev. H. K. *An Illustrated History of the State of Oregon.* Chicago, Lewis Publishing Co., 1883.

Hodge, Frederick Webb. *Handbook of American Indians North of Mexico.* 2 vols. Bureau of American Ethnology *Bulletin No. 30.* Washington, 1907–10.

———, and Theodore Lewis (eds.). *Spanish Explorers in the Southern United States, 1528–1542.* New York, Scribner's, 1907.

Hopkins, Sarah Winnemucca. *My Life among the Paiutes.* New York, G. P. Putnam's, 1883.

Huish, Robert (ed.). *A Narrative of the Voyages and Travels of Captain Beechey . . . to the Pacific and Behring's Straits . . . .* London, W. Wright, 1836.

Humboldt, Alexander von. *Political Essay on the Kingdom of New Spain.* Trans. by J. Black. 4 vols. London, Longman, Hurst, Rees, Orme, & Brown, 1811.

———. *Voyage aux regions equinoxiales du Nouveau Continent*

fait en 1799–1804 par Alexandre de Humboldt et Aimé Bonpland.
12 vols. Paris, la Librairie Grècque-Latine-Allemande, 1805–26.

Humphreys, Brigadier General A. A. *Preliminary Report Concerning Explorations and Surveys Principally in Nevada and Arizona.* Washington, Gov't. Printing Office, 1872.

Hunt, Rockwell D. *John Bidwell: A Prince of California Pioneers.* Caldwell, Idaho, Caxton, 1942.

Hussey, John A. *The History of Fort Vancouver and Its Physical Structure.* Portland, Oregon, Abbot, Kerns & Bell, 1957.

Innis, Harold A. *The Fur Trade in Canada.* New Haven, Yale University Press, 1930.

Irving, Washington. *The Adventures of Captain Bonneville, U.S.A., in the Rocky Mountains and the Far West.* New York, G. P. Putnam, 1868.

———. *Astoria.* New York, G. P. Putnam, 1849.

James, Edwin. *Account of S. H. Long's Expedition from Pittsburgh to the Rocky Mountains . . . 1819 and '20.* Vols. XIV–XVII of Thwaites' *Early Western Travels, q.v.*

Jefferson, Thomas. *Writings of Thomas Jefferson.* Ed. by H. A. Washington. 9 vols. Washington, Taylor & Maury, 1853–54.

Jesuit Relations and Allied Documents. 73 vols. Ed. by Reuben Gold Thwaites. Cleveland, Burrows Bros., 1896–1901.

Jesuit Relations. Ed. by Edna Kenton. New York, Vanguard Press, 1954.

Johansen, Dorothy O., and Charles Gates. *Empire of the Columbia.* New York, Harper & Bros., 1957.

Kelly, Charles. *Old Greenwood: The Story of Caleb Greenwood, Trapper, Pathfinder, and Early Pioneer of the West.* Salt Lake City, Western Printing Co., 1936.

———. *Salt Desert Trails.* Salt Lake City, Western Publishing Co., 1930.

King, Clarence (ed.). *Report of the Geological Exploration of the Fortieth Parallel.* 7 vols. Washington, Gov't. Printing Office, 1877–80.

Kino, Eusebio Francisco. *Kino's Historical Memoir of Pimeria Alta.* Trans. and ed. by Herbert Eugene Bolton. Berkeley, University of California Press, 1948.

Kroeber, Alfred L. *The Washo Language of East Central California and Nevada.* Berkeley, University of California Press, 1907.

Langsdorff, Georg Heinrich von. *Voyages and Travels in Various Parts of the World During the Years 1803, 1804, 1805, 1806, and 1807.* 2 vols. London, Henry Colburn, 1813–14.

Larocque, François Antoine. *Journal de Larocque de la rivière As-*

siniboine jûsqu'à la rivière "Aux Roche Jaunes." Ed. by Lawrence J. Burpee. Ottawa, Public Archives of Canada, 1911.

La Tourette, Kenneth S. *The History of Early Relations between the United States and China, 1784–1844.* New Haven, Yale University Press, 1917.

Leonard, Zenas. *Narrative of the Adventures of Zenas Leonard.* Ed. by Milo Milton Quaife. Chicago, R. R. Donnelley, 1934.

Lewis, Meriwether, and William Clark. *The Journals of Lewis and Clark.* Ed. by Elliott Coues. 4 vols. New York, F. P. Harper, 1893. Ed. by Reuben Gold Thwaites, 8 vols., New York, 1904–1905. Ed. by Bernard De Voto, Boston, Houghton Mifflin, 1953.

Loud, Llewellyn L., and M. R. Harrington. *Lovelock Cave.* Berkeley, University of California Press, 1929.

Lowie, Robert H. *Ethnographic Notes on the Washo.* Berkeley, University of California Press, 1939.

Lyman, George D. *Dr. John Marsh, Pioneer.* New York, Scribner's, 1930.

McGlashan, Charles F. *History of the Donner Party: A Tragedy of the Sierras.* Truckee, Calif., Crawley & McGlashan, 1879.

MacKay, Douglas. *The Honourable Company.* London, Cassell, 1937.

Mackenzie, Alexander. *Voyage from Montreal, on the River St. Lawrence, through the Continent of North America, to the Frozen and Pacific Oceans; in the Years 1789 and 1793 . . . .* 2 vols. Philadelphia, John Morgan & R. Carr, 1802.

Mackenzie, Cecil W. *Donald Mackenzie, King of the Northwest.* Los Angeles, I. Deach, Jr., 1937.

McLoughlin, John. *The Letters of John McLoughlin from Fort Vancouver to the Governor and Committee, First Series, 1825–38.* Ed. by E. E. Rich. *Publications* of the Hudson's Bay Record Society, IV. London, 1941.

——. *The Letters of John McLoughlin from Fort Vancouver to the Governor and Committee, Second Series, 1839–1844.* Ed. by E. E. Rich. *Publications* of the Hudson's Bay Record Society, V. London, 1944.

——. *The Letters of John McLoughlin.* Ed. by Burt B. Barker. Portland, Oregon, Binfords & Mort for the Oregon Historical Society, 1948.

Madsen, Brigham. *The Bannock of Idaho.* Caldwell, Idaho, Caxton, 1958.

Malloy, W. M., C. F. Redmond, and E. J. Treworth (eds.). *Treaties, Conventions, International Acts, Protocols, and Agreements between the United States and Other Powers, 1776–1937.* 4 vols. Washington, Gov't. Printing Office, 1910–38.

227

Maloney, Alice Bay (ed.). *Fur Brigade to the Bonaventura.* San Francisco, California Historical Society, 1945.

Marco Polo. *The Book of Ser Marco Polo, the Venetian, Concerning the Kingdoms and Marvels of the East.* Trans. and ed. by Colonel Henry Yule. 2 vols. London, J. Murray, 1871.

Merk, Frederick. *Albert Gallatin and the Oregon Problem.* Cambridge, Harvard University Press, 1950.

Merriam, C. Hart. *The Death Valley Expedition.* Washington, Gov't. Printing Office, 1893.

Michaud, E. (ed.). *Biographia Universelle, Ancienne et Moderne.* 52 vols. Paris, Michaud Frères, 1811–62.

Miller, David Hunter. *Treaties and Other International Acts of the United States.* 8 vols. Washington, Gov't. Printing Office, 1931–48.

Moraga, Gabriel. *The Diary of Ensign Gabriel Morago's Expedition of Discovery in the Sacramento Valley, 1808.* Trans. and ed. by Donald C. Cutter. Los Angeles, Glen Dawson, 1957.

Morgan, Dale L. *The Humboldt, Highroad of the West.* New York and Toronto, Farrar & Rinehart, 1943.

———. *Jedediah Smith and the Opening of the West.* Indianapolis, Bobbs-Merrill Co., 1953.

———. *The Great Salt Lake.* Indianapolis and New York, Bobbs-Merrill Co., 1947.

———, and Carl I. Wheat. *Jedediah Smith and His Maps of the American West.* San Francisco, California Historical Society, 1954.

Muir, John. *The Mountains of California.* New York, The Century Co., 1894.

Nasatir, A. P. (ed.). *Before Lewis and Clark; Documents Illustrating the History of the Missouri, 1785–1804.* 2 vols. St. Louis, St. Louis Historical Documents Foundation, 1952.

Nevins, Allan. *Frémont, the West's Greatest Adventurer.* New York and London, Harper & Bros., 1928.

Newell, Robert. *Robert Newell's Memoranda.* Ed. by Dorothy O. Johansen. Portland, Oregon, Champoeg Press, 1959.

Nidever, George. *The Life and Adventures of George Nidever.* Ed. by William Henry Ellison. Berkeley, University of California Press, 1937.

Nordenskiold, Nils Adolf Erik. *The Voyage of the Vega round Asia and Europe.* New York, Macmillan, 1882.

Nunis, Doyce Blackman. *Andrew Sublette, Rocky Mountain Prince.* Los Angeles, Dawson's Book Shop, 1960.

Nuttall, Zelia (ed.). *New Light on Drake: A Collection of Documents Relating to His Voyage of Circumnavigation, 1577–1580.* London, Hakluyt Society, 1914.

Ogden, Peter Skene. *Peter Skene Ogden's Snake Country Journals, 1824–25 and 1825–26.* Ed. by E. E. Rich and A. M. Johnson. With an introduction by W. Kaye Lamb. *Publications* of the Hudson's Bay Record Society, XIII. London, 1950.

———. *Peter Skene Ogden's Snake Country Journal, 1826–27.* Ed. by K. G. Davies and A. M. Johnson. *Publications* of the Hudson's Bay Record Society, XXIII. London, 1961.

Paden, Irene D. *Prairie Schooner Detours.* New York, Macmillan, 1949.

———. *The Wake of the Prairie Schooner.* New York, Macmillan, 1943.

Palou, Francisco. *Historical Memoirs of New California.* Trans. and ed. by Herbert E. Bolton. 4 vols. Berkeley, University of California Press, 1926.

Parks, George Bruner. *Richard Hakluyt and the English Voyages.* New York, American Geographic Society, 1928.

Pattie, James Ohio. *The Personal Narrative of James Ohio Pattie . . . .* Cincinnati, John H. Wood, 1831.

Paullin, Charles O., and John K. Wright. *Atlas of the Historical Geography of the United States.* Washington, Carnegie Institution, 1932.

Penrose, Boies. *Travel and Discovery in the Renaissance.* Cambridge, Harvard University Press, 1952.

Phillips, Paul Chrisler. *The Fur Trade.* With concluding chapters by J. W. Smurr. 2 vols. Norman, University of Oklahoma Press, 1961.

Pike, Zebulon. *Account of an Expedition to the Sources of the Mississippi and through the western parts of Louisiana . . . and a Tour through the Interior Parts of New Spain.* Ed. by Elliott Coues. 3 vols. New York, F. P. Harper, 1895.

———. *The Expeditions of Zebulon Montgomery Pike to the Headwaters of the Mississippi River, through Louisiana Territory, and in New Spain, During the Years 1805–6–7.* Ed. by Elliott Coues. 3 vols. New York, F. P. Harper, 1895.

Pinkerton, John, ed. *A General Collection of the Best and Most Interesting Voyages and Travels in All Parts of the World.* 17 vols. London, Longman, Hurst, Rees, & Orme, 1808–14.

Powell, John Wesley. *Exploration of the Colorado River of the West and Its Tributaries. Explored in 1869, 1870, 1871, and 1872 under the Direction of the Secretary of the Smithsonian Institution.* Washington, Gov't. Printing Office, 1875.

———, and G. W. Ingalls. *Report of the Special Commissioners on the Condition of the Ute Indians of Utah; the Pai-utes of Utah,*

Northern Arizona, Southern Nevada, and South-eastern California . . . . Washington, Gov't. Printing Office, 1877.

Powers, Stephen. *Tribes of California.* Washington, Gov't Printing Office, 1877.

Preuss, Charles. *Exploring with Frémont: The Private Diaries of Charles Preuss* . . . . Trans. and ed. by Erwin G. and Elisabeth K. Gudde. Norman, University of Oklahoma Press, 1958.

Priestley, Herbert I. *Franciscan Explorations in California.* Ed. by Lillian E. Fisher. Glendale, Arthur H. Clark, 1946.

Purchas, Samuel. *Hakluytus Posthumus; or Purchas, His Pilgrimes.* 4 vols. London, W. Stansby for H. Fetherstone, 1625.

Rich, E. E. *Hudson's Bay Company, 1670–1870.* 3 vols. New York, Macmillan, 1961.

Richman, Irving B. *California under Spain and Mexico, 1535–1847.* Boston and New York, Houghton Mifflin, 1911.

Roe, Frank Gilbert. *The Indian and the Horse.* Norman, University of Oklahoma Press, 1955.

———. *The North American Buffalo.* Toronto, University of Toronto Press, 1951.

Ross, Alexander. *Adventures of the First Settlers on the Oregon and Columbia Rivers.* London, Smith, Elder & Co., 1849.

———. *The Fur Hunters of the Far West: A Narrative of Adventures in the Oregon and Rocky Mountains.* 2 vols. London, Smith, Elder, & Co., 1855. A more recent edition has been edited by Kenneth A. Spaulding, University of Oklahoma Press, 1956.

Rundall, Thomas (ed.). *Narratives of Voyages towards the Northwest in Search of a Passage to Cathay and India; 1496 to 1631, with Selections from the Early Records of the Honourable East India Company and Mss. in the British Museum.* London, Hakluyt Society, 1849.

Russell, Israel Cook. *Geological History of Lake Lahontan.* Washington, Gov't. Printing Office, 1885.

Russell, Robert R. *Improvement of Communication with the Pacific Coast as an Issue in American Politics, 1783–1864.* Cedar Rapids, Iowa, Torch Press, 1948.

Sauer, Carl. *The Road to Cibola.* Berkeley, University of California Press, 1932.

Scrugham, James G. *Nevada.* 3 vols. Chicago and New York, American Historical Society, 1935.

Simpson, Sir George. *Fur Trade and Empire: The Journal of Sir George Simpson.* Ed. by Frederick Merk. Cambridge, Harvard University Press, 1931.

———. *Simpson's 1828 Journey to the Columbia.* Ed. by E. E. Rich and A. M. Johnson. *Publications* of the Hudson's Bay Record Society, X. London, 1947.

Simpson, James. *Report of Explorations across the Great Basin of the Territory of Utah for a Direct Wagon-Route from Camp Floyd to Genoa in Carson Valley in 1859.* Washington, Gov't. Printing Office, 1876.

Spurr, Josiah Edward. *Nevada South of the Fortieth Parallel and Adjacent Portions of California.* Washington, Gov't. Printing Office, 1903.

Stansbury, Howard. *Exploration and Survey of the Valley of the Great Salt Lake of Utah* . . . . Philadelphia, Lippincott, Grambo & Co., 1852.

Steward, Julian Haynes. *Basin-Plateau Aboriginal Socio-political Groups.* Washington, Smithsonian Institution, 1938.

———. *Nevada Shoshone.* Berkeley, University of California Press, 1941.

———. *Northern and Gosiute Shoshoni.* Berkeley, University of California Press, 1943.

Stewart, Omer Call. *Northern Paiute.* Berkeley, University of California Press, 1941.

———. *Ute–Southern Paiute.* Berkeley, University of California Press, 1942.

Stuart, Robert. *The Discovery of the Oregon Trail: Robert Stuart's Narratives.* Ed. by Philip Ashton Rollins. London and New York, Scribner's, 1935.

Sullivan, Maurice. *Jedediah Smith, Trader and Trail Breaker.* Santa Ana, Calif., Fine Arts Press, 1934.

Sunder, David E. *Bill Sublette, Mountain Man.* Norman, University of Oklahoma Press, 1959.

Tabeau, Pierre-Antoine. *Tabeau's Narrative of Loisel's Expedition to the Upper Missouri.* Trans. and ed. by Annie Heloise Abel. Norman, University of Oklahoma Press, 1939.

Talbot, Theodore. *The Journals of Theodore Talbot, 1843 and 1849–52.* Ed. by Charles H. Carey. Portland, Oregon, Metropolitan Press, 1931.

Taylor, E. G. R. *Late Tudor and Early Stuart Geography, 1583–1650.* London, Methuen & Co., 1934.

———. *Tudor Geography, 1485–1583.* London, Methuen & Co., 1930.

Thompson, David. *David Thompson's Narrative of Explorations in Western America, 1783–1812.* Ed. by Joseph Burr Tyrell. Toronto, University of Toronto Press, 1916.

Thomas, Alfred B. *After Coronado.* Norman, University of Oklahoma Press, 1935.

Thwaites, Reuben Gold (ed.). *Early Western Travels, 1748–1846.* 32 vols. Cleveland, Arthur H. Clark, 1904–1907.

Twitchell, Ralph Emerson (comp.). *The Spanish Archives of New Mexico.* Cedar Rapids, Iowa, Torch Press, 1914.

Tyrell, Joseph Burr. *A Brief Narrative of the Journeys of David Thompson in Northwestern America.* Toronto, University of Toronto Press, 1888.

Vancouver, George. *A Voyage of Discovery to the North Pacific Ocean, and round the World . . . Performed in the Years 1790, 1791, 1792, 1793, 1794, and 1795.* 3 vols. London, G. G. & J. Robinson & J. Edwards, 1798.

Venegas, Miguel, *Noticia de la California y de su Conquista temporal y espiritual hasta el tiempo presente.* 3 vols. Ed. by Andrés Marcos Burriel. Mexico City, Álvarez y Álvarez de la Cadeña, 1943–44.

Victor, Francis Fuller. *The River of the West.* San Francisco, R. J. Trumbull & Co., 1870.

Wagner, Henry Raup. *The Cartography of the Northwest Coast of America to the Year 1800.* 2 vols. Berkeley, University of California Press, 1937.

———. *Sir Francis Drake's Voyage around the World: Its Aims and Achievements.* San Francisco, John Howell, 1926.

Wallace, W. Stewart (ed.). *Documents Relating to the North West Company.* Toronto, Champlain Society, 1934.

Wallace, William Swilling. *Antoine Robidoux, 1794–1860: A Biography of a Western Venturer.* Los Angeles, Glen Dawson, 1953.

Waring, Gerald A. *United States Geological Survey, Water Supply Paper 231.* Washington, Gov't Printing Office, 1909.

Watson, Douglas Sloane. *West Wind: The Life Story of Joseph Reddeford Walker, Knight of the Golden Horseshoe.* Los Angeles, privately printed for friends by P. H. Booth, 1934.

Weld, Charles Richard. *History of the Royal Society.* 2 vols. London, J. W. Parker, 1848.

Wheat, Carl I. *Mapping the American West, 1540–1857, a Preliminary Study.* Worcester, Mass., American Antiquarian Society, 1954.

———. *Mapping the Trans-Mississippi West, 1540–1861.* 3 vols. San Francisco, Institute of Historical Cartography, 1957–58.

Wheeler, George M. *Preliminary Report Concerning Explorations and Surveys Principally in Nevada and Arizona.* Washington, Gov't. Printing Office, 1872.

Wilkes, Charles. *Narrative of the United States Expedition During the Years 1838, 1839, 1840, 1841, and 1842.* 5 vols. Philadelphia, C. Sherman, 1844.

Williamson, James A. *The Ocean in English History.* Oxford, Clarendon Press, 1941.

Willson, Beckles. *The Great Company.* New York: Dodd, Mead & Co., 1900.

Winship, George Parker (trans. and ed.). *The Journey of Coronado, 1540–1542.* New York, Allerton Book Co., 1922.

Winsor, Justin (ed.). *Narrative and Critical History of America.* 8 vols. New York and Boston, Houghton Mifflin, 1884–89.

Work, John. *The Journal of John Work.* Ed. by William S. Lewis and Paul C. Phillips. Cleveland, Arthur H. Clark, 1923.

ARTICLES AND ESSAYS IN PERIODICALS, ANNUALS, ETC.

Alter, J. Cecil. "Father Escalante's Map," *Utah Historical Quarterly,* Vol. IX (Jan., April, 1941), 64–72.

———. "W. A. Ferris in Utah," *Utah Historical Quarterly,* Vol. IX (Jan., April, 1941), 81–108.

Antevs, Ernst. "On the Pleistocene History of the Great Basin," *Quaternary Climates.* Washington, Carnegie Institution of Washington, 1925.

Applegate, Jesse. "A Day with the Cow Column in 1843," *Oregon Historical Quarterly,* Vol. I (Dec., 1900), 371–83.

Atkin, W. T. "Snake River Fur Trade, 1816–24," *Oregon Historical Quarterly,* Vol. XXXV (Dec., 1934), 295–312.

Auerbach, Herbert E. "Father Escalante's Route," *Utah Historical Quarterly,* Vol. IX (July, Oct., 1941), 109–28; Vol. XI (Jan., April, July, Oct., 1943), 1–132.

———. "Old Trails, Old Forts, Old Trappers and Traders," *Utah Historical Quarterly,* Vol. IX (Jan., April, 1941), 13–63.

Barrett, S. A. "The Washo Indians," *Publications* of the Museum of the City of Milwaukee, Bull. 2, No. 1 (1910).

Barrows, Henry Dwight. "William Wolfskill, the Pioneer," *Southern California Historical Quarterly,* Vol. V (Dec., 1903), 287–94.

Beattie, George William. "Reopening the Anza Road," *Pacific Historical Review,* Vol. II (March, 1933), 52–71.

Bidwell, John. "Address of John Bidwell to Society of California Pioneers in 1897," *Quarterly of the Society of California Pioneers,* Vol. III (March, 1926), 9–45.

———. "The First Emigrant Train to California," *The Century Magazine,* Vol. XLI (Nov., 1890), 106–30.

Bolton, Herbert Eugene. "Escalante in Dixie and the Arizona Strip," *New Mexico Historical Review,* Vol. III (Jan., 1928), 41–72.

————. "New Light on Manuel Lisa and the Spanish Fur Trade," *Texas Historical Quarterly,* Vol. XVII (July, 1913), 61–66.

Bonneville, General B. L. E. "Documents of General B. L. E. Bonneville," *Washington Historical Quarterly,* Vol. XVIII (Jan., 1927), 51–65; (July, 1927), 207–30.

Byington, Lewis F. "The Historic Expedition of Colonel John C. Frémont and Kit Carson to California in 1843–44," *Quarterly of the Society of California Pioneers,* Vol. VIII (Sept., 1931), 184–91.

Carey, Charles H. "Some Early Maps and Myths," *Oregon Historical Quarterly,* Vol. XXX (March, 1929), 14–32.

Cline, Gloria Griffen. "Jedediah Smith: Leading Contender in the Anglo-American Fur Rivalry," *The Pacific Historian,* Vol. V (Aug., 1961), 95–103.

————. "Peter Skene Ogden's Nevada Explorations," *Nevada Historical Quarterly,* Vol. III (July-Sept., 1960), 3–11.

Crampton, C. Gregory. "Humboldt's Utah, 1811," *Utah Historical Quarterly,* Vol. XXVI (July, 1958), 268–81.

————. "The Discovery of the Green River," *Utah Historical Quarterly,* Vol. XX (Oct., 1952), 299–312.

————. "The Myth of El Dorado," *The Historian,* Vol. XIII (Spring, 1951), 115–29.

————, and Gloria Griffen (Cline). "The San Buenaventura, Mythical River of the West," *Pacific Historical Review,* Vol. XXV (May, 1956), 163–71.

Dale, Harrison Clifford. "A Fragmentary Journal of William L. Sublette," *Mississippi Valley Historical Review,* Vol. VI (June, 1919), 99–110.

Dee, Henry Drummond. "An Irishman in the Fur Trade: The Life and Journals of John Work," *British Columbia Historcial Review,* Vol. VII (Oct., 1943), 229–68.

Donoghue, David. "Coronado, Oñate, and Quivira," *Mid-America,* Vol. VII (April, 1936), 88–95.

————. "Location of Quivira," *Panhandle-Plains Historical Review,* Vol. XIII (1940), 38–70.

Elliott, T. C. "The Fur Trade in the Columbia River Basin Prior to 1811," *Washington Historical Quarterly,* Vol. VI (Jan., 1915), 3–10.

———— (ed.). "Journal of the Snake Country Expedition, 1826–27," *Oregon Historical Quarterly,* Vol. XI (June, 1910), 201–22.

————. "Peter Skene Ogden, Fur Trader," *Oregon Historical Quarterly,* Vol. XI (Sept., 1910), 229–78.

———. "Wilson Price Hunt, 1783–1842," *Oregon Historical Quarterly*, Vol. XXXII (June, 1931), 130–34.

Ellison, William Henry. "From Pierre's Hole to Monterey: A Chapter in the Adventures of George Nidever," *Pacific Historical Review*, Vol. I (March, 1932), 82–102.

Emmons, S. F. "Wahsatch Range," *Report of the Geological Exploration of the Fortieth Parallel*, ed. by Clarence King, *q.v.*

Ermatinger, C. O. "The Columbia River under Hudson's Bay Company Rule," *Washington Historical Quarterly*, Vol. V (July, 1914), 192–206.

Espinosa, José Manuel. "The Legend of Sierra Azul," *New Mexico Historical Review*. Vol. IX (April, 1934), 113–58.

Farquhar, Francis P. "Exploration of the Sierra Nevada," *California Historical Quarterly*, Vol. IV (March, 1925), 3–58.

———. "Jedediah Smith and the First Crossing of the Sierra Nevada," *Sierra Club Bulletin*, Vol. XXVIII (June, 1943), 36–53.

———. "Walker's Discovery of Yosemite," *Sierra Club Bulletin*, Vol. XXVII (Aug., 1942), 35–49.

Fletcher, F. N. "Eastbound Route of Jedediah S. Smith, 1827," *California Historical Quarterly*, Vol. II (Jan., 1923–24), 344–49.

"Fur Trader," *Traits of American Indian Life and Character*. London, Smith & Elder, 1853.

Galbraith, John S. "The Little Emperor," *The Beaver*, Oufit 291 (Winter, 1960), 22–28.

Gallatin, Albert, "A Synopsis of the Indian Tribes Within the United States East of the Rocky Mountains, and in the British and Russian Possessions in North America," *Transactions and Collections of the American Antiquarian Society*, II. Worcester, Mass., 1836.

Gentleman's Magazine. London. 1744–54.

Gilbert, Sir Humphrey. "A Discourse of a Discovery for a New Pasasge to Cataia," in volume VII of *Hakluyt's Voyages* (ed. by E. E. Speight).

Hafen, LeRoy R. "Armijo's Journal of 1829–30: The Beginning of Trade between New Mexico and California," *Colorado Magazine*. Vol. XXVII (April, 1950), 120–31.

———. "Armijo's Journal," *Huntington Library Quarterly*, Vol. XI (Jan., 1947), 87–101.

———. "Mountain Men before the Mormons," *Utah Historical Quarterly*, Vol. XXVI (Oct., 1958), 307–26.

Haines, Francis D., Jr. "The Relations of the Hudson's Bay Company with the American Fur Trade in the Pacific Northwest," *Pacific Northwest Quarterly*, Vol. XXXX (Oct., 1949), 273–94.

Hammond, George P. "The Search for the Fabulous in the Settlement of the Southwest," *Utah Historical Quarterly,* Vol. XXIV (Jan., 1956), 1–19. Reprint.

Heizer, Robert F. "Aboriginal California and Great Basin Cartography," University of California *Archaeological Survey Report No. 41.* Berkeley, University of California Press, 1958.

Hill, Joseph J. "Ewing Young in the Fur Trade of the Far Southwest, 1822–1834," *Oregon Historical Quarterly,* Vol. XXIV (March, 1923), 1–35.

——. "Free Trapper: The Story of Old Bill Williams," *Touring Topics,* Vol. XXII (March, 1930), 18–27.

——. "Spanish and Mexican Explorations and Trade Northwest from New Mexico into the Great Basin, 1765–1853," *Utah Historical Quarterly,* Vol. III (Jan., 1930), 3–23.

——. "The Old Spanish Trail," *Hispanic American Historical Review,* Vol. IV (Aug., 1921), 444–73.

Hodge, Frederick Webb. "Pioneers and Prices, 1829–32," *Southern California Historical Quarterly,* Vol. XXVIII (Sept., 1946), 99–102.

Holman, Frederick V. "Life and Services of Peter Skene Ogden," *Oregon Historical Quarterly,* Vol. XXIV (Dec., 1923), 363–79.

Howay, F. W. "Authorship of Traits of Indian Life," *Oregon Historical Quarterly,* Vol. XXXV (March, 1934), 42–49.

Hubbs, Carl L., and Robert R. Miller. "The Zoological Evidence: Correlation Between Fish Distribution and Hydrographic History in the Desert Basins of Western United States," *The Great Basin* (ed. by Eliot Blackwelder), Salt Lake City, University of Utah Press, 1948.

——. "Early Navigation of the Straits of Fuca," *Oregon Historical Quarterly,* Vol. XII (March, 1911), 1–32.

Ireland, Willard E. "James Douglas and the Russian American Fur Company, 1840," *British Columbia Historical Review,* Vol. V (Jan., 1941), 53–66.

Jones, Claude J. "Geologic History of Lake Lahontan," *Quaternary Climates.* Washington, Carnegie Institution of Washington, 1925.

Kelly, Charles. "The Hastings Cutoff," *Utah Historical Quarterly,* Vol. III (July, 1930), 67–82.

——. "Jedediah Smith on the Salt Desert Trail," *Utah Historical Quarterly,* Vol. III (Jan., 1930), 23–27, 35–52.

——. "The Salt Desert Trail," *Utah Historical Quarterly,* Vol. III (April, 1930), 34–52.

Kittson, William. "William Kittson's Journal Covering Peter Skene Ogden's 1824–25 Snake Country Expedition," ed. by David E. Miller, *Utah Historical Quarterly,* Vol. XXII (April, 1954), 125–42.

Lawrence, Eleanor. "Mexican Trade between Santa Fe and Los

Angeles, 1830–1848," *California Historical Quarterly*, Vol. X (March, 1931), 27–39.

Lowie, Robert H. "Cultural Connections of California and Plateau Shoshoneans," University of California *Publications in American Archaeology and Ethnology*, Vol. XX. Berkeley, University of California Press, 1925.

McGregor, D. A. "Old Whitehead, Peter Skene Ogden," *British Columbia Historical Review*, Vol. XVII (July–Oct., 1953), 161–95.

McKelvie, B. A. "Sir James Douglas: A New Portrait," *British Columbia Historical Review*, Vol. VII (April, 1943), 93–101.

Maloney, Alice Bay (ed.). "Peter Skene Ogden's Trapping Expedition to the Gulf of California, 1829–30," *California Historical Quarterly*, Vol. XIX (Dec., 1940), 308–16.

Merk, Frederick (ed.). "The Snake Country Expedition Correspondence, 1824–1825," *Mississippi Valley Historical Review*, Vol. XXI (June, 1934), 63–75.

———. "Snake Country Expedition, 1824–25: An Episode of Fur Trade and Empire," *Mississippi Valley Historical Review*, Vol. XXI (June, 1934), 46–62.

——— (ed.). "Snake Country Expedition, 1824–25," *Oregon Historical Quarterly*, Vol. XXXV (June, 1934), 93–122.

Merriam, C. Hart. "Earliest Crossing of the Deserts of Utah and Nevada to Southern California: Route of Jedediah S. Smith in 1826," *California Historical Quarterly*, Vol. II (Oct., 1923), 228–36.

———. "Jedediah Smith's Route across the Sierras in 1827," *California Historical Quarterly*, Vol. III (April, 1924), 25–29.

Miller, David E. "Peter Skene Ogden's Explorations in the Great Salt Lake Region: A Restudy Based on Newly Published Journals," *The Western Humanities Review*, Vol. VIII (Spring, 1954), 139–50.

———. "Peter Skene Ogden's Journal of His Expedition to Utah, *Northwest Historical Quarterly*, Vol. LI (Jan., 1960), 16–25.

Niles' Register, Dec. 9, 1826.

Nute, Grace Lee. "The Papers of the American Fur Company: A Brief Estimate of their Significance," *American Historical Review*, Vol. XXXII (Oct., 1926–July, 1927), 519–38.

Ogden, Peter Skene. "Ogden's Report of His 1829–30 Expeditions," ed. by John Scaglione, *California Historical Quarterly*, Vol. XXVIII (June, 1949), 117–24.

———. "The Peter Skene Ogden Journals: Snake Country Expedition, 1827–28 and 1828–29," ed. by T. C. Elliott, *Oregon Historical Quarterly*, Vol. XI (Dec., 1910), 355–99.

———. "Peter Skene Ogden's Journal of His Expedition to Utah,

1825," ed. by David E. Miller, *Utah Historical Quarterly*, Vol. XX (April, 1952), 160–86.

Rickard, T. A. "The Strait of Anían," *British Columbia Historical Quarterly*, Vol. V (July, 1941), 161–83.

Rolle, Andrew F. (ed.). "Jedediah Strong Smith: New Documentation," *Mississippi Valley Historical Review*, Vol. XXXX (Sept., 1953), 305–308.

Ross, Alexander. "Journal of Alexander Ross—Snake Country Expedition, 1824," ed. by T. C. Elliott, *Oregon Historical Quarterly*, Vol. XIV (Dec., 1913), 366–88.

Rudy, Jack R. "An Archeological Survey of Western Utah," *Anthropological Papers* of the University of Utah, No. 12. Salt Lake City, University of Utah Press, 1953.

Russell, Carl P. "Trapper Trails to the Sisk-kee-dee," *Annals of Wyoming*, Vol. XVII (July, 1945), 88–105.

———. "Early Years in Yosemite," *California Historical Quarterly*, Vol. V (Dec., 1926), 328–41.

———. "Wilderness Rendezvous Period of the American Fur Trade," *Oregon Historical Quarterly*, Vol. XLII (March, 1941), 1–47.

Sage, Walter N., and T. C. Elliott. "Governor George Simpson at Astoria in 1824," *Oregon Historical Quarterly*, Vol. XXX (June, 1929), 106–10.

Sample, Laetitia. "Trade and Trails in Aboriginal California," University of California *Archaeological Survey Report No. 8*. Berkeley, University of California Press, 1950.

Sauer, Carl O. "The Discovery of New Mexico Reconsidered," *New Mexico Historical Review*, Vol. XII (July, 1937), 270–87.

Snow, William J. "Utah Indians and Spanish Slave Trade," *Utah Historical Quarterly*, Vol. II (July, 1929), 67–75.

Steward, Julian Haynes. "Culture Element Distributions: XIII. Nevada Shoshoni," *Anthropological Records*, Vol. IV, No. 2. Berkeley and Los Angeles, University of California Press, 1941.

———. "Ethnography of the Owens Valley Paiute," University of California *Publications in American Archaeology and Ethnology*, Vol. XXXIII, No. 3. Berkeley, University of California Press, 1933.

Stewart, Omer Call. "Northern Paiute Bands," University of California *Publications in Anthropological Records*, Vol. II, No. 3. Berkeley, University of California Press, 1939.

Teggart, Frederick J. "The Approaches to California," *Southwestern Historical Quarterly*, Vol. XVI (July, 1912), 63–74.

———. "Notes Supplementary to Any Edition of Lewis and Clark," American Historical Association *Annual Report* (1908), 188–93.

Thwaites, Reuben Gold (ed.). "American Fur Company, 1821–22," *Wisconsin State Historical Collections,* Vol. XI (1888), 370.

Trudeau, Jean Baptiste. "Trudeau's Description of the Upper Missouri," ed. by Annie Heloise Abel, *Mississippi Valley Historical Review,* Vol. VIII (June, Sept., 1921), 149–79.

Tyler, S. Lyman. "The Myth of the Lake of Copala and Land of Teguayo," *Utah Historical Quarterly,* Vol. XX (Oct., 1952), 313–29.

———. "The Spaniard and the Ute," *Utah Historical Quarterly,* Vol. XXII (Oct., 1954), 343–61.

Wagner, Henry Raup. "Apocryphal Voyages to the Northwest Coast of America," *Proceedings* of the American Antiquarian Society, Vol. XLI. Worcester, Mass., 1931.

———. "California Voyages, 1539–41," *California Historical Quarterly,* Vol. III (Dec., 1924), 307-97.

———. "The Descent on California in 1683," *California Historical Quarterly,* Vol. XXVI (Dec., 1947), 309–19.

———. "Early Franciscan Activities on the West Coast," *Southern California Historical Quarterly,* Vol. XXIII–XXIV (Dec., 1941), 115–26.

———. "Fr. Marcos de Niza," *New Mexico Historical Review,* Vol. IX (April, 1934), 184–229.

———. "Some Imaginary California Geography," *Proceedings* of the American Antiquarian Society, XXXVI. Worcester, Mass., 1926.

———. "Spanish Voyages to the Northwest Coast," *California Historical Quarterly,* Vol. VI (Dec., 1927), 293–331.

———. "Spanish Voyages to the Northwest Coast: the Voyage of Juan Rodríguez Cabrillo," *California Historical Quarterly,* Vol. VII (March, 1928), 20–77.

Warren, Gouverneur K. "Bonneville's Expedition to the Rocky Mountains, 1832–33, '34, '35, '36," *Annals of Wyoming,* Vols. XV–XVI (1943–44), 220–28.

———. "Memoir to Accompany the Map of the Territory of the United States from the Mississippi River to the Pacific Ocean ...," *Reports of Explorations and Surveys to Ascertain the Most Practicable and Economical Route for a Railroad from the Mississippi River to the Pacific Ocean,* Vol. II. Washington, B. Tucker, 1859. (Commonly referred to as the *Pacific Railroad Survey.*)

Wissler, Clark. "The Influence of the Horse in the Development of Plains Culture," *American Anthropologist,* Vol. XVI (1914), 1–25.

Woodbury, A. M. "The Route of Jedediah S. Smith in 1826 from the

Great Salt Lake to the Colorado River," *Utah Historical Quarterly,* Vol. IV (April, 1931), 34–46.

Work, John. "Journal of John Work . . . April 30 to May 31, 1830," ed. by T. C. Elliott, *Oregon Historical Quarterly,* Vol. X (Sept., 1909), 296–313.

———. "Journal of John Work . . . Covering Snake Country Expedition of 1830–31," ed. by T. C. Elliott, *Oregon Historical Quarterly,* Vol. XIII (Sept., 1912), 363–71; Vol. XIV (Sept., 1913), 280–314.

Yount, George C. "The Chronicles of George C. Yount," ed. by Charles L. Camp, *California Historical Quarterly,* Vol. II (April, 1923), 3–74.

INDEX

246

101, 147; Sanpete Nation of, 56; "Bearded," 56

Valle, André: 70
Valmy, Nev.: 117
Vancouver, George: 62–63, 75, 76; geographical ideas of, 66, 69, 193
Vandenburg & Co.: 82
Vargas, Diego de: 26
Vejil, Josef Santiago: 55
Velásques, Josef: 55
Venegas, Miguel: 50
Verrazano, Giovanni: 22
Victorville, Calif.: 38, 39
Villa de Santa Cruz de la Cañada: 55
Virgin River: 155, 165, 199, 206, 213, 214
Virgin, Thomas: 159
Virginia Canyon: 175
Vizcaíno, Sebastián: 34
Vopellius: 19

Wadsworth, Nev.: 188, 212
Wager, Charles: 30
Walker-Bonneville party: 168ff., 174ff., 198; at Humboldt Sink, 8, 9; name Humboldt River, 116; contributions of 179–80
Walker, Don Juan Pedro: 193, 194
Walker, Joseph Reddeford: 8, 9, 15, 168ff., 187, 188, 198
Walker Lake: 126, 158, 176, 185, 187
Walker Pass: 198; Indian knowledge of, 14; Walker's use of, 176; Walker-Chiles use of, 187; Frémont uses, 213
Walker River: 8, 198; Ogden on, 126; Smith on, 157–58; Walker on, 174, 177, 179; Bidwell-Bartleson on, 184–85; Frémont on, 212
Walla Walla River: 90, 94
Walnut River: 25
Walton, A.: 181
Walton, Maj.: 181
Warner Lake: 211
War of 1812: 76ff., 81
Warren, Lt. G. K.: 203, 204
Wasatch Mountains: 4, 7, 8, 32, 49, 140, 166, 168, 188, 215
Washo Indians: 12, 13
Weaver, Charles: 182
Weber, Capt. John: 138, 139, 146
Weber River: 6, 8, 31, 206; Kittson's

map of, 106; Ogden on, 106, 119n., 141; Ogden-Gardner clash on, 142, 145; Ashley on, 146ff.; Smith on, 159
Wells, Nev.: 7, 118, 129, 188
Western Emigration Society: 181
Wheeler Peak: 158
White River: 38, 44, 45
Wlikes, Lt. Charles: 160, 205, 207ff.
Willamette River: 64–65, 101, 107n., 120, 204; *see also* Multnomah River
Willes, Richard: 21
Williams, Richard: 182
Wilson, John: 154
Wimmulche River: 157, 200
Wind River: 179; W. P. Hunt on, 69; Smith on, 83, 133, 134; rendezvous on, 162–63
Wind River Range: 133, 148, 209
Winnemucca, Nev.: 116, 123, 124, 129, 184
Wisconsin River: 29, 51n.
Wolfskill, William: 59, 166, 168, 186
Work, John: 127ff., 172, 179, 203
Workman, William: 186
Wyld, James: 22n.
Wyoming: 83; as part of the Great Basin, 3, 4; Indians of, 11; Astorians in, 73; Donald Mackenzie in, 98

Yampa Plateau: 44
Yampa River: 210
Yellowstone Expedition: 149
Yellowstone Lake: 158
Yellowstone River: 60, 64, 81, 82, 179, 193n., 207; Larocque on, 79; Missouri Fur Company on, 93–94; Rocky Mountain Fur Company on, 133, 149
Yosemite National Park region: Indians of, 13–14; Walker in vicinity of, 175, 180
Young, Ewing: 165, 168
Young's Bay: 64
Yount, George C.: 59, 166, 168
Yuma, Ariz.: 36, 54, 57n.
Yuma Indians: 35
Yuma Massacre: 54, 57n.

Zacatecas, Mexcio: 25ff.
Zaltieri, Bolognio: 20
Zárate Salmerón, Father Gerónimo de: 27, 50
Zuñi Indians: 24, 25, 41n., 43, 48